The Psychotherapy Relationship

The Psychotherapy Relationship

Theory, Research, and Practice

Charles J. Gelso
and
Jeffrey A. Hayes

JOHN WILEY & SONS, INC.

New York • Chichester • Weinheim • Brisbane • Singapore • Toronto

Library of Congress Cataloging-in-Publication Data:

Gelso, Charles J., 1941–
    The psychotherapy relationship: theory, research, and practice/
Charles J. Gelso and Jeffrey A. Hayes.
        p.   cm.
    Includes bibliographical references and index.
    ISBN 0-471-12720-5 (cloth : alk. paper)
    1. Psychotherapist and patient.   2. Psychotherapy.
3. Transference (Psychology).   4. Counter-transference (Psychology).
I. Hayes, Jeffrey A. Ph. D.   II. Title.
    [DNLM: 1. Psychotherapy.   2. Professional-Patient Relations.
3. Transfer (Psychology)   WM 420 G321p 1998]
RC480.8.G45   1998
618.89′14—dc21
DNLM/DLC
for Library of Congress   98-10212

Printed in the United States of America.

10 9 8 7 6 5 4 3 2 1

To my clients, who have taught me much about
therapeutic relationships over the years.

CJG

To Janet, who teaches me continually about relationship.

JAH

Preface

THE RELATIONSHIP that develops between psychotherapists and clients or patients is, by any yardstick, a vital part of the psychotherapy experience. As we conceive of and participate in psychotherapy, a good relationship is likely to be an enormously valuable contributor to positive outcomes; conversely, good outcomes rarely occur in the context of a poor client-therapist relationship.

This book is about the client-therapist relationship in psychotherapy—what that relationship consists of, how it develops during treatment, how it varies for different systems of psychotherapy, how it operates in and affects treatment. The book consists of two parts. Part One uses previous theoretical work on the therapy relationship presented by the first author and Jean Carter (Gelso & Carter, 1985, 1994a) as a takeoff point, and refines, modifies, and extends that work. In keeping with Gelso and Carter, all therapy relationships are seen as consisting of a working alliance, a transference configuration (including therapist countertransference), and a real relationship component. After providing an introduction to the therapy relationship (Chapter 1), Part One examines each of these components in depth and explores how each operates in different therapies (Chapters 2 through 5). We conclude Part One by exploring in Chapter 6 how these components interact in the context of the therapy relationship, and how the relationship and therapist techniques interrelate during treatment.

In these chapters on the components of the therapy relationship (Chapters 2 through 6), we explicitly state theoretical propositions and discuss how those propositions are informed by theory, research, and practice. Our aim in making these statements is at once to foster research and theory while providing a theoretical guide to practitioners of therapy.

In Part Two, we examine what is made of the therapy relationship—what it looks like and how it operates—in four major theory clusters: psychoanalytic (Chapter 7), cognitive-behavioral (Chapter 8), humanistic (Chapter 9), and feminist (Chapter 10). Each organized theory of psychotherapy has its own vision of the client-therapist relationship. We analyze the vision offered by these theories in terms of four dimensions: (a) the centrality of the relationship; (b) the extent to which the relationship is seen as curative in itself versus helpful because of something done to or because of it; (c) the relative emphasis on what we call the real relationship versus the transference configuration (the "unreal" relationship, so to speak); and (d) the therapist's conceptualization and use of power in the relationship. The organization of the chapters in Part Two varies somewhat, to take into account how the four major theories themselves vary in certain ways. Specifically, for the psychoanalytic and humanistic chapters, we explore how the psychotherapy relationship is envisioned by different theoretical approaches within the general theory cluster, and then we look at the entire cluster in terms of the dimensions of centrality, relationship as a means vs. an end, real vs. transference relationship, and use of power. For the feminist and cognitive-behavioral clusters, on the other hand, we believe that the subtheories within these general clusters "hang together" in terms of visions of the relationship, so we do not analyze those subtheories separately. Instead, we examine the general theory cluster (cognitive-behavioral and feminist) with respect to its vision of the relationship on the four aforementioned dimensions.

Our most basic hope in writing this book has been to benefit both science and practice in the field of psychotherapy—to offer some clear-cut theoretical statements that would foster empirical research and theory development about the relationship, and to present material that would be useful to therapy practitioners in furthering their thinking about therapy relationships. Thus, we intend this book for, and hope it will be useful to, students, researchers, and practitioners of the art and science of psychotherapy. Because of our dual emphasis on science and practice, we have sought to incorporate research (when it exists) into all of the chapters, to express views developed from our own practice and supervision of psychotherapy, and to provide case material when it might clarify certain points. Just as we have used theory, research, and practice in writing the book, we hope, in turn, that the book serves to benefit theory, research, and practice.

Our investment in reaching both scientists and practitioners likely stems from our own involvement as scientists and practitioners. Both of us have been involved in teaching, studying, and practicing psychotherapy throughout our careers, and we have been intellectually and emotionally sustained by all of these professional activities. This book surely comes out of and reflects each of these different parts of our experience.

The focus of the book is individual psychotherapy. Although we believe that much of what we have to say pertains to other modes of intervention (e.g., group therapy, couples therapy), individual therapy is the central concern about which we have deliberately theorized.

Although the material on the components of the therapy relationship (working alliance, transference, countertransference, and real relationship) emanated from psychoanalytic theory, we have sought to be even-handed theoretically throughout the book. In this, we were aided by the differences in our theoretical approach: one of us is psychoanalytically oriented (CJG), and the other leans toward humanistic theory (JAH). Nevertheless, both of us seek to integrate diverse perspectives into our therapy. We think we have been good at "catching" each other's theoretical prejudices—at pointing out any "cheerleading" for one or another theory, or any antagonism against a particular viewpoint. Our readers will, of course, be the final judges of whether we have succeeded in these efforts.

We are grateful to and want to acknowledge many individuals who have helped us with the book. Dr. Jean Carter's thinking and writing as part of the Gelso and Carter team have been deeply influential and are credited throughout the book. We also owe her a debt of gratitude for her thoughtful critiques of several of our chapters. Dr. Janet McCracken and Ms. Sarah Knox read and provided invaluable feedback on several chapters. We express our appreciation to the following people who each read and gave extremely helpful input into one or another of our chapters: Dr. Alicia Chambers, Mr. James Fauth, Ms. Suzanne Friedman, Dr. Shirley Hess, Dr. Clara Hill, Mr. Jonathon Mohr, and Mr. Eric Rosenberger.

CHARLES J. GELSO
JEFFREY A. HAYES

Contents

PART ONE

CHAPTER 1

The Psychotherapy Relationship and Its Components: An Introduction

SYCHOTHERAPY MAY be thought of as consisting of a technical part and a relationship part. The technical aspect includes the techniques used by the therapist in an effort to modify client behavior, and the theoretically prescribed roles taken on by the participants. The relationship aspect consists of the feelings and attitudes the participants hold toward one another, and the psychological connection between therapist and client, based on these feelings and attitudes. This latter aspect, the client-therapist relationship, is our central concern in this book. As we have seen over the years, of the two aspects, the relationship is the part that is harder to grasp theoretically and clinically. One quality of its elusiveness is that it means different things to different practitioners and theoreticians. It is an understatement to say that the relationship has been difficult to study empirically.

Psychotherapy is a highly complex and multifaceted process. Even after many years of scientific research, few assertions can be made about psychotherapy on which there would be general agreement. One assertion that can be made pertains to the relationship that develops between therapist and client or patient. Despite the elusiveness of the relationship, noted above, nearly all psychotherapy practitioners, theoreticians, and researchers agree that the relationship that develops between therapist and

3

client is important—that is, it has a significant effect on the process and outcome of treatment.

Current beliefs about the impact of the relationship are summarized nicely by Lambert (1983), in the opening paragraph of his book on client-therapist relationships:

> Human beings are social animals. They live through a series of interrelationships, forming and being formed by interactions with other people. Much of what people come to feel and be is directly and indirectly related to the quality of the associations they have had with others. Much has been written about the quality of these formative relationships. If relationships help form troubled lives (in the natural environment), then new relationships are needed to change troubled lives. . . . the relationship that develops between patient and psychotherapist can be especially powerful in stimulating personality change. Despite the long history of successful and unsuccessful relationships the patient has had, the relationship that develops with the therapist, quite apart from the techniques the therapist uses, can facilitate the patient's growth. (Lambert, 1983, p. 1)

Although there is general agreement that the relationship importantly influences treatment, open to debate are questions such as: Just how important is this relationship? What elements of the relationship are important? How do those elements interact with each other and influence the treatment? Just how does the relationship exert its impact on process and outcome? Answers to these questions are very difficult to come by. Furthermore, the answers one gets depend to an important extent on the therapist's theoretical orientation. For example, generally speaking, psychoanalytic, humanistic, and feminist therapists will contend that the relationship is a vital element of treatment, perhaps the sine qua non of psychological intervention. On the other hand, the behavioral and cognitive therapists, while admitting that the relationship is important, will tend to view it as less vital than will the analytic and humanistic practitioners.

Similarly, as will be discussed in detail later in this book, one's theory tends to dictate conceptions of the ways in which the relationship influences treatment. Following Prochaska's (1979) observation, one may see the relationship as (a) one of the *preconditions* for therapy to proceed (as in the cognitive and, probably, the behavioral therapies); (b) an *essential process* that itself creates change (as in person-centered therapy, feminist therapy, and some versions of gestalt therapy); or (c) as a fundamental *source of content* to be talked about and processed in therapy (as in most psychoanalytically based therapies and some humanistic approaches).

While these questions (just how important, in what ways, are what elements) are open to debate, as we have noted, the agreed-on view, well supported by research and theory, is that the relationship is indeed a very significant aspect of psychotherapy of every theoretical persuasion.

The present book seeks to extend the theoretical formulations on the psychotherapy relationship originally developed by Gelso and Carter (1985, 1994a). It has been well over a decade since publication of their first lengthy treatise on the relationship and how it works during treatments of diverse orientations (Gelso & Carter, 1985). During the intervening time, a number of empirical studies have been conducted on the components of the client-therapist relationship, and further theoretical work has been put forth. Gelso and Carter's conception of the components of the therapy relationship has been used to analyze extensively the existing research on the topic (Sexton & Whiston, 1994); and Gelso and Carter's work advanced to the point that theoretical propositions have been possible about more complex aspects of the relationship than had been previously considered (Gelso & Carter, 1994a, 1994b). Because of these developments, the time seemed ripe for a book-length treatment of this subject matter.

In the remainder of this chapter, we give an overview of the material to come. As part of our introduction to Part One of the book, the therapy relationship is defined, the conceptualization of the therapy relationship as being comprised of three fundamental components is discussed, and these components are defined and briefly examined. As part of defining the relationship, we give a brief overview of an uncharted territory—how the relationship and therapist techniques interact with one another during treatment. Subsequently, in our introduction to Part Two, we offer some general statements about how the relationship operates within the four most prominent general systems of psychotherapy. We briefly discuss each theory cluster in terms of its status on four key concepts or dimensions, along with how the theories vary in their respective visions of the client-therapist relationship.

THE RELATIONSHIP AND ITS COMPONENTS

Because the therapy relationship has been given such a central place in our field over such a long period of time, one might expect that many definitions of the relationship have been put forth. In fact, there has been very little definitional work. The client-centered therapy group led by Carl Rogers (e.g., Rogers, 1957, 1975; Patterson, 1984) seemed to provide a definition when the relationship was equated with therapist-offered conditions such as empathic understanding, unconditional positive re-gard, and congruence. Upon reflection, though, it becomes clear that therapist-offered conditions, however important (and we maintain that they are deeply important), cannot be equated with the relationship it-self. These conditions were thought of by the client-centered group as prerequisites for effective treatment or constructive client change. Rela-tionship conditions for effective treatment cannot serve as definers of the relationship. What the therapist does to promote an effective relationship is simply not of the same order as a definition of what constitutes a ther-apy relationship. In addition, therapist conditions pertain to only one side of the relationship—the therapist side. Any definition of the relationship must include both sides: the client (or clients) and the therapist.

THE PSYCHOTHERAPY RELATIONSHIP DEFINED

Things are never as easy to define as they might seem at first glance, and the psychotherapy relationship is no exception. After struggling with the issue of definition for some time, Gelso and Carter (1985, 1994a) settled on the following:

> The relationship is the feelings and attitudes that therapist and client have toward one another, and the manner in which these are expressed. (Gelso & Carter, 1985, 1994)

We use this as our working definition of the relationship in this book.

Just about any definition the theoretician can cook up is going to gen-erate some controversy when the construct is as complex as the psy-chotherapy relationship. In response to an extensive review of empirical research on the therapy relationship (Sexton & Whiston, 1994), Hill (1994) has raised questions about the definition we use. Specifically, she takes issue with including *"the manner in which these are expressed"* as part of the definition of relationship, stating that this inclusion "muddies the water and opens up the relationship to include everything" (p. 90). Although we recognize the general nature of our working definition, we believe any definition must include the manner in which feelings and attitudes are expressed (or, by implication, withheld). This expression need not be clear and direct, and the manner of expression can be tremendously vari-able. It may be, and often is, very subtle, nonverbal, and indirect. Thus, what one experiences about the other—the feelings and attitudes one pos-sesses—may creep out, slip out, or be directly shared; and this process both reflects and further informs the relationship. The point is: The manner of expressing what is felt and perceived is a necessary part of any relationship definition.

The complex and elusive nature of the psychotherapy relationship, and thus the difficulty in capturing it with a single definition, is beautifully highlighted by Barrett-Lennard (1985) when he states:

> One may think of a [dyadic] relationship as being centered on the qualities and contents of experiencing of the two participant individuals with, and toward, one another. This covers a lot of territory but it does not fully encompass the ways in which the participants communicate with each other, the messages that are passed back and forth, the moment-by-moment or generalized image that A has of B's awareness of A, or of B's feeling toward A, and likewise in respect to B's image of A's interperceptions. Neither of these levels fully encompasses "a relationship" as an emergent entity that develops a life and character of its own, existing in intimate *inter*dependence with the single-person components, a "we" in the consciousness of member persons and a distinctive "you" or "they," or the like, as seen from the outside. Any of these levels of relationship can be viewed in terms of what is present or typical at a given time in the life of the relationship, or from a developmental standpoint; and interest may center on the interior process of the relationship or on the ways the relationship system maintains itself or is altered under the influence of external forces. (p. 282)

Among other things, what Barrett-Lennard reminds us is that when considering what constitutes the psychotherapy relationship, the "we" of the relationship must be taken into account, as well as the two separate "I's," or the two individuals. Thus, a third force is present in a relationship, and it transcends or at least is different from the individuals who are involved.

THE RELATIONSHIP AND THERAPIST TECHNIQUES

Returning to our definition of the psychotherapy relationship, in line with Hill's (1994) concerns, the very general nature of this definition requires that we address what the relationship *does not* include. As Gelso and Carter (1985, p. 159) noted, "if the relationship consists of *all* things, then there is nothing else—and a definition would be beside the point."

At the start of this chapter, we suggested that psychotherapy has a relationship part and a technical part. The latter consists of the techniques used by the therapist in order to bring about change, as well as the theoretically prescribed roles in which the therapist and client engage. Generally speaking, therapists' techniques emanate from their theories of how to bring about constructive change. Thus, a person-centered therapist uses reflection of feeling; an analytic therapist employs certain kinds of interpretations; and a cognitive-behavioral therapist uses conditioning and persuasive techniques in order to induce the types of change dictated by the relevant theory. Regarding roles, for example, an analytic therapist *and his or her client* more or less follow certain roles dictated by the particular version of analytic therapy being adhered to by the therapist. In classical analysis, the analysand reclines on a couch and free associates while the analyst quietly listens and offers interpretations when the time is right. Each theory of therapy contains its prescribed roles.

Although we differentiate the technical aspects of therapy from the relationship aspects, it must be understood that, in practice, the two parts constantly interact with and influence one another. There is a profound synergism between the two. The techniques used by the therapist, for example—and certainly the manner in which they are used—influence the kind of relationship that unfolds. Likewise, how the therapist feels toward the client will have a profound effect on the techniques he or she uses and the manner in which they are used with each client. For example, if the therapist is analytically oriented and places a premium on interpretation, how and what the therapist feels toward his or her client will have an impact on the nature, depth, frequency, length, content, and emotional tone of the interpretations that are presented (Gelso & Carter, 1985; Gelso & Fretz, 1992). The client, in turn, will experience the therapist's interpretations in certain affective and intellectual ways and will react accordingly, which will affect the relationship and create the conditions for the therapist's subsequent internal reaction and technical response. This cycle will repeat itself continually as long as the relationship lasts.

COMPONENTS OF THE CLIENT–THERAPIST RELATIONSHIP

A number of years ago, the psychoanalyst, Ralph Greenson, discussed how the analytic relationship consisted of a working alliance and a "real relationship," as well as the transference relationship that was nearly universally agreed on as a vital part of psychoanalytic theory (Greenson, 1967). The view held throughout Gelso and Carter's writing, and the one that we espouse, is that all psychotherapies, regardless of theoretical orientation, consist of these three components. At the same time, the centrality of the individual components varies importantly with the theory guiding the work, as will be examined in Part Two.

In much of the remainder of Part One, we shall provide an in-depth analysis of the components: the working alliance, what we call the transference configuration (including client transference and therapist countertransference), and the real relationship. We offer here our basic definitions of these components, as well as a preliminary discussion of their operation in therapy.

The Working Alliance

The most fundamental component of the therapy relationship, we suggest, is the working alliance that develops between client and therapist. It is hard to imagine therapy being successful in the absence of a sound working alliance; indeed, empirical research supports the importance of the alliance to treatment outcome (Horvath & Symonds, 1991). Stronger alliances are associated with more positive outcomes.

The working alliance may be defined as *"the alignment or joining of the reasonable self or ego of the client and the therapist's analyzing or 'therapizing' self or ego for the purpose of the work"* (italics added; Gelso & Carter, 1994a, p. 297). The alignment or joining of these parts allows the participants to observe, understand, and do therapeutic work in the face of many obstacles and resistances that inevitably impinge on probably all therapies. Related to Bordin's (1979, 1994) seminal writing, it is suggested that the strength of the working alliance both affects and is affected by the degree to which the therapist and client (a) agree on the goals of treatment and the in-session or out-of-session tasks that are useful or necessary to attain those goals, and (b) experience an emotional bond with each other. In contrast to Bordin, we do not think that agreement on goals and tasks, and the existence of a bond constitute a *definition* of the working alliance. Rather, as noted, they influence and are influenced by it.

Over the years, somewhat different terms have been used to capture the alliance. Terms such as *working alliance* (Bordin, 1979; Greenson, 1967), *helping alliance* (Luborsky, 1976), *therapeutic alliance* (Marmar, Horowitz, Weiss, & Marziali, 1986; Zetzel, 1956), or simply *alliance* (Horvath, Gaston, & Luborsky, 1993) have all been employed, each with somewhat different meaning. We prefer the term *working alliance* because it more clearly and specifically refers to the concept of the participants' joining together to foster the working element of therapy, and it helps us separate this element from other components of the overall relationship. Of the relationship components, the working alliance has received the greatest research attention, and, during the past decade, research on the alliance has occurred at a fast pace. (Research on the working alliance will be examined in Chapter 2.)

The Transference Configuration

In contrast to the general agreement that the working alliance is a key factor in treatment, the importance and role of transference remain controversial. Generally speaking, psychoanalytic therapists view transference
as a key concept, whereas humanistic, cognitive-behavioral, and many
feminist therapists view the concept with skepticism. Our position is that
transference (and therapist countertransference) is an important element
of all therapy (and probably all relationships), and, as we shall discuss
in Chapter 2, we believe this position is well supported by empirical
research.

Not only are the existence and importance of transference controversial, but so too is its definition. When the theoretical literature is
scanned, three definitions seem most salient. The first views transference
as a reliving of Oedipal issues within the therapeutic relationship. Thus,
the therapist is reacted to as if he or she were any or all participants in the
client's early Oedipal situation (see E. Singer, 1970). This is the conception of transference embedded in classical psychoanalytic drive theory.

The second definition of transference is broader than the first. Transference is seen as a repetition of past conflicts with significant others, so
that feelings, attitudes, and behaviors belonging rightfully in those earlier relationships are displaced onto the therapist. This definition does
not restrict the source to the Oedipal situation; instead, transference is
viewed as a manifestation of early experience in crucial interpersonal relationships. Often espoused by interpersonally oriented therapists (e.g.,
Fromm-Reichmann, 1950; Sullivan, 1954), this definition is also broader
than the classical view in the sense that transference is seen as entailing
reactions that were appropriate and adaptive at an earlier time and place.
These reactions protected the child's emerging self-esteem (rather than
avoiding castration) and served to make otherwise intolerable situations
tolerable.

A fundamental aspect of both of the above definitions is that transference is seen as an error. The client distorts the reality of the therapist,
projecting and displacing objects (people) or parts of objects from the
client's past onto the person of the therapist. The third and most recent
definition goes beyond this concept of transference as distortion. Transference is seen as an intersubjective process, contributed to by both
client and therapist, and the therapist's job is to understand, and help
the client understand, the reality that both have constructed. Although
the therapist contributes to the transference, it is still the client's
construction that is of central interest. Thus, Stolorow and Lachmann

(1984/1985), the leading proponents of this third view, define transference as referring to "all the ways in which the patient's experience of the analytic relationship is shaped by his own psychological structures—by the distinctive, archaically rooted configurations of self and object that unconsciously organize his subjective universe" (p. 26). In this sense, transference is seen as an unconscious organizing activity. The client assimilates the therapeutic relationship into the thematic structures of his or her personal subjective world (Stolorow, 1991).

As Pulver (1991) has nicely clarified, within current-day psychoanalysis there is a trend to see both positions (transference as distortion, and transference as co-constructed reality) as useful and truthful, and to choose between them according to clinical circumstances. Our view, in keeping with Gill (1982, 1984), is that, although the therapist certainly contributes to the client's transference by virtue of his or her person and behavior, and although it is crucial that the therapist struggle to understand that contribution, the ways in which the client distorts the therapist (and others in his or her life) that are tied to early conflictual relationships and are still vital elements of the concept of transference and what is to be done with it. Transference is indeed an unconscious organizing activity, and it is important to understand that the portion of it that represents displacement is an error driven by unresolved issues. Thus, we maintain the traditional view of transference as distortion, while incorporating the intersubjective position in which the therapist's stimulus value is seen as vital to a full understanding of transference. Our working definition of transference is: *the client's experience of the therapist that is shaped by his or her own psychological structures and past, and involves displacement, onto the therapist, of feelings, attitudes, and behaviors belonging rightfully in earlier significant relationships.* As we have discussed, the person and activity of the therapist always figure into the transference (often in very subtle ways) and ordinarily must be considered when trying to understand the client's transference.

Within what we call the transference configuration also resides the construct of therapist *countertransference*. Like perhaps all high-level constructs emanating from psychoanalytic theory, the definition of countertransference has been controversial. The classical psychoanalytic definition essentially views countertransference as the therapist's transference to the client's transference (Singer & Luborsky, 1977). A more recent position is called the totalistic view: countertransference is seen as all of the therapist's emotional reactions to the client. Each of these definitions has serious limitations, in our opinion. The classical view seems narrow and restrictive; the totalistic view is so broad and encompassing as to have limited utility. *All* of the therapist's emotional reactions are important, we would offer, but to consider all of them countertransference badly muddies the construct.

We think it is useful to differentiate a therapist's reactions that are based on his or her conflictual issues from those that are a natural and realistic response to the stimulus of the client (granted that there is overlap between these two types of reactions). At the same time, we also believe that whether the therapist's reactions might be seen as countertransferential should be independent of whether the reaction is to the client's transference or nontransference material. Thus, our working definition of countertransference is *"the therapist's transference to the client's material—both the transference and nontransference communications presented by the client"* (see Gelso & Carter, 1994a, p. 297). As elaborated in Chapter 4, if understood and worked through by the therapist, countertransference feelings can be extremely useful to the work. If they are ignored or remain ununderstood, they can literally destroy the work.

Within these conceptions of transference and countertransference, expectations are given a key role. For example, in addition to having some feelings toward the therapist that were not "earned" by this therapist, clients will have fundamentally inaccurate, or transference-based, expectations of the therapist's feelings and behavior and of themselves with the therapist. Thus, it is not just clients' affective reactions to the therapist that compose the transference. Transference also involves what the client expects from the therapist and how the client expects to behave and feel. In response to a particular client behavior or to the client in general, a given client may expect any of a range of therapist emotional or behavioral reactions. The client may expect the therapist to love, hate, abuse, understand, attack, seduce, and so on. Clients will tend to distort their therapists so as to make them consistent with those expectations, and will alter their own behavior and feelings to conform to those expectations. In fact, based on transference expectations, clients may react to their therapist in a way that actually produces the expected reaction from the therapist. This is the basis for the defense mechanism of projective identification, which has been linked to psychodynamic therapy, with clients suffering from borderline personality disorders.

In summary, both transference and countertransference occur in all therapies, from the first moment of contact. They may even occur before actual contact and then might be called preformed transferences: the client experiences feelings, attitudes, and expectations of his or her imagined therapist, and these represent unresolved issues from the past. Both transference and countertransference may be helpful, neutral, or destructive to the therapy, depending on their nature, their valence, the central thrust of the therapy, and the therapist's beliefs about these processes and ways of handling them.

Empirical research on both transference and countertransference has progressed at an exceedingly slow pace since Freud coined the terms during the early part of the 20th century. The pace has somewhat quickened, however, since about the mid-1980s. The development of transference measures based on session evaluations by outside judges (Luborsky et al., 1993) and therapists' reports (Gelso, Kivlighan, Wine, Jones, & Friedman, 1997; Multon, Patton, & Kivlighan, 1996) should help accelerate this process. In the area of countertransference, several lines of research are emerging (e.g., Gelso, Fassinger, Gomez, & Latts, 1995; Hayes, Riker, & Ingram, 1997; Lecours, Bouchard, & Normandin, 1995; McClure & Hodge, 1987). Research on transference and countertransference will be discussed in Chapters 3 and 4, respectively.

The Real Relationship

In an obvious and profound way, the client-therapist relationship is always fully real. Thus, it seems ironic that what we call the real relationship has been the most theoretically neglected and least understood of the relationship components.

In accord with Greenson's (1967) thinking, we use the term *real relationship* in a particular way. Real relationship pertains to *"that dimension of the total relationship that is essentially nontransferential, and is thus relatively independent of transference"* (italics added; Gelso & Carter, 1994a, p. 297). This usage dictates a certain philosophical position about reality— namely that, in some sense, reality does exist and is not simply a function of the perceiver. If there were no belief in reality independent of the observer, any definition of transference as a distortion of reality would be meaningless. A use of the term *real relationship* to connote the nontransferential part of the total relationship would also be meaningless.

Although our views on this matter have clashed most pointedly with staunch phenomenological and social constructionist positions, we must add that the perceptions and constructions of the observers and the participants are vitally important in the relationship. Perceptions of what is real and true do depend profoundly on the observers, and there is no simple reality out there. Yet we do maintain the position that there is a complex reality and that perceptions do contain degrees of accuracy and inaccuracy.

Our discussion of real relationship in this book centers on those aspects of the relationship that are primarily undistorted by transference.

The real relationship, we suggest, contains two defining features: *genuineness* and *realistic perceptions*. Genuineness is seen as the tendency to be what one truly is in the relationship—honest, open, authentic, congruent with one's inner experiencing. Realistic perceptions, as implied above, refer to those perceptions that are uncontaminated by transference distortions and other defenses that may not directly implicate transference. Thus, for example, if the client is high on the realistic perceptions feature, he or she sees the therapist in an accurate, realistic way.

Gelso and Carter (1985, 1994a, 1994b) have suggested that all therapeutic encounters contain a real relationship component, although the importance of this component certainly varies according to one's theoretical orientation. For example, the humanistic therapist typically places a premium on the real relationship, whereas many psychoanalytic therapists may even question whether such a construct truly exists or is useful.

Not only do we propose that all therapy relationships contain a real relationship component, but we suggest that the real relationship has an important impact on all encounters, theoretical differences notwithstanding. Thus, even in classical psychoanalysis, which maximizes the importance of transference, a real relationship (a degree of genuineness and realistic perceptions) exists and is contributed to by both participants, and this component exerts an important influence on process and outcome.

Generally speaking, the stronger the real relationship (greater genuineness and more realistic perceptions), the more effective the treatment, although this proposition must be qualified in a number of ways. For example, many psychoanalytic treatments seek a buildup of transference, which may then be usefully interpreted and worked through. This may suggest that high transference (and perhaps low realistic perception) is a positive element at some points in some therapies. However, whether an increase in transference leads to a reduction in realistic perceptions is as yet unknown. Although transference entails distortion, it is quite conceivable that high transference and high realistic perception may occur simultaneously.

As will be discussed in Chapter 5, there has been almost no research on the real relationship as we have defined it. The genuineness element has been extensively studied in terms of therapist genuineness, and the findings have generally been supportive of its positive effects (Beutler, Crago, & Arizmendi, 1986; Orlinsky & Howard, 1986). However, research on client genuineness is virtually nonexistent. The construct of realistic perceptions, too, has been given very limited empirical scrutiny.

THE PSYCHOTHERAPY RELATIONSHIP AND THEORETICAL ORIENTATION

Each major theory of therapy has a particular vision—usually explicit but at times implicit—of the psychotherapy relationship. Thus, psychotherapists' theoretical orientations are deeply connected to their views of the psychotherapy relationship—its role in the treatment; what is to be done with and to the relationship; and the overall importance of the relationship. At the same time, it is not clear what causes what, regarding a therapist's theoretical orientation and his or her beliefs about the relationship. Each orientation contains statements about the therapy relationship, and these will affect how a therapist behaves with clients. At the same time, beliefs about the relationship draw particular therapists to particular theoretical orientations. Thus, the causal influence probably goes both ways.

Relationship Dimensions

In seeking to delineate how theories of therapy differ from one another in their visions of the relationship, we suggest that there are four salient dimensions along which formulations of the psychotherapy relationship vary (see Gelso & Carter, 1985). Following our descriptions of each of these dimensions, we will discuss how four major theory clusters (psychoanalytic, cognitive-behavioral, humanistic, and feminist therapy) may be situated and evaluated on these dimensions.

1. We call the first dimension a *centrality dimension*. Its defining feature is the extent to which the client-therapist relationship is seen as a crucial element of client change. Theoretical orientations vary widely in terms of how central the relationship is seen to be.
2. The *means-end dimension* is defined by the extent to which a theory of therapy views the relationship as an end in itself as opposed to a means to an end. Theories that view the relationship as an end in itself, or that at least lean toward that side of the continuum, tend to view the client-therapist relationship, in and of itself, as the mechanism through which client change occurs. In other words, the relationship itself, when it possesses certain desired qualities, produces constructive change.

Theories that envision the relationship more as a means to an end suggest that it is what we do about, to, or because of the relationship that produces change. The relationship itself is not the cause or mechanism of positive change. The relationship may effect change, for example, through providing an impetus for the client to follow the therapist's instructions, which themselves are the mutative elements; or the relationship that unfolds must be transformed through interpretation, the mutative element, if constructive change is to occur; or the relationship may allow the client to reveal more about self, which in turn permits the therapist to devise more effective techniques and procedures, and these are the major change agents.

3. The *real-unreal relationship dimension* is defined in terms of whether the real relationship or the transference relationship is given primacy in a particular theoretical perspective. As discussed below, theories differ substantially in which of the two components is most vigorously addressed in theory and treatment.

4. The *power dimension* is defined in terms of the manner in which power is conceptualized and used by the therapist. Therapists' power derives from many sources, including socially ascribed and legislated authority, command of a knowledge base, technical expertise, and, for some therapists (e.g., members of dominant cultural groups in a society), particular cultural characteristics. Whereas the power that therapists possess at the outset of therapy may not vary appreciably as a function of therapists' theoretical orientation, the manner in which power is conceptualized, garnered over time, shared, used to affect change, and potentially abused differs widely among the major theoretical approaches. Thus, for each theory that is examined, we shall address questions about power dynamics in the therapy relationship, such as: How is power conceived and attended to theoretically? What are the sources of power within the therapist and client? How much power does the client possess, especially relative to the therapist? How is power used and potentially misused?

THEORY CLUSTERS AND RELATIONSHIP DIMENSIONS

Depending on how specific one wants to be, the current theoretical scene may be divided into many or a few theories of psychotherapy. Some years ago, Harper (1959) wrote about 36 different systems of therapy. Others have divided the pie into even smaller slices. In considering how the therapy relationship is envisioned, we find it useful to think in terms of four general theory clusters: (a) psychoanalytic, (b) cognitive-behavioral, (c) humanistic, and (d) feminist. Each of these broad clusters contains many more specific theories, and the theories within a cluster may seem quite divergent from one another. Yet we believe that these clusters hang together in terms of their visions of the basic client mechanisms through which change occurs and, very much related to these mechanisms, the role of the psychotherapy relationship in facilitating change.

The Psychoanalytic Cluster

The psychoanalytic cluster is very complex; it includes many different theories, which are often reduced to four groups: (a) Freudian drive theories, (b) ego analytic theories, (c) object relations theories (including interpersonal theory), and (d) psychoanalytic self psychology (Mishne, 1993; Pine, 1990). Within all or nearly all of these psychoanalytic theories, the central mechanism through which client change occurs is *insight* (Gelso & Fretz, 1992). Insight is usually described as the understanding, emotionally as well as intellectually, of how the client distorts and misperceives in his or her present life and in her or his relationships as a result of unresolved conflicts from earlier times—usually childhood, and most often early childhood.

How do psychoanalytic theories in general stack up on the four dimensions we use to differentiate conceptions of the client-therapist relationship? Given that insight, as defined above, is the key mechanism for client change in the psychoanalytic theories, it makes sense that the analytic therapist would view the relationship as highly central. Thus, the relationship, as conceived of in psychoanalytic treatments, is high on the centrality dimension. But the psychoanalytic vision of the relationship is of a particular sort. The transference relationship is key: the relationship to a large extent involves distortions of the therapist based on unresolved issues in earlier relationships. Thus, the psychoanalytic relationship clearly is situated on the "unreal" side of our real-unreal continuum. Because of this focus on the unreal (qua transference) relationship, the relationship cannot be an end in itself, but rather is a means to an end. For the analytic therapist, something must be done to the relationship if it is to be curative. In Prochaska's (1979) terms, the relationship is a "source of content" to be talked about and processed. Usually, this implies that the transference relationship must be interpreted by the therapist so that the client acquires insight into how his or her distortions occur, where they come from, and how they also occur in other relationships. These misperceptions, through repeated interpretations of how they are enacted in the therapy relationship and many other situations, are then worked through or resolved.

Regarding how power is used and conceptualized in psychoanalytic treatments, the analytic therapist generally aims to have the client run the ship. The client takes the lead, and the therapist is careful not to advise, persuade, or push the client. At the same time, and paradoxically, the therapist's or analyst's role of providing interpretations of what is causing what—in the client's psyche and in the therapeutic relationship—imbues this role with a great deal of subtle power in the relationship.

The Cognitive-Behavioral Cluster

This cluster includes the many versions of cognitive and behavioral therapy currently on the scene. We put cognitive and behavioral theories together because of the compatibility of the two approaches, because of their very similar vision of the therapy relationship, and because, in practice, most therapists who lean toward this cluster also use both cognitive and behavioral techniques.

In virtually all cognitive and behavioral approaches, the most fundamental client mechanism through which change occurs is *learning*. Further, learning is usually seen as taking the form of classical conditioning, instrumental conditioning, and modeling. The therapist helps the client change through the use of techniques that revolve around these forms of learning, and techniques of cognitive persuasion, which help to change faulty or maladaptive thinking. Such cognitive change is also seen in learning terms, although conditioning and modeling are not as commonly implicated as the bases for cognitive learning.

How does the cognitive-behavioral approach rank on the four dimensions? Given the cognitive-behavioral therapists' focus on techniques, the relationship has not been seen as highly central, although its centrality to change surely has increased in recent years. In terms of the real-unreal continuum, the portion of the relationship that has been of interest to cognitive-behavioral therapists is most often the real relationship. The unreal or transference relationship is probably of less concern to the cognitive-behavioral therapist than to therapists of any other major persuasion. Furthermore, the relationship is very clearly a means to an end rather than an end in itself. A sound working alliance and real relationship are seen as somewhat helpful in themselves, but mostly as providing the therapist with leverage that will help him or her gather client information and use cognitive-behavioral techniques most effectively. If the relationship is good, the client is more likely to cooperate with the treatment regimen, to be responsive to techniques, and to carry out assignments. In Prochaska's (1979) terms, the relationship in the cognitive-behavioral therapies is a "precondition" for therapy to proceed effectively. Finally, regarding the conceptualization and use of power, perhaps more than in any other approach, cognitive-behavioral therapists explicitly use their power to educate and persuade clients and directly influence clients' behavior.

The Humanistic Cluster

Within the humanistic cluster are theories such as person-centered, gestalt, experiential, relationship, and some versions of existential therapy. Theories within this cluster place a premium on the client's (and therapist's) here-and-now functioning, the client's phenomenological/perceptual world, and the client's capacity for self-actualization. The fundamental mechanism through which change occurs is the client's *emotional experiencing or awareness* in the moment. Immediacy, a kind of emotional being in the present in the relationship, is a part of this central mechanism. The therapist and the client are to work toward genuineness, a state of being true to oneself and honest with the other.

Given the central mechanism of experiencing/awareness in the here-and-now, it makes sense that the therapist would seek to capitalize on the client-therapist relationship, particularly on the feelings that are alive in the moment, regardless of the content. In terms of our four dimensions, it follows that the relationship is highly central for the humanistic therapist. Furthermore, given the premium placed on genuineness and realness in the moment, the clearly real relationship, rather than the unreal or transference relationship, is viewed as key. Regarding the third dimension, the relationship tends to be an end in itself rather than a means to an end in most humanistic treatments. It is the relationship, not something done to it or because of it, that causes constructive change. In Prochaska's (1979) terms, in the humanistic cluster, the relationship is an "essential process" that creates change. Finally, in terms of power, a pervasive theme in the humanistic therapies is that the client and therapist are viewed as coequals in the therapy process.

Feminist Therapy

Disagreement exists as to whether feminist therapy constitutes a separate system of therapy or is best viewed as a theoretical approach that can be used to evaluate and inform other approaches. We take the position that both stances are possible. Feminist therapy may be conceptualized and practiced in pure form, or, like almost any other approach, it may be integrated with other theories. When viewing feminist therapy as a system of therapy in itself, the question arises as to what, if any, central mechanism of client change is posited by this orientation. The central mechanism for each of the three theory clusters just summarized seemed relatively easy to specify, but such a mechanism is not so easily identified with feminist therapy. The feminist literature, to our knowledge, is not clear about such a mechanism. At the same time, one construct that does appear to stand out as vital in all statements of feminist therapy is *client empowerment*. This concept (like insight, learning, and experiencing, for the three other theory clusters) appears to represent a client process that mediates desired outcomes. The client in feminist therapy is seen as growing and changing essentially through internalizing a healthy sense of personal power and overcoming personal and internalized societal disempowerment. This internal shift itself promotes a host of desired outcomes in feminist therapy.

How does the feminist therapy vision of the client-therapist relationship rank on the four dimensions we use to assess theories? Because of the general importance of relationships to women, feminist therapists tend to view the therapy relationship as a highly central element of their treatment. The relationship tends to be situated on the end side of the means-end continuum because the relationship is one way through which feminist therapists empower their clients. That is, feminist therapists seek to "give away" their power to clients within the context of a relationship in which egalitarianism is the ideal. However, there are other ways in which feminist therapists seek to empower clients (e.g., advocacy, consciousness raising, political activism), so the therapy relationship is conceptualized as less significant as an agent of change in and of itself than in, say, person-centered therapy.

Regarding the real-unreal dimension, we would rank feminist therapy toward the real relationship end of the continuum. At the same time, whether the real relationship or the transference configuration is the focus of therapy varies greatly, depending on whether, for example, a particular feminist therapist subscribes to psychoanalytic or humanistic theory, to both, or to neither. As discussed in detail in Chapter 10, there is, within the feminist cluster, a wide range of views on the utility of emphasizing transference or the real relationship in therapy, although, as noted, there does appear to be a relatively greater emphasis on the real relationship among feminist authors. Finally, in terms of our fourth dimension, an analysis of power dynamics in the therapy relationship is

Table 1.1

Status of Humanistic, Psychoanalytic, Cognitive-Behavioral, and
Feminist Theory Clusters on the Centrality, Real-Unreal, Means-End,
and Therapist Power Dimensions

Theoretical Cluster	Dimensions			
	Centrality	Real-Unreal	Means-End	Therapist Power
Humanistic	High	Real	End	Low
Psychoanalytic	High	Unreal	Means	Medium
Cognitive-behavioral	Medium	Real	Means	High
Feminist	High	Mixed	End	Low

one of the hallmarks of feminist approaches. More than any other theoretical system, feminist therapy attends to the ways in which power is
acquired, utilized, and potentially mishandled by therapists. The fundamental goal of feminist therapy, and the central change mechanism, is
client empowerment.

The role of the relationship in each of the four theory clusters will be
examined in much greater detail in Chapters 7 through 10. Table 1.1 summarizes the status of these four theory clusters in terms of the centrality,
real-unreal, means-end, and use-of-power continuua discussed in this
chapter. Regarding our fourth dimension—conceptualization and use of
power—each system is evaluated in the table in terms of the extent to
which the therapist employs overt and covert power as a means of promoting change.

CHAPTER 2

Working Alliance:
The Foundation of the
Psychotherapy Relationship

O F ALL aspects of the psychotherapy relationship, the working alliance seems most fundamental. In fact, it is difficult to envision a psychotherapy relationship in which something like a working alliance is absent. Yet the specific concept of the working alliance is relatively recent in the psychotherapy field. Although its roots date back to the early part of the century, not until more recent times has the working alliance been addressed as such and examined across diverse theoretical approaches and treatments. In recent years, and especially since Bordin's (1979) integrative theoretical statement, the working alliance has been the topic of a large amount of theory and empirical scrutiny. In fact, from about the middle of the 1980s onward, it is hard to find a construct in the psychotherapy field that has been as vigorously investigated.

Just what is the working alliance? How does it operate during therapy? And how does it affect the process and outcome of treatment? These are some of the central questions we address in this chapter. After providing a background discussion of this construct, we discuss its relationship to other key constructs that pertain to the therapy relationship, and then present nine theoretical propositions aimed at both guiding clinical practice and promoting research.

WORKING ALLIANCE: DEFINITION
AND HISTORICAL SKETCH

The working alliance has been variously defined over the years since Ralph Greenson, the psychoanalyst, first used the term (Greenson, 1965, 1967). Some definitions include the client's transference; others exclude it, viewing the working alliance as essentially synonymous with the real relationship that develops between client and therapist (e.g., Bordin, 1994). Our conception is that the alliance is primarily reality based but is also influenced by the transference relationship.

As stated in Chapter 1, we define the working alliance as *the alignment or joining of the reasonable self or ego of the client and the therapist's analyzing or "therapizing" self or ego for the purpose of the work.* In developing this definition, we rely on the psychoanalytic concept of split in the ego, pointed to many years ago with respect to analytic treatment (Sterba, 1934). In this split, the ego is seen as dividing into an experiencing side and an observing side. The experiencing side allows the person to unreflectively feel and experience; the observing side permits the person to stand back from the experiencing and observe, reason, and understand. Both sides are necessary for effective therapy, although different theoretical systems would tend to differentially emphasize one or the other. Each of the participants, in other words, needs to both affectively experience and stand back from that experience, reasonably observing it.

The reasonable and observing side of the ego comes into play in the working alliance, allowing therapist and client to join together, often in the face of obstacles (e.g., client resistance, therapist countertransference). This joining together is stimulated most fundamentally by the client's wish to heal and grow in one way or another, and by his or her rationally based willingness to cooperate. It also is determined by the therapist's aim of helping the client in his or her quest.

In keeping with Bordin's (1979, 1994) theory, we suggest that the alliance is influenced by the therapist's and client's agreement on (a) the goals of the work—that they are worthwhile and attainable; and (b) the tasks that are to be performed in order to attain those goals. The alliance is also influenced by (c) the bond between the participants.

Four points deserve particular note regarding this formulation. First, the agreement on goals and tasks need not be explicit. At times, the therapist and client do not even discuss goals or tasks explicitly, at least not in any systematic way; but there may be a sense of shared mission, as well as a tacit agreement that the tasks make sense.

A second point is that the tasks of therapy may be either in-session or extra-session. For example, for a psychoanalyst, free association is the major task of treatment; for a cognitive-behavior therapist, out-of-session homework may be the major task.

A third point to be noted about the goals-tasks-bond concept is that not only do these influence the developing alliance, but they themselves are affected by the alliance. In other words, the alignment or joining together for the purpose of the work has an impact on the extent to which participants agree on goals and tasks, and it surely has an impact on the developing bond between therapist and client.

The fourth point to be made about the goals-tasks-bond concept is that the bond part may be best seen as a working bond. Because the working alliance exists for the sole purpose of furthering the work of therapy (what Gelso & Carter, 1994a, refer to as the "mandate of the working alliance"), the bond that is part of it is a bond or attachment that reflects most fundamentally the participants' trust and belief in each other as members of a working team. In Chapter 5, we differentiate the bond that is tied to the working alliance from what we call a "liking bond," which is part of the real relationship between therapist and client.

In forming a basic definition of the working alliance, two concepts seem most fundamental: *collaboration* and *attachment or bonding.* Regarding collaboration, the therapist and the client must conjointly invest in the work. The collaborative element, however, need not be the bottom line for all clients during all phases of therapy. Clients are likely to differ, for example, in the extent to which they prefer an alliance in which the collaborative element is the fundamental feature (see Proposition 8, later in this chapter). In addition, the collaborative element of the working alliance is likely to deepen as the work progresses, as Luborsky's (1976) research suggests (see Proposition 3). Very early in the work, there probably needs to be at least an emerging sense of collaborativeness on the part of both the therapist and the client, if the alliance and the overall relationship are to build. The early absence of a collaborative spirit and the failure of it to develop are likely indications that therapy will not be successful.

Regarding the attachment or bonding element, the therapist and the client must form an attachment with each other for the purpose of furthering the work (see our later discussion of attachment theory). As noted above, we think of the bond that is connected to the working alliance as a working bond, because the fundamental reason for existence of the working alliance itself pertains to how the client and therapist further the work of therapy. In sum, we suggest that these two elements, collaboration and attachment, must be part of any definition of alliance. It is interesting, in this respect, that a review of all major measures of alliance, variously defined, has revealed both elements as common across all measures (Horvath, Gaston, & Luborsky, 1993). Below, we provide a historical sketch of thought about the working alliance and examine some of its current definitions and conceptions.

FROM NEUROTIC TRANSFERENCE TO HEALTHY ALLIANCE

The working alliance concept grew out of psychoanalysis, but, like so many such constructs, was fed by discontent with psychoanalytic orthodoxy. From the time of Freud's discovery of transference (S. Freud, 1905/1959, 1913), much of psychoanalysis seemed to focus on the analysand's neurotic transference and the development of the transference neurosis. Yet, from the beginning of psychoanalysis, there also existed a strand of thought suggesting that there was something more to the therapy relationship than the neurotic transference. As early as 1912, in his seminal paper on transference, Freud alluded to a particular kind of transference that he believed was necessary for success in analysis—the friendly and affectionate aspects of the analysand's transference to the analyst. Freud believed that such reactions should not be interpreted to the analysand as transference (i.e., neurotic distortions), but allowed to exist as an aid to the work of interpreting the more neurotic transferences that were at the core of the analysand's problems.

Part of this "something more" pertained to the feeling of rapport that developed in the relationship. A concept that has become common to diverse therapies (e.g., Brammer & Shostrom, 1968), rapport was seen by Freud as reflective of the client's attachment to the therapist and the treatment. Witness the following: "It remains the first aim of the treatment to attach him [the client] to it and to the person of the doctor" (S. Freud, 1913, pp. 139–140). Freud believed that giving the patient time, showing interest, "clearing away resistances," and avoiding technical errors would allow for this attachment. He further suggested that one sure way to undermine initial successes in forming this attachment was to take any approach other than one of "sympathetic understanding" (S. Freud, *id.*).

During the 1940s and 1950s, a number of influential psychoanalysts furthered this idea of "something more." For example, Fenichel (1941) talked about "rational transferences"; Zetzel (1956) discussed therapeutic alliances; and Stone (1961) wrote about "mature transferences." It remained for Greenson (1965, 1967), however, to put forth the term *working alliance,* in his attempt to get at the notion of the participants' joining together for the purpose of the therapeutic work, in a kind of relationship in which transference was not a central element.

Yet the concept of working alliance remained embedded in psychoanalysis until Bordin's (1979) seminal paper, in which he sought to generalize working alliance beyond psychoanalytic interventions. He suggested that the working alliance is a key part of all therapies. As noted above, he defined the working alliance as the client's and therapist's agreement on the goals of treatment (including an agreement that the goals are attainable); an agreement on the in-therapy and extra-therapy tasks useful to attain those goals; and an emotional bond between the two.

Even before Bordin's theoretical article, empirical research had begun on the alliance within psychoanalytically oriented treatment (Luborsky, 1976). Since that time, a number of measures of alliance have been developed. The review by Horvath et al. (1993), for example, reveals the existence of eleven major measures that may be broken down into five clusters of measures. Each cluster of measures seems to tap somewhat different aspects of the alliance. All except the Working Alliance Inventory (WAI; Horvath, 1982; Horvath & Greenberg, 1989) are heavily influenced by psychodynamic theory. The WAI, in contrast, is based on Bordin's pantheoretical concept, and because of this has perhaps wider applicability than other measures.

THE CURRENT SCENE

As mentioned earlier, the working alliance currently is one of the most vigorously investigated constructs in psychotherapy. What has made this concept so appealing to researchers, theoreticians, and practitioners? It seems to us that a number of factors have come together to create this interest. As Horvath and Greenberg (1994) point out, the research literature over a period of more than 30 years has seemed to clearly suggest that diverse treatments produce approximately equal results. Researchers and theoreticians therefore searched for common factors among treatments that might account for efficacy. The therapist-client relationship appeared to be a likely candidate, but the main existing pantheoretical notion of the relationship—Rogers' (1957) notion of the necessary and sufficient conditions—seemed too tied to only the therapist's contributions and too embedded in client-centered therapy (Gelso & Carter, 1985).

Bordin's (1975, 1979) theory of the working alliance seemed truly pantheoretical and integrative, and, in a profound way, included the therapist and client as cocreators of the alliance. Because of these features, the notion had wide appeal. From a research standpoint, in our view, the greatest impetus to interest in the working alliance was the creation of measures. When a measure is at once reliable, valid, *and* convenient, it stirs the minds and hearts of researchers; among the existing measures, the WAI (Horvath, 1982; Horvath & Greenberg, 1989) seems to have had that effect. The fact that it is pantheoretical has only added to its appeal.

As is so common in the life of a theoretical construct, as the concept of alliance has mushroomed, multiple meanings and terms have also emerged. In particular, the terms *working alliance, therapeutic alliance* (e.g., Henry & Strupp, 1994), *helping alliance* (e.g., Luborsky, 1976), or simply *alliance* (Horvath et al., 1993) all seem to be part of our current language—often meaning the same thing and yet often meaning somewhat different things (see Gaston, 1990). In keeping with Greenson (1965, 1967), Bordin (1979, 1994), and others, we prefer the term *working alliance* to other terms because it better gets at the idea of the participants' coming together for the purpose of the work of therapy. Other concepts, such as transference (Chapter 3), countertransference (Chapter 4), and real relationship (see Chapter 5), address components of the total relationship that do not include the idea of joining for the purpose of the work.

As the general concept of alliance has gained prominence, some authors have equated alliance with relationship, as if the alliance was the relationship in its totality. In our view, conceptual lumping of this sort is not useful; ultimately, it hinders understanding of important distinctions about the therapy relationship (see Horvath & Greenberg, 1994, for a similar view).

THE WORKING ALLIANCE AND OTHER RELATED CONCEPTS

Although the major components of the psychotherapy relationship, including working alliance, have connections to a number of other theoretical constructs and conceptions, there are two conceptions to which these components are most intimately related: Carl Rogers' conception of the "necessary and sufficient conditions" for constructive change in psychotherapy (Rogers, 1957), and John Bowlby's theory of attachment (Bowlby, 1969/1982, 1973, 1980). We consider these related constructs in this section.

(In Chapters 3–5, we also examine the role of the Rogers conditions and Bowlby's attachment theory in the development of transference, counter-transference, and real relationship.)

FACILITATIVE CONDITIONS AND THE WORKING ALLIANCE

Carl Rogers' (1957) statement of the necessary and sufficient conditions for constructive change in therapy has perhaps been the most heuristically valuable theory ever presented in the field of psychotherapy. It has generated a huge amount of research over the more than 40 years since it was first offered. It speaks to practitioners, and it has deeply influenced therapy training and practice. As we read the current scene, its influence on practice is still very strong.

Although Rogers actually specified six conditions that were necessary and sufficient for change, the bulk of research and clinical attention (including Rogers' own work) was given to the three therapist conditions: (a) empathic understanding, (b) unconditional positive regard (or, simply, positive regard), and (c) congruence. These conditions were seen by Rogers as both attitudes of the therapist and qualities to be communicated by the therapist to the client. When considering Rogers' conception, we prefer the term *facilitative conditions*, because most now agree that the conditions are generally not sufficient, and there is some evidence that, at times, the conditions are not all necessary (Gelso & Carter, 1985; Gelso & Fretz, 1992).

It seems clear that these facilitative conditions are related to the working alliance, and such a relationship has been solidly documented for at least one of the conditions. Horvath and Greenberg (1989) found that therapist empathy was strongly related to a measure of the alliance, with the overlap between the two generally around 50%. Our view is that there is a reciprocal and synergistic relationship between the conditions and the alliance (cf. Gelso & Carter, 1985). Therapist empathy, regard, and congruence serve to build and strengthen the working alliance, and the alliance in turn deeply influences how the work of therapy proceeds. What may be less obvious is that the alliance also influences the client's perceptions of the conditions. For example, when the working alliance is strong, the client is more likely to perceive or to "take in" the therapist's empathy and regard. Also, as the alliance strengthens, it is likely that the therapist will in fact experience and communicate more empathy and regard, and will be freer to be *congruent*, in the sense that Rogers intended, i.e., a consistency between inner experience and outer expression—genuineness.

Although we are suggesting an important relationship between Rogers' conditions and the working alliance, there are also important differences (Gelso & Carter, 1985; Horvath & Greenberg, 1989). The major difference is that whereas the conditions are therapist-offered and client-received, the working alliance is by definition an interactional construct. The parties come together to form the alliance interactively. Although either the therapist or the client may contribute more to this alliance building (or deterioration), the concept itself is inherently interactive.

As will be amplified in subsequent chapters, clinical experience suggests that the necessary and sufficient conditions are related to the transference configuration and the real relationship, as well as to the working alliance. Thus, all three relationship components are influenced by and have an impact on the conditions. The nature of this influence will be discussed in Chapters 3–5.

ATTACHMENT AND THE WORKING ALLIANCE

Originated by John Bowlby (1969/1982, 1973, 1980, 1988), and furthered by the landmark empirical studies on mothers and infants by Mary Ainsworth (Ainsworth, Blehar, Waters, & Wall, 1978), attachment theory has become one of the most vigorously investigated theories in developmental and personality psychology in recent years. Because the psychotherapy relationship is an interpersonal attachment—often, a profound one—it is not surprising that therapy researchers and practitioners have also shown great interest in a theory with the label "attachment theory" (cf. Dolan, Arnkoff, & Glass, 1993; Farber, Lippert, & Nevas, 1995). The working alliance also represents a two-person attachment, so it is useful to consider how the alliance relates to attachment theory.

Attachment theory contains several key concepts that have a bearing on the formation and maintenance of client-therapist working alliances. The need to seek and form attachments, as a way of enhancing felt security, is seen as inherent in human beings. Attachment theory revolves around such needs. Infants seek attachments with their primary caregivers—usually, their mothers. Based on these caregivers' responses, infants' attachment experiences become represented as *working models of self and others* (the extent to which self is worthy of love and care, and others are loving, dependable caregivers). Infants and children who have healthy, secure attachments are able to explore their worlds with confidence and effectively regulate their emotions. By being emotionally responsive and accessible, their early attachment figures have provided them with a *secure base*.

Based on her infant research, Ainsworth and her colleagues (Ainsworth et al., 1978) identified three basic attachment styles that infants seem to develop: (a) secure, (b) anxious-ambivalent, and (c) avoidant. Main, Kaplan, and Cassidy (1985) have suggested a fourth style: (d) disorganized/disoriented. Generally, research supports the stability of these styles throughout early childhood and within middle-class families (Elicker, Englund, & Stroufe, 1992; Main et al., 1985).

Attachment theory would suggest that these styles emanate from the emerging working model of self and others in the infant and child. Recent work has focused on adult attachment styles, which appear, in turn, to emanate from the infant/child styles. For example, Bartholomew and Horowitz (1991) have theorized and empirically supported the following four-group taxonomy of adult attachment styles, based on working models of self and others: (a) secure style (positive self, positive other); (b) preoccupied style (negative self, positive other); (c) dismissing style (positive self, negative other); and (d) fearful style (negative self, negative other). One can readily see the infant counterparts to these adult styles (preoccupied = anxious/ambivalent; dismissive = avoidant; fearful = disorganized/disoriented).

How does attachment theory relate to the concept of working alliance? Can attachment theory help inform our understanding of working alliance in therapy? To begin with, it is critical that the therapist provide the client with a secure base. In doing so, the therapist strengthens the working alliance. In turn, a strong working alliance allows for the secure base the client must have if she or he is to explore difficult, threatening affects and experiences in the session, as well as behaviors outside the session.

How the therapist provides a secure base is, in fact, part and parcel of how one promotes a sound working alliance. Witness Holmes's (1993) summary of what makes for a secure base in therapy:

> . . . to be available regularly and reliably; to be courteous, compassionate, and caring; to be able to set limits and have clear boundaries; to protect the therapy from interruptions and distractions; and not to burden the patient with his own [the therapist's] difficulties and preoccupations. (p. 153)

An additional way in which attachment theory can help us understand working alliance is through our clients' current attachment styles, as well as their histories of attachments. One may expect, for example, that clients with less secure attachment histories (e.g., with their parents) will have more trouble forming and maintaining a sound alliance. Likewise, clients with secure current attachment styles would more readily develop sound alliances than would those with preoccupied, dismissive, or fearful styles. Relatedly, although certain responses from the therapist ought to enhance alliance for clients of any attachment style, some methods of alliance building by the therapist may also need to vary according to the attachment style of the client. Clients with any one of the four styles may differ in what they will need from their therapists in order to experience therapy as a secure base. This question is worth examination by researchers and practitioners.

The therapist's attachment history and style also enter into the equation in the development and maintenance of the working alliance. Because of this, therapists would do well to reflect on their attachment behavior and issues, and on how these relate to the development of working alliances with individual clients. The connection of therapist attachment style and history to both working alliance and other aspects of the therapist's contribution to the relationship (e.g., countertransference) is a fertile ground for research.

Some research, most notably the work of Mallinckrodt and his associates, has recently examined the relationship of attachment to working alliance. Mallinckrodt, Coble, and Gantt (1995b), for example, found that attachment memories (of parents' caring and overprotection) held by women clients, as well as current attachment styles of these clients, related significantly to the quality of working alliance during brief psychotherapy. Mallinckrodt, Gantt, and Coble (1995), in a second study, found that clients' patterns or styles of attachment to therapists were similar to clients' attachment styles as children and adults. They also found that these patterns of adult attachment and attachment to therapist were related to strength of working alliance. Such research gives therapists and researchers a sound beginning in trying to understand how attachment relates to working alliance.

BUILDING THE WORKING ALLIANCE

As we have noted, the working alliance is an interactional concept; both the therapist and the client contribute a share. From the first moment of their interaction, both are involved in the roles of their joint venture. The therapist adheres to his or her theoretically prescribed role, using the techniques suggested by his or her theory (whether the theory is formal or informal), and seeks to portray the attitudes that are important according to the therapist's theory (e.g., investigative attitude, empathic attitude). The client must more or less adhere to the role asked of him or her by the therapist. He or she must find this role agreeable in general terms, although some aspects of the client's role may be experienced as disagreeable. As these roles are enacted, the working alliance develops, often imperceptibly.

THE THERAPIST'S ROLE IN BUILDING AND PRESERVING THE ALLIANCE

The therapist's techniques and attitudes are important in developing the alliance. The effective use of techniques that are experienced as acceptable and helpful to the client is important in the formation and maintenance of the working alliance. For example, most clients would find some techniques acceptable and helpful, and other techniques not acceptable or helpful. The techniques used by psychoanalysts and behavior therapists are likely to appeal to different clients who experience different problems. As an example of efficacy in usage, the consistently effective use of the technique of *interpretation* communicates to the client that the therapist knows what he or she is doing and understands the client. This surely enhances the client's investment in the alliance.

As noted, the therapist also contributes to the alliance through certain attitudes. Among these are: respect for the client; the facilitative conditions of empathy, regard, and congruence; an abiding interest in the client's well-being; a sincere desire to be of help therapeutically; and, last but not least, patience.

As the work proceeds, the therapist needs to pay close attention to the unfolding alliance; the aim, initially, is to build and strengthen it. As therapy continues, the therapist seeks to maintain the working alliance. This alliance, once formed, generally tends to recede into the background, coming forth under conditions of threat. For example, lapses in the therapist's empathic attunement may produce ruptures in the alliance (Safran, Muran, & Samstag, 1994). Or, the client's negative transference may present a threat to the alliance. When the alliance is thus ruptured or threatened, the therapist needs to take steps to repair it.

The repair may come through either technical intervention or the expression of certain attitudes. In our supervision, we have noticed a tendency, especially among less experienced therapists, to view alliance formation and repair as simply a function of the kinds of attitudes noted above. In fact, we would offer that, at times, technical intervention is critical in preserving the working alliance. For example, when the client's transference-based negative feelings toward the therapist or therapy are invading the work, effective interpretations may be vital to the alliance. Although the therapist surely must empathically grasp the client's feelings, the client may also need to understand that he or she is reacting negatively to unresolved issues from another time and place. This assumes that the culprit is transference, and not some actual error (attitudinal or technical) on the part of the therapist. When the client's negative reaction is a response to the therapist's error, the therapist needs to face and address the error with the client.

In sum, when the therapist does his or her job (including the attitudinal part) competently, he or she contributes crucially to the alliance formation and preservation. This goes beyond Freud's "sympathetic understanding," although surely that must be part of it.

The Client's Role in the Alliance

Because the working alliance is an interactional concept, the client's contribution must also be understood. As discussed early in this chapter, the bases for the client's participation in the working alliance are: his or her desire to heal and grow in one way or another, and his or her willingness to cooperate with the tasks that are asked of him or her in the treatment and as a result of the treatment. Because the working alliance includes a bonding or attachment between the participants, the client must have the willingness and basic ability to form a *healthy* working bond. The qualities needed by the client in order to do so will be discussed later in the chapter, in our theoretical Proposition 6, regarding clients' contributions to the working alliance.

THEORETICAL PROPOSITIONS ABOUT THE WORKING ALLIANCE

Against the background of the preceding discussion, we are now ready to offer theoretical statements about the operation of the working alliance in brief and longer-term psychotherapy. In this section, we suggest nine basic propositions about the role and impact of the working alliance in different therapies; its unfolding during the treatment process; client and therapist contributions to the alliance formation and maintenance; the different types of alliance that are possible; and the interaction of working alliance with both transference and real relationship.

Our theoretical propositions are based on many sources: our own experience in conducting brief and long-term psychotherapy; our work in supervising graduate student trainees as well as more experienced therapists; existing theoretical papers; and empirical research on the working alliance and related constructs. Our aims in presenting these propositions are: to guide practitioners as they work with their clients to develop and maintain healthy alliances; and to provide a stimulus to research on the working alliance. Whenever possible, we have sought to connect our propositions to research findings.

Prior to presenting the propositions, we state, as an overarching theoretical proposition: *The working alliance has a significant positive impact on the outcomes of both brief and longer-term psychotherapy.* In many ways, this proposition comes from the fact that it is hard to imagine effective therapy occurring in the absence of a sound alliance. In this sense, the alliance is seen as a necessary, although probably insufficient, condition for successful treatment. Research support for this general proposition is substantial, as indicated by the meta-analysis conducted by Horvath and Symonds (1991). These researchers synthesized the results of 24 studies and found clear evidence for the positive effects of the working alliance on outcome, regardless of duration of treatment.

In what ways does the alliance affect outcome? We suggest that there are at least three salient ways. First, as proposed by Gaston and Marmar (1994), the alliance has an effect in and of itself, just as a good relationship between the therapist and the client will have an effect above and beyond the technical interventions of the therapist. The curative effect of the working alliance was one of the major findings of the classic Menninger study of 42 patients in various forms of psychoanalytic therapy over a period of 20 years (Horwitz, 1974). In contrast to the expectations of the researchers, the alliance in and of itself was one of the most potent sources of constructive change.

In addition to its direct curative effects, the working alliance also affects outcome through helping clients become more receptive to the therapist's technical interventions. Thus, when the working alliance is strong, the client is more likely to "take in" the therapist's interpretations in analytic therapy (Gaston & Marmar, 1994), or to follow the therapist's homework instructions in behavior therapy.

A third way in which the working alliance influences success in therapy is through serving as a buffer against the many stresses and strains that will occur during treatment. Perhaps the most influential, although at times the subtlest, stress derives from the client's negative transferences. Transference-based negative reactions can poison any therapy if they are not checked or mollified by a strong working alliance. In this sense, the working alliance immunizes the client from "infections" caused by negative transference and other stresses.

Let us now move on to our formal propositions about the working alliance.

1. *It is important that a "good enough" working alliance be established relatively early, if treatment is to be successful.*

In many cases, therapists and clients experience an initial "clicking"; they sense they are on the same wavelength, both personally and in their efforts to help resolve the clients' miseries. Although we conceptualize this clicking as emanating largely from the real relationship (see the discussion in Chapter 5), and, to a lesser extent, from transference, such initial clicking is usually indicative of the speedy development of a sound working alliance. The participants have a sense of joining together in their efforts, and there tends to be agreement on the goals of the work as well as the tasks that will move the client toward those goals. At least the rudiments of interpersonal attachment and collaboration are present. Bordin (1994) has offered that, in his experience, a viable initial level of alliance is almost invariably formed within a single session for clients who do not have severe pathology. Our experience, similar to Bordin's, suggests that a "good enough alliance" is generally formed at least within the first few sessions. Conversely, the existence of a very weak alliance in the first few sessions appears to be an ominous sign, unless both the therapist and the client have great amounts of motivation and time to accomplish the work.

In long-term psychotherapy, authors often note that more extended periods of time are needed to develop sound working alliances. Greenson (1967), for example, marked the first six months as the time line for sound alliance formation in classical psychoanalysis. Our clinical experiences suggest an alternative view: that even in long-term, exploratory therapy, a "good enough alliance" (similar to Bordin's viable alliance) needs to be established very early. This alliance may need to deepen, to allow for the difficult work of long-term uncovering therapy, but the good enough alliance must still be there early if the work is to move forward in an effective way. Within this good enough alliance, the parties must agree on the goals and tasks of therapy, and the working bond must have a sound beginning.

This general proposition is moderated by several variables; among them are the client's capacity to form healthy attachments, the nature of the psychotherapy being conducted, and the duration of the treatment. We shall explore these more complex interactions in some of the following propositions.

The research literature provides substantial support for this early-alliance proposition. Most notably, Horvath and Symond's (1991) meta-analysis of 24 outcome studies indicated that the alliance as measured in the first few sessions (up to the fifth session) correlated significantly with the outcome. Also, the alliance as measured in the first few sessions was just as predictive of outcome as were the alliance measures taken near the end of therapy. Similarly, Henry and Strupp (1994, p. 78), when integrating findings from their research program, suggested that "the alliance is either well-formed or fails to form early in therapy (the first three sessions)."

2. *Although the early formation of a sound alliance is important in all therapy, it is especially important in brief therapy.*

In long-term therapy, the therapist has the luxury of time. If the initial alliance is weak, time allows for the cultivation of a stronger alliance, provided both parties are motivated for this often arduous task. In brief therapy, by definition, there is limited time to strengthen a weak working alliance. Given the variability in definitions of the term *brief* (e.g., from a few sessions up to about 25 sessions), we also suggest that, within the parameters of brief therapy, the briefer the work, the earlier the appearance of a viable or good enough working alliance is needed. If, for example, an agency requires the establishment of a six-session duration limit, the appearance of a viable alliance is probably necessary within about the first session. On the other hand, with a six-month treatment (24 weekly sessions), more time is available for the development of the alliance.

Although this second proposition has never been tested directly, there is indirect support for it. For example, in one of the studies in the University of Maryland's Time-Limited Therapy Research Program (Gelso & Johnson, 1983), intensive, semistructured interviews were conducted with a small number of clients (n = 4) who appeared to have profited a great deal from 12 sessions of time-limited therapy. When an effort was launched to find out what made for success in the brief therapy, the pervasive themes among these former clients were: the existence of a very strong working alliance, and the absence of negative power struggles or more general negative reactions that the authors noted may appear and be worked through in long-term work (Adelstein, Gelso, Haws, Reed, & Spiegel, 1983).

In another study (Gelso, Mills, & Spiegel, 1983), it was found that therapists' expectations of enjoyment in working with clients, when rated after a first session, were significantly related to client-rated outcome 18 months after termination, when the clients had received time-limited therapy. The same relationship was not found among those in open-ended counseling (which lasted about twenty sessions, as opposed to

seven or eight sessions for the time-limited group). To the extent that expected "enjoyment" is indicative of working alliance, this study supports
the idea that early alliance is more important in briefer work.

What can the therapist do to foster speedy alliances with various types
of clients in brief, symptom-oriented therapy? This is a high-priority
question for researchers and practitioners, especially in the current
sociopolitical climate's emphasis on brevity and symptom remission in
psychological treatment.

We do know some of the ingredients in a positive early alliance. For example, Al-Darmaki and Kivlighan (1993) found that counselor and client
congruence in expectations for their relationship (around issues of spontaneous self-disclosure, egalitarianism, etc.) was related to early measures of working alliance. Many other ingredients have been noted
earlier in this chapter. As Bordin (1994) has told us of his experience, viable alliances are readily formed within one session with mildly to moderately neurotic clients. But we know little about how to successfully
develop speedy alliances with the more difficult and more disturbed
clients. Can the expected alliance difficulties with more profoundly disturbed and/or less securely attached clients be overcome by therapist intervention (see Gelso, 1992; Steenbarger, 1992)? Clinical observation,
theory, and research are badly needed here.

3. *Especially in treatments that abbreviate duration, an initially sound alliance will subsequently decline, but in successful therapy this decline will be followed by an increase to earlier high levels of alliance.*

Clinical experience and research both suggest that, in successful therapy, an early sound alliance is followed by conflicts that cause the alliance to deteriorate somewhat. The reasons for this decline are many. For
example, after the initial formation of the alliance, and due to an increase
in the therapist's evolving understanding of the client's issues, the therapist begins to deal more directly, perhaps more confrontationally, with
what might variously be labeled the client's resistances, problematical
way of relating, neurotic style, pathogenic habits, or core conflictual
theme. In time-abbreviated treatments, after an initial sense that all is
going well, the client confronts the reality of ending therapy soon. The
warm initial glow dims somewhat when this occurs (see, e.g., Mann,
1973). The therapist's confrontation of the client's issues—and, in abbre-
viated therapies, the added issue of time limitation—causes the alliance
to decline after the initial positive experience.

In successful therapy, however, the decline is temporary. As the therapist continues to do his or her work—empathically dealing with the

client's issues from the therapist's theoretical position—the core issues become at least better understood and placed into a healthier perspective, if not resolved. The client in time-abbreviated treatment comes to accept the reality of time limitation and of ending therapy. As the client accepts these realities, the alliance again strengthens.

In less successful treatments, different patterns may occur. An initially weak alliance may never strengthen; there may be a decline in the alliance without a return to a higher level, or the decline may never occur. The latter, rather than being a healthy sign, may suggest that the therapist and client are not properly confronting difficult issues. The therapy may be coasting (Horvath et al., 1993), or the therapist and client may be defensively colluding to avoid the difficult core problems, or the client's resistances may be too strong to allow the necessary working through.

The return to former, higher levels in successful therapy does not imply that early and later working alliances are the same. Luborsky (1976), in one of the first empirical studies of alliance, suggested two types of helping alliances. Type 1 occurred in the early phase of the work and was based on the patient's perception of the therapist as supportive and helpful. Type 2 occurred later and was based on a sense of mutual collaboration—the two participants were seen as working together to overcome the patient's problems. A greater sense of "we-ness" occurs in the second type. Horvath and Greenberg (1994) discuss "mature alliances" occurring in the later stages of therapy.

Research support for the high-low-high pattern of working alliance, at least in time-limited interventions, comes from several sources. In one of the studies in the University of Maryland Time-Limited Therapy Research Program (J. M. Miller et al., 1983), it was found that client resistance, as assessed by therapists of various theoretical orientations, increased during the middle phase of therapy and subsequently decreased. Similarly, Golden and Robbins (1990) intensively studied two cases of time-limited therapy and found that, from the viewpoint of both the therapist and the client, alliance dropped during the middle phase of therapy but rose again later on. This finding also occurred in Horvath and Marx's (1990) study of four cases. Kivlighan and Shaugnessy (1995) were able to connect the high-low-high pattern to outcome. They found that when the initial level of working alliance was statistically controlled, the high-low-high pattern of alliance was more predictive of positive therapy results than were other patterns. More research is needed on how variations in the alliance across treatment are related to outcomes.

4. *The importance of the working alliance waxes and wanes during various phases of treatment, and the alliance is especially important during crises in the relationship.*

As Greenson (1967) noted, the working alliance generally emerges silently, although therapists often sense its development—or, perhaps more accurately, sense when something is amiss in the working alliance. After the initial development, it appears that the alliance recedes into the background. The therapist and client experience a positive working connection, and the therapy proceeds from some explicit or implicit theoretical position adhered to by the therapist and agreeable to the client.

The alliance only becomes salient again when problems or crises occur in the relationship. At such points, the alliance again emerges as figure rather than ground. Crises in the relationship generally come from two often related sources. First, negative transference can seriously undermine the relationship and the working alliance. Paradoxically, just as the alliance can be injured by negative transference, so can the alliance be a crucial source of buffering the relationship against the potential injuries inflicted by negative transference. Thus, when the client-therapist relationship is threatened by the client's negative feelings and projections stemming from the transference, the working alliance allows the client to stand back from these feelings and projections, and to try to understand what they are about. This task of "standing back" and seeking to understand is aided greatly by an already existing solid alliance, which is why very early and strong negative transference can be so damaging. The alliance has not had a chance to strengthen sufficiently beyond the early "good enough" development to preserve the relationship in the face of such onslaughts.

A second and related source of crises is the ruptures in the alliance due to therapist errors. These may entail technical errors (e.g., inaccurate or premature interpretations), but in our experience they most often revolve around empathic failures on the part of the therapist (cf. Safran, Crocker, McMain, & Murray, 1990). In fact, we would suggest that technical errors, such as poorly timed interpretations or homework assignments, arise from the therapist's empathic failures more than from any other source.

Here we must add that we do not use empathy in the sense of a communication skill; we regard it as an internal experience—specifically, the therapist's understanding of the client, arising from vicarious partial identification with the client. This understanding becomes expressed in some form, if only vaguely and indirectly, and that expression gets transmitted to the client. Misunderstanding, or empathic failure, can be similarly transmitted. Such empathic failures can profoundly injure the alliance, but if the emerging alliance is healthy enough, and if the therapist is able to grasp the empathic failure, the rupture in the alliance can generally be healed. The healing or resolution of ruptures, ironically, can have a strengthening effect on the alliance. But, again, during the crisis, the alliance surely becomes figure rather than ground.

This second source of crises in the relationship—therapist error, generally due to empathic failures—is related to negative transference because transference issues are likely to be involved in the client's response to the error. Empathic failures may be most painful and difficult for the client when they involve areas of unresolved conflict or trauma—areas from which transference is most likely to also arise. For example, the therapist's failure to empathically grasp the client's deep feelings around an area of intense trauma is most likely to stir up in the client not only negative feelings but negative transference. The client may then project a range of negative feelings and motives onto the therapist, and may be pained by the misunderstanding in a way that seems to go far beyond the actual event. Thus, the therapist's empathic error, painful in itself, may also stir up negative transference. Together, they seriously threaten the working alliance.

The ideas we have discussed under this proposition are related to a number of theoretical concepts and studies of what has been called the "strain or rupture and repair" of the working alliance. Led by investigators such as Bordin (1989, 1994) and Safran (Safran et al., 1990; Safran et al., 1994), therapy has been seen as a series of strains or ruptures in the alliance, which are then repaired by the therapist's efforts. Safran's work focuses on therapist-induced strains (e.g., through empathic failures), and he has been able to empirically identify markers for strains in the relationship, and ways in which therapists can repair the alliance. In an important qualitative study, Rhodes, Hill, Thompson, and Elliott (1994) found that therapist misunderstandings could seriously damage the alliance, and such misunderstandings were best resolved if the relationship was solid to begin with, if clients were willing to assert themselves, and if therapists maintained a flexible and accepting stance.

Bordin (1989, 1994) has been more concerned with strains or ruptures in the working alliance due to the manifestation of clients' issues and defenses rather than therapist factors. Bordin's focus is similar to our idea of the relationship being invaded by transference. In both Bordin's and our conceptions, it is essential that therapists seek to help clients understand how their issues are playing out in the therapy in a way that is hindering the alliance. Helping clients gain such understanding requires empathy, skill, and a sense of timing on the part of therapists. Working on the sort of rupture that is due to client issues can help clients work through pathogenic styles or patterns both in and outside of therapy. Moreover, the waxing and waning of the alliance in terms of importance or salience, and the idea of strains/ruptures and repairs, are some of the most vital areas of emerging research and thought on the working alliance.

5. *Within and between different kinds or genres of therapy, the strength of the alliance that is required for successful treatment varies according to the difficulty of the treatment.*

Bordin (1979) has asserted that therapies from different theoretical orientations (e.g., dynamic versus behavioral) require different types of working alliances. As earlier noted, Gelso and Carter (1985) go a step beyond Bordin and suggest that therapies vary in their "difficulty level" for clients, in terms of both the goals of the therapy and the client tasks required to attain those goals. Some therapies place greater, more difficult demands on clients than do others. *Difficulty,* as we use the term, refers to a range of phenomena, such as the psychological threat to or vulnerability required of the client, the extensiveness of the therapy's goals, the compatibility of the treatment's demands with the emotional capabilities of the client, the overall effort required of the client, and so on.

Following this definition of difficulty, we would predict that briefer therapies would be less difficult than longer therapies, more intensive therapies (greater frequency of visits) would be more difficult than less intensive therapies, and perhaps more uncovering therapies would be more difficult than less uncovering therapies within the same theoretical orientation. In their earlier work, Gelso and Carter (1985) had suggested that insight-oriented therapies would generally require stronger alliances than action-oriented therapies because the insight therapies would demand more of their clients. Demand would be greater in the insight therapies because the deep self-exploration that is a hallmark of such treatments would require greater vulnerability from the client and would be much more threatening to the client. Subsequent research and clinical experience, however, have not supported this hypothesis. In retrospect, action may be just as "difficult" for some clients as insight is for others. Which of the two is more difficult, in other words, is likely a matter of individual differences.

Virtually no research exists on the topic of strength of alliance needed for therapies of varying "difficulty levels." Regarding the insight-vs.-action distinction, results clearly indicate that working alliance is equally important to outcome in the different approaches (Horvath, 1991; Krup-nick, Stotsky, Simmens, & Moyer, 1992). Furthermore, at least one study indicates that, if anything, alliances in the cognitive-behavioral therapies are stronger than those in dynamic-interpersonal therapies (Raue, Cas-tonguay, & Goldfried, 1993); another found no difference in strength of alliances among expressive, cognitive, and supportive therapy (Salvio, Beutler, Wood, & Engle, 1992). No studies to date have directly examined the level of alliance needed for successful outcome in therapies of differ-ing theoretical orientations, e.g., insight-vs.-action therapies.

6. *Clients vary in their ability to form working alliances, and certain client factors are related to strength of alliance.*

Research and clinical experience are in accord in suggesting a range of client qualities that are important in forming and maintaining a sound working alliance. Most fundamentally, the working alliance requires that clients have a desire to heal and grow, as well as a willingness to cooper-ate with the therapist. Clients who have these qualities to a high degree are surely more likely to form a sound alliance, and clients who have too little or too conflicted a desire to grow or a willingness to cooperate surely have at least two strikes against them in the work of therapy. If suc-cess is going to occur with these clients, other positive client qualities are needed, as well as therapists of extraordinary skill.

Our reading of the research and our clinical experience suggest three interdependent clusters of client predisposing characteristics that fig-ure most basically into the formation and maintenance of a sound al-liance (see reviews by Horvath, 1991; Horvath & Greenberg, 1994). First and perhaps foremost, because the working alliance requires the client's willingness/ability to form an interpersonal attachment, clients need to have had at least some positive attachment experiences in their lives, and thus a working model of others (see the earlier review of attachment theory) as "safe enough" to allow for a working bond. Those with the poorest histories of attachment will be the most difficult; their connec-tion with early figures is filled with mistrust, anxiety, and rage. This early attachment notion has received empirical support from a number of studies (e.g., Kokotovic & Tracey, 1990; Mallinckrodt, Coble, et al., 1995b; Piper et al., 1991).

A second cluster relates to the client's cooperativeness. The client needs at least a modicum of cooperation, or at least not such profound op-positionalism that developing agreement on goals and tasks is impossi-ble. Relatedly, we have already noted the finding by Horvath et al. (1993)

that willingness to collaborate (similar to cooperativeness or low opposi-tional behavior) undergirded all extant measures of alliance.

A third cluster of client predisposing factors for the formation and maintenance of a sound working alliance revolves around the construct of self-efficacy. In particular, if clients are to form an alliance, they need to have a sufficient belief that they can grow from therapy, that the work of therapy can be done with "sufficient" success, and, most basically, that they themselves are capable of growth in therapy. This sense of efficacy regarding treatment and self may be very tentative and precarious to begin with. The client may possess initial doubt, but there has to be, at the core, a degree of optimism that he or she can "succeed" in therapy. In contrast, we suggest that when the client has a pervasive disbelief or doubt that he or she can grow from therapy, the prognosis for the develop-ment of a viable working alliance is dire. Research supports the idea that when patients have little initial hope for success in therapy, poorer al-liances are likely (Ryan & Cicchetti, 1985).

Although a number of other client factors have been documented as being related to quality of working alliance (see Horvath & Greenberg, 1994, p. 274), it seems to us that the above factors are most fundamental, can incorporate most other factors, and account for much of the variance in alliance determined by client factors. A major therapeutic task revolves around how therapists can foster at least "good enough" working al-liances with clients who are low on any or all of the above three clusters. That is, are there approaches that will help develop and maintain effec-tive alliances in clients who appear to be low on a scale of potential for al-liance? This question would also be a key one for researchers to address.

7. *Therapists, too, vary in their ability to form working alliances, and certain therapist factors are related to strength of alliance.*

Just as with the client, a range of therapist factors are likely to be im-plicated in alliance formation and maintenance. First, and perhaps fore-most, the therapist's possession of Rogers' (1957) necessary and sufficient conditions, or what we refer to as the facilitative conditions—empathic understanding, positive regard, and congruence—must play a major role in the formation and maintenance of a working alliance. It is essential that these facilitative conditions be both experienced within the therapist and communicated to the client. It is hard to imagine a sound alliance being established or preserved when these conditions are present to a low degree. Studies are available (e.g., Bachelor, 1995) that powerfully docu-ment the importance clients place on such facilitative conditions in their working alliances. Also, as noted earlier, there is evidence of a substantial relationship between at least one of the facilitative conditions (empathic understanding) and a working alliance (Horvath & Greenberg, 1989; Safran et al., 1990).

A second therapist ingredient that seems important in alliance formation and maintenance is what might be called a willingness to take appropriate responsibility for the therapist's own contributions to problems in the alliance. It is all too easy for therapists to focus on the client's issues, which will surely exist, and bypass or defend against an awareness of their own issues and limitations. We believe that taking appropriate responsibility is of fundamental importance for the working alliance. A qualitative study of therapist misunderstandings, by Rhodes and her colleagues (1994), is telling in this respect. In clients' eyes, one of the most important things a therapist can do to resolve misunderstandings that occur in the relationship is to accept the client's feelings and own his or her share of the misunderstandings. A therapist's denial of his or her share was found to have a deteriorative effect on the alliance.

A third therapist factor pertains to the therapist's past object relations. Like clients, therapists vary in the quality of their past object relations; those with sound working models of self and others, based on their history of attachments, should be more likely to form and maintain healthier alliances with clients. Henry and Strupp (1994) strongly support this therapist factor. They found that therapists' internal representation of past relationships (working models, in attachment terms) had a pronounced effect on the alliances they formed. We should note that the therapists' personal therapy may play a vital role for those who have had a history of poor interpersonal relationships and attachments. Attachment patterns can be modified by therapy, and the importance of such modification for therapists with attachment issues can be deeply important for the quality of working alliances of which the therapist is capable.

Other therapist factors that are very hard to measure are also likely to play an important role in alliance development. It seems to us that the therapist's abiding investment in the work, and his or her commitment to the patient, must affect alliance. Also, a factor that might be labeled "skillfulness" would appear to be at work in alliance formation and maintenance, although this concept has been a hard one for researchers to pin down. Skill in the use of techniques, in handling the session, and in understanding what the client is about would all seem to influence the alliance.

Research on therapist contributions was conducted at a high rate during the 1960s and 1970s, as a response to Rogers' (1957) theoretical pronouncements about the facilitative conditions. Since then, relatively little has been done. As Horvath and Greenberg (1994) note, this decline may have been due to an increased interest in manualizing therapy and, in effect, designing the therapist factor out of the equation. Recently, though, interest in therapist factors has revived, corresponding perhaps to attention to the working alliance. We believe that therapist factors cannot be "manualized away"; they need to remain of central interest in theory and research on the working alliance. Continued research on therapist factors will be important in helping us understand what goes into alliance formation and preservation.

8. *Type as well as strength of working alliances will vary for different clients, depending on these clients' needs.*

In the preceding material, we have discussed working alliance as if it meant the same thing to all clients, and as if the same elements constituted the alliance for all clients. In fact, some preliminary evidence (Bachelor, 1995) suggests that there may be different types of alliances, based on clients' needs. Although nearly all clients may need some common ingredients in their working alliances (e.g., a climate of trust, understanding), Bachelor's (1995) qualitative-phenomenological study of clients' reports suggests that there may be three types of stable and relatively distinct working alliances: (a) nurturant alliances, (b) insight-oriented alliances, and (c) collaborative alliances. *Nurturant* alliances were marked by therapist facilitativeness as well as active directiveness; *insight-oriented* alliances, by the client's self-understanding, which was stimulated by the therapist's insight-oriented approach (e.g., clarification, interpretation); and *collaborative* alliances, by the sense of therapist and client working together and sharing joint responsibility for the work.

Although this research requires replication, it certainly makes clinical sense that different clients need different types of alliances. In addition, it seems likely to us that the type of working alliances that clients need or want will depend, to some extent, on the phase of treatment. As mentioned previously, early alliances are likely to incorporate some different features from later or more "mature" alliances. A growing edge of research and clinical understanding may be trying to understand what types of clients and client issues require what types of alliances at what points in treatment.

9. *The working alliance interacts with the transference configuration and real relationship in affecting process and outcome.*

Although our definitions of the three components of the psychotherapy relationship appear to suggest that the components operate independently, and while at times they may in fact do so, most often the three are in constant interaction with one another in a system of mutual influence. Thus, the working alliance is influenced by, and in turn influences, the transference configuration and the real relationship. This system of interacting processes forms the total relationship, and, together, the interacting processes affect the unfolding and outcome of treatment. The nature of the interactions of the working alliance, transference configuration, and real relationship will be explored in greater detail in Chapter 6.

CONCLUSION

As we have conceptualized it, the working alliance that emerges between the therapist and the client is the bedrock of therapy. All other processes depend on this alliance, and therapy could hardly proceed without a good enough alliance. The alliance is an interactive concept, formed by the joint and evolving contributions of client and therapist. Since Gelso and Carter's (1985) first theoretical work on the working alliance, a substantial amount of research and theory has been produced, and, in virtually all systems of therapy, the alliance has taken its place among the key concepts of psychotherapy (as indicated by Horvath & Greenberg's, 1994, major book). Understanding of the working alliance is now most likely to be furthered by the study of complex interactions and relationships involving the client, the therapist, and the treatment factors that serve to form and preserve different kinds of alliances.

CHAPTER 3

Transference and Its Many Faces: The Unrealistic Relationship in Psychotherapy

T HE COMPONENT of the overall psychotherapy relationship that we address in this chapter has been, over many decades, a source of great controversy among psychotherapists. The construct, transference, also is undoubtedly among the most complex concepts in psychotherapy, as we shall discuss below.

The term *transference* seems to produce a visceral reaction in more therapists than perhaps any other construct in the field. In our experience, those who react in a highly negative way are usually responding to what they see as undesirable elements of the system out of which transference emanates more generally: psychoanalysis. Their reactions may be directed toward its historical tendencies to pathologize; to use too much jargon, with the effect of obfuscating rather than clarifying; to imbue the analyst with seeming omniscience; and to place too great an emotional distance between analyst and analysand. The concept of transference, however, need not be burdened with these difficulties.

Reflecting its controversial nature, on one side of the continuum some therapists see transference as a vital part of all psychotherapy relationships (indeed, all relationships) and a phenomenon that must be dealt with if treatment is to be effective. Therapists holding this viewpoint usually align themselves with one or another version of psychoanalytic theory. On the other side of the continuum are therapists who view transference as an artifact—a next-to-useless construct; a phenomenon that is manufactured by therapists and exists only in the minds of therapists. Therapists in this group are likely to define themselves theoretically as humanistic, experiential, or cognitive-behavioral.

The viewpoint we maintain is that transference is an ever present component of the psychotherapy relationship, and is present in all therapies, regardless of theoretical orientation. In contrast to psychoanalytic theories, we propose that there is no best way of dealing with client transference; it may be dealt with in a range of ways, or deliberately not dealt with at all. These views will be elaborated later in this chapter.

Perhaps because of the manifold reactions to transference, as well as the concept's inherent complexity, an enormous amount of theoretical and clinical material has been written about transference since Freud first discovered it. Yet, until recent years, there has been almost no empirical research aimed at understanding the process and the impact of client transference. The sheer complexity of the concept is the likely culprit here, along with the fact that psychoanalysis, the system to which transference has been tied, historically has exhibited notable indifference toward empirical research.

Transference is a concept that arises from and is embedded in psychoanalytic theory. It is seen by most analytic therapists as one of Freud's most central, profound, and creative discoveries (Fine, 1990; Schwaber, 1985). Even within psychoanalytic circles, however, just what is meant by the term is not clear; controversy about the basic definition persists.

In this chapter, we provide a historical sketch of the development of the construct of transference; clarify the contrasting definitions of transference; provide our own definition; and show how transference is related to other constructs in psychotherapy. We then offer eight theoretical propositions about how transference operates in psychotherapy and affects the therapy process and its outcomes in a range of treatment situations, in brief and longer-term therapy, and in therapies of varying theoretical persuasions. Findings from recent research are integrated into the discussion of these propositions.

HISTORICAL SKETCH AND CURRENT CONCEPTIONS: TOWARD AN INCLUSIVE DEFINITION OF TRANSFERENCE

Although Freud was occupied with the role and meaning of transference in psychoanalysis throughout his career, his earliest and most influential papers (S. Freud, 1905/1953, 1912/1959) provided the basis for subsequent statements. In his 1905 work, Freud gave an eloquent account of how his failure to recognize transference in his analysis of Dora resulted in a therapeutic failure. At that time, he offered the following views of transference:

> What are transferences? They are new editions or facsimiles of the impulses and phantasies which are aroused and made conscious during the progress of the analysis; but they have this peculiarity, which is characteristic of their species, that they replace some earlier person by the person of the physician. To put it another way: a whole series of psychological experiences are revived, not as belonging to the past, but as applying to the person of the physician at the present moment. Some of the transferences have a content which differs from that of their model in no respect whatever except for the substitution. These then—to keep the same metaphor—are merely new impressions or reprints. Others are more ingeniously constructed; their content has been subjected to a moderating influence—to *sublimation*, as I call it—and they may even become conscious, by cleverly taking advantage of some real peculiarity in the physician's person or circumstances and attaching themselves to that. These, then, will no longer be new impressions, but revised editions. (S. Freud, 1905/1953, p. 116)

As noted in Chapter 1, Freud's conception of transference was that the client material transferred to the person of the analyst was rooted in the client's Oedipal situation. That is, the Oedipus complex forms the nucleus out of which transference projections emerge, and what is transferred pertains to unresolved issues with mother or father, beginning in that early period of life.

It would be a mistake, however, to view Freud's conception of transference as consisting of only that singular viewpoint. Luborsky and Crits-Christoph (1990), for example, discuss 22 observations that Freud made about transference, many of which did not implicate the Oedipus Complex. Most fundamentally, Freud saw transference as a template or a central relationship pattern that serves as a prototype or a scheme for shaping subsequent relationships.

As we have noted, there is much current debate within psychoanalysis as to the definition of transference. Out of this debate, three fundamental definitions seem most prominent. The first, which is embedded in classical Freudian theory, views transference as a repetition and reliving of Oedipal issues in the current therapeutic relationship. The therapist is reacted to as if he or she were any or all of the participants in the client's early Oedipal situation (E. Singer, 1970).

The second definition is broader than the first. Transference is defined as a repetition of past conflicts with significant others, in such a way that feelings, attitudes, and behaviors belonging rightfully in those earlier relationships are displaced onto the therapist. This view is broader than the classical definition in that the source is not restricted to the Oedipal situation, but includes any crucial interpersonal relationships occurring at any point in the person's childhood. Relationship conflicts occurring before and after the Oedipal period may be the source, as may relationship difficulties with significant figures other than the person's parents. Within this conception is also the view that transference reactions have a reality base in the person's past; they may have been appropriate and adaptive at an earlier time and place. The original reactions (e.g., to one or both parents) served to protect the child's emerging self-esteem, rather than to avoid castration, as in classical theory. They served to make otherwise intolerable situations tolerable. The broadened view of transference is characteristic of interpersonal and neo-analytic theoreticians such as Sullivan (1954) and Fromm-Reichmann (1950). It is also consistent with many ego-analytic and object relations conceptions (Mishne, 1994).

Although the second definition is broader than the first, it still maintains the view of transference as an error, a distortion of sorts. The client reacts to the therapist in a way that is not befitting of the therapist, but is instead a carryover from past perceptions and unresolved issues with significant others.

The third view is more recent. Rooted in postmodern constructivist thought (Rabin, 1995), this view seeks to go beyond the conception of transference as distortion or error. Transference is an intersubjective process to which the client and the therapist contribute, and the therapist's job is to help the client understand the reality that both have created. The therapist contributes to the transference, but the client's construction is still of most fundamental interest. Thus, Stolorow and Lachmann (1984/1985) define transference as referring "to all the ways in which the patient's experience of the analytic relationship is shaped by his own psychological structures—by the distinctive, archaically rooted configurations of self and object that unconsciously organize his subjective universe" (p. 26). Seen from this perspective, transference is an unconscious organizing activity. The client assimilates the therapy relationship into his or her personal and subjective world. More than the other two definitions of transference, Stolorow (1991) contends: "This concept of transference as an organizing activity, rather than the client's distortion, explicitly invites attention to the activities of the therapist and the recurrent meanings these acquire for the patient" (p. 180).

The intersubjective view has the benefits of: directing therapists' attention to their contributions to the transference, and fostering attention to the ways in which the client's psychological structure shapes his or her experience of the therapeutic relationship. It also fosters a climate of collaboration: the therapist and client work together to understand the client's experience of the therapist, whether or not distortions are involved. However, at times, the intersubjective conception of transference seems too broad to be of optimum value scientifically. (The counterpart to this very broad conception in the area of countertransference is what has been referred to as the totalistic definition of countertransference, which is examined in Chapter 4.) Transference, according to the intersubjectivists, appears to encompass *all* of the ways in which the client experiences and makes meaning of the therapist that are shaped by that client's psychic structures. Because transference is so encompassing, it becomes difficult to determine what is *not* transference. We believe that more theoretical work is needed to differentiate patient reactions that represent transference from those that do not.

Our conception of transference maintains the concept of distortion, although not in any simple linear way. It is consistent with the second definition above, but also seeks to incorporate intersubjective thought. We define transference as: *the client's experience of the therapist that is shaped by the client's own psychological structures and past and involves displacement, onto the therapist, of feelings, attitudes, and behaviors belonging rightfully in earlier significant relationships.* Although in our conception transference does involve distortion of the therapist to some degree, this does not imply that the therapist should search for these distortions or even work directly with transference in all or nearly all cases. Furthermore, although distortion is involved, transference is never just distortion. In keeping with the intersubjective position, transference may be seen as the engagement of therapist and client such that old psychodynamic configurations in the client are activated within the context of the current relationship (see Richardson, 1997). As shall be discussed below, the person and activity of the therapist are always involved in the formation and expression of transference reactions.

Client perceptions, feelings, and attitudes in regard to the therapist that do not involve distortion are surely important; however, we believe it is most useful to view these as nontransference reactions. Such reactions are best seen as residing within the *real relationship,* as discussed in Chapter 5.

Several aspects of our conception of transference should be noted. First, as mentioned when discussing the intersubjective view, transference can be seen as an *unconscious organizing activity:* the client assimilates the therapeutic relationship into the thematic structures of his or her personal subjective world (Stolorow, 1991). This concept of thematic structures is very close to what Freud referred to as templates, or to what may be considered schemata the client uses to organize his or her world, including the therapy relationship. Luborsky and Crits-Christoph's (1990) work on what they call the Core Conflictual Relationship Theme is also closely connected to this intersubjective view. In essence, most clients' lives witness a significant relationship theme or pattern that is learned early in life and reflects unresolved conflicts in early relationships. This theme becomes enacted in a multitude of ways in the therapy and in the client's perception of the therapist that is considered transference.

A second aspect of our conception is that transference, in some way, includes a repetition within the therapy relationship of past issues with significant others, as well as a repetition of past attempts to achieve secure relationships. The client learned certain relationship patterns, themes, and defenses in an effort to achieve security with significant others. To achieve some semblance of security within dangerous or traumatizing relationships during childhood, for example, the client learned certain ways of interacting with significant others—most centrally, parents. These patterns were then carried over into current relationships, including psychotherapy. They impel the client to see the therapist through certain lenses (carryovers from the past), to interact with the therapist in certain ways (again, carryovers aimed at protecting self-esteem and attaining security), and to experience certain feelings toward the therapist (repetitions from the past, but also tied to responses that the client stirred in the therapist). Unfortunately, these efforts do not work in the present. In carrying over the past into the present, the patterns impede accurate perception of present objects and seek gratification of needs that cannot be satisfactorily met in present relationships, including the therapy relationship. But the patterns did make sense in an earlier time and place; they protected the vulnerable child and created security to the extent possible, given the traumatizing or excessively frustrating situation and the child's naturally limited psychic tools.

A third aspect of our conception pertains to the role of the therapist in transference. In the classical psychoanalytic conception of transference, the therapist's ambiguity in terms of his or her own personhood is seen as allowing transference to emerge in nearly pure form, untainted by the therapist's actions, beliefs, and feelings. It is as if the client's transference inclinations are stored up and will come out as they truly are, if the therapist does not contaminate them with his or her reactions. To the contrary, we assert that *all* of what the therapist does, including being ambiguous, influences the transference—the feelings and attitudes that are projected onto him or her. Thus, the therapist's activity when addressing the transference needs to at least be along the lines of "When I do this, you feel that," rather than operating from the assumption that, as a blank screen, the therapist has nothing to do with the client's reactions. As Gill (1985) has pointed out, transference always has at least a degree of plausibility and is thus understandable in terms of the current interpersonal context of the therapist-client relationship. Although, as we conceptualize it, transference always involves some degree of distortion, Gill (1985) also points out, and we agree, that transference is not a distortion in any simple sense of the word, even in grossly maladaptive responses. It always incorporates the therapist's responses and reactions and is connected to current reality to some degree (and usually complexly).

A fourth significant aspect of transference is that the displacement it entails (from early figures to the therapist) is rarely simple and straightforward. It is true that, at times, as S. Freud (1905/1953) incisively states, transference does involve a straightforward substitution; e.g., the client experiences the therapist as, in effect, the depriving mother of his or her childhood. More often than not, however, transferences are more complex and subtler. The client may experience the therapist as, and seek to make the therapist into, a figure the client needed but never had (e.g., the good mother); the client may develop an idealizing transference in which the therapist is the all-powerful parent who was needed but unavailable at critical periods in childhood; the client projects onto the therapist both good and bad objects, and the transference contains mixtures of both maternal and paternal sources; or the client may steadfastly resist the development or emergence of any transference, thus attempting to maintain the therapeutic relationship as entirely realistic. Transference-based feelings are repressed, and thus maintained as an unconscious experience. (See our later discussion of transference as an intrapsychic event versus an overt expression.) Weiss and Sampson (1986) also discuss how transference may be manifested by the client's "turning passive into active." The client behaves as he or she experienced a parent behaving toward him or her, and in this way reproduces in the relationship with the therapist parental behavior that was experienced as conflictual or traumatic. In other words, the client does to the therapist what was once done to him or her. These are but a few of the infinite ways in which transference may be involved in the therapeutic work in a complex and often nonlinear fashion.

A fifth point we wish to emphasize is that, although transference involves distortion, it is not distortion alone that makes the phenomenon transferential. In fact, it can easily be argued that all perceptions of present figures in our lives are distortions to one degree or another—carryovers from both our immediate and our distant past. The quality that makes an experience transferential is that the client clings to the perception or experience of the therapist, failing to let go of it in the face of contrary evidence. The empathic therapist is still mistrusted and experienced as rejecting; the kind therapist is experienced as omnipotent; the cool therapist is experienced as warmly receptive. Considerable efforts are required to change transference reactions, when change is desirable.

WHY TRANSFERENCE?

What makes someone maintain his or her perceptions or experience in the face of contrary evidence? Asking this vital question is similar to asking why transference occurs at all. Over the years, many answers have been given. At various points, Freud himself gave several reasons for transference: (a) to seek satisfactions of which the client had earlier been deprived; (b) to enact humans' basic and conservative tendency to repeat (the repetition compulsion); and (c) as a means of avoiding memory (S. Freud, 1912/1959, 1914/1958). Regarding this latter reason, in one of Freud's most important papers, "Remembering, Repeating and Working-Through" (S. Freud, 1914/1958), he offered the revolutionary idea that transference is a reflection of the patient's unconsciously rooted attempt *not* to remember the traumatizing past. Thus, in experiencing the therapist in a certain way, the client is able to avoid re-experiencing affects that had to be hidden from consciousness because they were too painful.

Another reason that perceptions and experiences within the transference are maintained, despite evidence to the contrary, is that they are familiar ways of dealing with stressful situations. Even though not an ideal solution, the client's way of perceiving and reacting, as displayed in the transference, earlier provided some mode of coping when few options were available (e.g., during childhood). These ways of perceiving and experiencing others are maintained out of familiarity and a feeling of safety. The problem now is that this safe and protective way of perceiving and experiencing relationships does not work well. The present safety is thus attained at a great cost.

As offered so compellingly by Weiss and Sampson (1986), yet another reason for the occurrence and maintenance of transference is that the client tests a pathogenic belief about how he or she will be reacted to, and unconsciously hopes that the therapist will disconfirm that belief. Whether the client enacts attitudes and behaviors from the past or does to the therapist what was done to him or her (turning passive into active), the client *expects* a negative or otherwise unhealthy response from the therapist, but *hopes for* a disconfirmation of this expectancy. By responding therapeutically (e.g., empathically comprehending; not being critical, defensive, or upset), this negative expectancy is disconfirmed, and the client begins to change perceptions, and/or remember hidden feelings.

As can be seen from this brief review, transference has many roots. Each of the factors we have noted above deserves attention. Clinically, we have found it useful to try to understand these roots on a case-by-case basis.

Is Distortion a Necessary Element?

Much of the current debate about the definition of transference centers on whether the concept of distortion should be or must be a necessary element (Pulver, 1991). Our answer to this question is a qualified Yes. Distortion is a necessary element, but distortion should not be seen in a simple, straightforward manner, and distortion is not the only basic defining feature. Instead, the distortion involved in transference is often very subtle and complex. Such complexity is especially evident in what are referred to as self-object transferences, as examined by psychoanalytic self psychologists. Idealizing transferences, in which the client imbues the therapist with omnipotence, or mirror transferences, in which the therapist is put into the role of the empathic mirror the client needed but did not have, are by no means simple in how they involve distortions. In such narcissistic transferences, self and other are partly fused, and the therapist is not experienced as a fully separate person. Yet, the critical point for this discussion is that the person or role of the therapist is perceived and responded to in terms of the client's needs and deprivations, and such reactions are not fully befitting of the person of the therapist. Some significant distortion has taken place.

Two main problems have been noted with the concept of distortion. First, it has been argued that because everyone has his or her own reality, there is no absolute reality that reflects who the therapist really is and whether a distortion of the therapist has taken place. The concept of distortion, in other words, requires a corresponding concept that there is a reality "out there," and this is untenable to some. Relatedly, only the client is in a position to determine his or her reality. In response, our view is that each of us, of course, has his or her own reality, but there is indeed a reality of the therapist, and the therapist may be and often is seen, experienced, and responded to in a way that does not befit him or her. Given a reasonably clear working definition of transference, evidence also suggests that outside judges can reliably detect transference phenomena (Gelso et al., 1997; Luborsky, Popp, Luborsky, & Mark, 1994). Furthermore, we would add that it is important that therapists be trained to detect transference, as well as to decide wisely how it should be dealt with. At times, this entails helping clients see and understand their distortions.

A second argument against the concept of distortion is that it places the therapist in a one-up position relative to the client. He or she becomes the arbiter of reality, and this diminishes the client. In response, we maintain that, although there is an inevitable power imbalance in the therapeutic relationship due to the roles played by the participants, the extent to which the therapist responds to the client with empathy, respect, and humanity (and not whether the therapist believes the client distorts or not) keeps this imbalance in check and helps the client feel prized and empowered.

DETECTING AND RESPONDING TO TRANSFERENCE

How is the therapist to know when client reactions are transferential? Given that, in most cases, the client does not present reactions that are clear-cut indications, it would be useful to have a set of guidelines for drawing clinical inferences.

In his classic work on transference and resistance, Greenson (1967) discusses several interrelated characteristics of clients' reactions that are indicative of transference. Although there have been some changes in thinking about what constitutes transference, we believe Greenson's guidelines are still quite helpful. Below we discuss each of the characteristics.

INAPPROPRIATENESS

A female client becomes angry with her therapist. To determine whether this reaction is transferential, we first need to assess whether the reaction is realistic—whether the therapist's behavior justifies the reaction of anger. If, for example, the therapist is not properly attending to the client (e.g., answering the phone during sessions, dozing off, being late for sessions, not seeming to listen to what the client says), the client's annoyance is unlikely to be transferential. It is still an important reaction that ought to be explored, but it is appropriate to the therapist's behavior. On the other hand, if the client becomes furious if the therapist answers the phone in the context of an imminent or ongoing emergency, such a reaction is likely to be transference-based. Greenson (1967) gives an interesting example of inappropriateness:

> . . . My telephone rings repeatedly during an analytic hour and I answer, thinking it is an emergency. To my dismay it turns out to be a wrong number and I indicate my annoyance by inadvertently mumbling "Goddam it" under my breath. Then I am silent. The patient resumes talking where he left off. After a few minutes I interrupt him and ask him how he felt about the phone call. He replies: "How am I supposed to feel? It was not your fault." Silence. He tries to return to the earlier conversation, but it seems strained and artificial. I then point out how he seems to be trying to cover up certain of his emotional reactions by acting how he imagines he is "supposed to." This leads the patient to recall a momentary flash of anger as he heard me answer the phone. This was followed by a picture of me shouting at him angrily. The patient then recalls a host of memories of how he was forced to submit to his father's ideas about how he was "supposed" to behave. (p. 156)

Although it is often arguable whether a reaction is "inappropriate," when the data convincingly indicate that the reaction does not fit the therapist's behavior or feelings, transference is a likely suspect. Inappropriateness may be seen as the most fundamental indication of transference, because it reflects reactions to and experiences and perceptions of the therapist that do not befit the therapist. The remaining four characteristics of transference (intensity, ambivalence, capriciousness, and tenacity) all involve inappropriateness.

Intensity or Lack of Emotions

On the whole, highly intense emotional reactions to the therapist are suggestive of transference. Such reactions may be positive or negative; they may involve love, as well as hate and fear. A general rule of thumb is to help the client explore and understand intense reactions to the therapist. At times, when these reactions are highly negative, it is important that the therapist help the client see that they are rooted in another time and place. Not doing so may allow the feelings to destroy the working alliance.

We must underscore, however, that whether intense reactions are indicative of transference depends largely on whether the therapist earned such intensity. Major empathic failures on the part of the therapist, and otherwise traumatizing behavior, may warrant intense reactions; such reactions may well be realistic. In such cases, a nonintense reaction on the part of the client is likely to be transferential.

On the other side of the continuum, the absence of emotional reactions to the therapist is just as indicative of transference—in this case, a resistance to transference—as are intense reactions. The client may be consciously withholding feelings toward the therapist because of embarrassment; or such feelings may be genuinely repressed. The client may have a psychological investment in keeping the relationship rational, and may fear that his or her emotions will hinder the therapy. How the therapist should deal with such nonreactions depends on the theoretical basis of the therapy, the client's overall progress, the therapist's assessment of the kinds of material the client is capable of working with in the time allotted, and so on. Generally, if the therapy is insight-oriented, it is important to explore what makes the client maintain his or her rational stance and what stops him or her from experiencing emotional reactions to the therapist. The therapist's sense of timing (regarding when to explore) is critical.

HIDDEN AMBIVALENCE

Greenson (1967) states that all transference reactions are characterized by ambivalence, the coexistence of opposite feelings. We would suggest, on the other hand, that all human relationships are marked by some degree of ambivalence, and what is suggestive of transference is actually repressed ambivalence. Here, one side of the ambivalence is split off from consciousness, and the client experiences only the other side. Which side is conscious may oscillate. For example, a client with a borderline personality disorder may fluctuate between idealizing and condemning the therapist without obvious provocation. In other clients, one side of the ambivalence may be conscious for long periods of time, and the other may be repressed. The client may compulsively maintain loving feelings toward the therapist and repress hateful feelings. The repressed side of the ambivalence may also show itself in terms of the client's reactions to other people who might resemble the therapist and his or her role. For example, the client may respond to the therapist in a consistently positive manner but often express hostile reactions to authority figures in roles similar to the therapist's role.

CAPRICIOUSNESS

Many years ago, Glover (1955) referred to "floating transferences," a term he used to capture the erratic, highly changeable nature of some transference reactions. Feelings toward the therapist and projections of feelings and attitudes onto the therapist may be especially changeable early in the work and are more likely to occur in intensive therapy (therapy occurring twice a week or more). In our experience, such capriciousness is also more likely in clients with certain personality disorders (e.g., borderline or hystrionic personalities), but this is a question that deserves empirical study. Greenson (1967) uses as an admittedly extreme example of capriciousness a hysterical patient who, in the course of four consecutive sessions, shifted from (a) being in love with her analyst, who was seen as an idealistic dreamer, to (b) feeling overwhelmed with guilt that her love caused her to neglect her daughter, to (c) feeling the analyst was cold and disdainful, to (d) feeling that the analyst was endearingly clumsy in his work.

TENACITY

This characteristic may be seen as the flip side of capriciousness. Whereas capricious reactions will more likely occur early in the work, tenaciously stable transference reactions are more common after the initial stages. A client will develop a particular way of experiencing and reacting to the therapist that is indicative of that client's core conflictual relationship theme, to use Luborsky and Crits-Christoph's (1990) term. This theme or template may reflect an infinite array of ways in which one person can experience and react to another who is in a help-giving capacity: the therapist is experienced and/or responded to as the critical father, the ungiving mother, or the nurturant mother or father the client never had. Furthermore, through the defense often referred to as projective identification, the client may stir the therapist to enact the theme that the client projects onto the therapist; e.g., the therapist in fact becomes overcritical or overgratifying.

Whether this transference template should be explored, in our opinion, once again depends on the nature of the therapy, the therapist, the client, and the kind of transference itself. If the transference is injurious to the working alliance and the client's progress, it ought to be examined carefully, regardless of the therapist's theory. Not doing so, in our experience, is one of the major reasons for unsuccessful treatments. We say more about this below.

USING THE GUIDELINES IN PRACTICE AND RESEARCH

Detecting transference in practice is often not easy, unless the therapist is trained to do so. As we have mentioned earlier, the signs are usually not so pronounced that the therapist who is not oriented toward transference can readily point to client reactions as indicative of this phenomenon. The guidelines we have presented above can help; but even when transference is detected, the question of what to do about it remains. For the psychoanalyst or the psychoanalytic therapist conducting psychoanalytic psychotherapy, the answer is fairly straightforward: Transferences are to be examined and explored, most often through interpretive activity wherein the nature and timing of interpretations are guided by the therapist's conceptual and empathic comprehension of the client.

For the nonanalytic therapist, or the therapist who uses psychoanalytic principles to understand the client but then is eclectic in the use of techniques (what we could call *psychoanalytically informed therapy*), what to do with transference is a much more complex question without uniform answers. Our conception is that how the therapist should treat transference depends on the theory of therapy he or she is using, the client's issues and dynamics, the practical constraints on the treatment (e.g., time limitations), and, perhaps most importantly, the nature of the transference. It is surely true that effective therapy can occur in the absence of direct examination of the transferences. For example, Carl Rogers and the person-centered adherents certainly attended to problems in the relationship, but they rarely addressed transference as such—nor do the cognitive-behavioral therapists. Yet the data overwhelmingly support the efficacy of those approaches to treatment (Lambert & Bergin, 1994). At the same time, it seems likely that problems in the therapeutic relationship are often connected to unaddressed and unresolved transference reactions. This view has been empirically supported; it has been found that misunderstandings and impasses that bring therapy to a halt typically involve transference, defined in a way that is almost identical to our conception (Hill, Nutt-Williams, Heaton, Thompson, & Rhodes, 1996; Rhodes, Hill, Thompson, & Elliott, 1994). In these follow-ups of psychotherapy, such transference-based difficulties occurred from the vantage point of both the client (Rhodes et al., 1994) and therapist (Hill et al., 1996). It is notable that the therapists in these studies had a range of theoretical orientations—they were not exclusively psychoanalytic in their orientation.

Our suggestion is that, whatever the therapist's theoretical orientation, it is wise for him or her to be attentive to clients' overt and often covert reactions to the therapist; and it is also wise to address these reactions when the work is not moving forward or when the reactions threaten to disrupt the working alliance. The manner in which they are dealt with, and even whether these reactions are seen as transference in the way we define it, may not be the most important issue. The most vital issue is that the therapist should be sensitive to the client's reactions within the therapeutic relationship, not avoid those reactions, and seek to explore them with the client when they may become an issue or impede movement in the treatment.

Regarding research on the guidelines proposed by Greenson (1967), Multon et al. (1996) recently developed the Missouri Identifying Transference Scale (MITS), a 43-item measure consisting of adjectives derived from Greenson's discussion of the above five clinical criteria for transference. Multon and her colleagues asked therapists to rate, after each session, the extent to which their clients had unrealistic reactions to them in terms of the 43 adjectives, which could be divided into two factors: negative transference (e.g., annoyance) and positive transference (e.g., love). The scale demonstrated sound reliability and beginning validity. For example, the MITS correlated with therapists' direct ratings of transference during the hour and with clients' ratings of their mothers and fathers in terms of control, affiliation, sociability, and trust. In other words, the more controlling and untrustworthy, and the less affiliative and sociable, were ratings of mothers and fathers, the more transference clients exhibited on the MITS. This work represents an extremely positive beginning in studying transference from the therapist's perspective, using the five criteria we have discussed.

TRANSFERENCE AND OTHER RELATED CONCEPTS

In this section, we examine how transference is related to three constructs: one derived from a learning perspective, a second from a humanistic perspective, and a third from a psychodynamic perspective.

Transference as an Instance of Stimulus Generalization

Although the concept of transference arose out of psychoanalysis and has tended to be associated with that theoretical orientation, it was shown long ago that this phenomenon could readily be explained on the basis of learning principles. Dollard and Miller (1950) provided what is perhaps the clearest attempt to explain psychoanalytic treatment in general, and transference in particular, in learning terms. For them, transference is an instance of *stimulus generalization*. The client, in effect, makes the same responses to different but similar stimuli; he or she inappropriately generalizes reactions to and perceptions of parents in childhood onto the therapist and the therapy situation, as well as other relationships in his or her life. Therapist ambiguity fosters this generalization, and, through interpretive activity, the therapist teaches the client to properly discriminate stimuli—to see how the therapist and other figures in the client's life are to be differentiated from parents.

Although the attempt to translate psychoanalysis into learning principles and to explain psychoanalytic content through the use of learning principles is intellectually appealing, it is difficult to see what concrete gains occur from this attempt. Treatment may be essentially identical to treatment in the absence of such translations. At the same time, the use of learning concepts for some has the appeal of not requiring the use of high-level abstractions that are too far removed from the level of observation to be scientifically or clinically useful. One can use familiar Hullian and Skinnerian concepts of positive and negative reinforcement, stimulus generalization, and discrimination to explain transference events and how they are to be resolved. One need not resort to classical drive theory concepts such as instinct. Again, though, the use of learning terms merely represents the translation of theoretical constructs from one theory into another, and perhaps demonstrates simply that learning principles are so general that they may be used to explain a wide range of phenomena.

FACILITATIVE CONDITIONS AND TRANSFERENCE

As discussed in Chapter 2, Carl Rogers' (1957) statement of the necessary and sufficient conditions for constructive change to occur in therapy had a profound effect on psychotherapy practice and research. In particular, the therapist-offered conditions of empathic understanding, unconditional positive regard (or simply positive regard), and congruence (or genuineness) are synergistically connected to the therapeutic relationship. In Gelso and Carter's earlier thinking (Gelso & Carter, 1985), these facilitative conditions were seen as influencing and being influenced by the working alliance, as discussed in Chapter 2. Although we concur with Gelso and Carter's formulation, we do not think that it goes far enough. We suggest that the facilitative conditions also relate to the transference (and real relationship) component of the psychotherapy relationship. In our conceptualization, the conditions are seen as influencing and operating through transference, and transference in turn is seen as influencing the client's receptivity to the facilitative conditions.

There are many ways in which transference connects to the facilitative conditions. High levels of empathy, regard, and genuineness not only enhance the working alliance, but also likely foster the development and expression of transference in a complex way. For example, expressed levels of the facilitative conditions that are consistently and extremely high may affect transference in an undesirable manner. The client may consequently experience a chronically positive transference: he or she may be too ashamed to accept or unable to experience and/or express negative feelings toward the therapist that need to be experienced and expressed for the most beneficial outcomes. Relatedly, although the facilitative conditions have almost always been conceptualized as positive qualities, we suggest that, at times, they may be used defensively or neurotically by the therapist. So-called positive regard (and warmth, which is part of it), for example, may be used seductively by the therapist, with the unconscious aim of winning the client over, being loved and appreciated by the client, and so on. On the other hand, a level of facilitativeness that is appropriately high, and expressed in a manner that accords with the client's needs and experience, is likely to foster the resolution of transference, even if that transference is not directly dealt with by the therapist. In this way, facilitativeness often has a helpful effect on the transference.

Moreover, how, when, and to what degree the facilitative conditions are offered may need to be informed by the transference relationship (and by the working alliance and real relationship). Assessment of the transference may help guide how facilitative the therapist ought to be, as well as the manner in which facilitativeness is expressed. For example, the degree and manner of the empathy that is offered should take into account the particulars of the transference relationship, and empathy offered in some standard way (e.g., reflection of feeling) may be experienced by the client as intrusive and ingenuine rather than facilitative. Consider the client who experiences closeness as assaultive. For such a client, continual, accurate, and deep reflections of feeling may be damaging to the relationship. Silence, on the other hand, may be experienced as highly empathic by that client. Bozarth (1984) presents a wonderful case example in which his telling a seemingly trivial story about his car was experienced as deeply empathic by his very regressed client.

Not only do the facilitative conditions influence the development, awareness, and expression of transference, but the transference relationship itself affects the client's receptivity to the therapist-offered conditions. Consider the following case example:

> From essentially the first session with this narcissistically injured 27-year-old woman, the therapist [CJG] felt empathically attuned, experienced himself as congruent, and experienced regard for the client. Consultations with colleagues served to confirm these perceptions. The client, however,

felt chronically misunderstood and devalued in the therapy. Many months of exploration revealed that this socially and vocationally competent client experienced very profound deprivation from parents whose energies seemed constantly devoted to themselves. It was only after a year of therapy, as the client began to understand the transference implications of these relations with the parents, that she was able to *begin* experiencing the therapist's facilitativeness.

The connection between therapist-offered facilitativeness and the development, awareness, and expression of transference reactions has rarely been explored theoretically or empirically. The clinical literature, too, is almost devoid of case examples of this connection, although the work of Kohut (1971, 1977, 1984) and other psychoanalytic self psychology theorists (e.g., Wolf, 1998) on empathy and narcissistic transferences is certainly a beginning. This is a potentially fruitful area for clinical theory and research. Clinically, though, the link between the facilitative conditions and transference points to the importance of therapists' considering carefully how and to what extent they implement the facilitative conditions, and how this bears on the client's developing transference.

TRANSFERENCE AND ATTACHMENT

In Chapter 2, we discussed some of the fundamental tenets of Bowlby's (1973, 1980, 1988) attachment theory and how it related to the client-therapist working alliance. Here, we briefly examine its connection to transference.

Attachment theory is attaining a significant place in the psychotherapy literature, and its influence is profound and fundamental. This theory speaks to the very early and lasting press for relatedness and proximity to some desired other(s). According to attachment theory, the need for relatedness is ubiquitous and essential. The need continues throughout life. At the same time, early experiences with significant attachment figures (usually parents) result in the creation of internal *working models* for relatedness, and of self and others in relationships. This conception seems highly similar to the notion of transference as schema, template, or working model of a significant other in a relationship. In addition, according to attachment theory, internal working models bias an individual's perception, information processing, and interpersonal behavior in ways that produce schema-consistent experiences, so that early attachment models are assumed to function as prototypes for later social relationships (Farber et al., 1995). This sounds very much like transference as we conceptualize it. In fact:

> Viewed from the perspective of attachment theory, transference may be understood as a misperception of the therapist and of the therapeutic relationship resulting from the client's use of long-established working models of self and others to resolve ambiguities in the new caregiving (therapeutic) attachment and to anticipate the motives and behavior of the new attachment figure (therapist). (Mallinckrodt, Gantt, & Coble, 1995, p. 316)

Therefore, we would assume that research on attachment theory and models of attachment would be very directly relevant to the understanding of transference. Because attachment behavior is "any form of behavior that results in a person attaining or retaining proximity to some other differentiated and preferred individual, who is usually conceived as stronger and/or wiser" (Bowlby, 1979, p. 129), one would expect that patterns of attachment would be a significant factor in a therapy relationship. These patterns of attachment are understood to be internal working models of self in relation to others (Lopez, 1995), and these models bias the client's perception, information processing, and interpersonal behavior in ways that produce schema-consistent experiences.

Beyond the general statements above, how might attachment patterns relate to transference? As discussed in Chapter 2, Bartholomew and Horowitz (1991) have theorized and empirically supported the existence of four adult attachment styles: (a) secure, (b) preoccupied, (c) dismissive, and (d) fearful. We also noted in Chapter 2 the counterparts to these adult styles in terms of infant attachment patterns. As regards transference, it is likely that clients form transference patterns that reflect both the styles they formed as infants and the styles they now enact as adults. In fact, some highly significant empirical work suggests that clients form attachment styles to therapists that are very similar to infant attachment styles and adult styles (Mallinckrodt, Gantt, & Coble, 1995). Both the investigators (Mallinckrodt, Coble, & Gantt, 1995; Mallinckrodt, Gantt, & Coble, 1995) and a reactor (Robbins, 1995) have commented on the relevance of these styles for transference patterns. For example, Robbins notes that an attachment-to-therapist subscale (developed by Mallinckrodt and his collaborators) labeled Fearful-Avoidant ought to reflect negative transference, whereas a subscale labeled Preoccupied-Merger ought to detect positive transference. Mallinckrodt and his coauthors also comment that clients with secure attachment patterns may be likely to form positive transferences and that, indeed, attachment styles themselves, including the working models of self and others that they carry with them, may be seen as suggestive of transference inclinations.

In sum, in our conception, the working models of self and others that clients develop are indicative of what might be called transference proclivities—tendencies to perceive and experience others in certain ways, and to behave with others in a way related to those perceptions and experiences. The therapy relationship, with its emphasis on giving and receiving help and its potential stirring up of related issues around dependency, magnifies these tendencies. As clinicians, discerning clients' attachment styles helps us understand the emerging transferences and how to respond to them. As researchers, the likelihood of empirical connections between retrospective and current attachment styles, on the one hand, and transference manifestations, on the other, presents some intriguing possibilities.

THE MEASUREMENT OF TRANSFERENCE: APPROACHES AND ISSUES

Transference and its counterpart, therapist countertransference, are inarguably two of the most complex constructs that psychotherapy theoreticians have conceived of. If it were not for the meaning and significance of these constructs in the eyes of many (including the authors), it might be best simply to do away with them and substitute much simpler constructs. Regarding the complexity, consider Gelso, Hill, and Kivlighan's (1991) observation that virtually any traditional definition views transference as: (a) at least partly an unconscious process; (b) implicating a number of internal states; (c) requiring the deployment of defenses; and (d) basically an error in perception. Empirically measuring a process with these features is more than difficult, and this, more than anything, is what has impeded measurement over decades of study. At the same time, within the past few years, the study of transference has gradually increased, and we expect this increase to continue in the years ahead.

Basically, three viable approaches to measurement have been used, and each has its own set of advantages and weaknesses. The first approach involves structured or semistructured interviews with former clients (Adelstein, Gelso, Haws, Reed, & Spiegel, 1983; Horwitz, 1974; Rhoads & Feather, 1972; Ryan & Gizynski, 1971). Although we cannot ask clients directly about transference (the concept is technical and at least part of the process is unconscious), we can ask them about their reactions to therapists, their perceptions of therapists' reactions to them, and perhaps even how these perceptions related to earlier experiences. Based on the interview data, clients' responses may be quantified, and/or judges can make inferences about transferences. The resulting data can then be either quantitatively or qualitatively analyzed. Although methodological questions may always be raised about such data, the client perspective is critical and helpful, as long as we remember that it is only one perspective.

The second approach, the flip side of the client report approach, involves the therapist's ratings of transference, directly or indirectly. Some studies have required that therapists rate the amounts of total transference, of positive transference, and of negative transference after every session of long-term psychoanalytic interventions (Graff & Luborsky, 1977) or brief, time-limited therapy (Gelso et al., 1997; Patton, Kivlighan, & Multon, 1997). Others (Gelso et al., 1991) have used therapist ratings after a single session. In these studies, researchers provide therapists with a definition of transference, to which therapists presumably adhere in the ratings.

Therapists may also rate the extent to which clients had unrealistic (transference) reactions to them in terms of a series of adjectives often associated with transference. As noted above, this is essentially how the Missouri Identifying Transference Scale is used (Multon et al., 1996). Therapists may rate clients on these adjectives after every session or some designated number of sessions. The advantage of therapist ratings is that therapists are in a unique position from which to judge transference matters. They are the professionals who are treating the clients, they are the persons closest to the clients, and their transference judgments guide their behavior with clients. The downside is that therapists' views are biased by their own defenses and by their immersion in the work. Therapists' immersion is both a strength and a weakness of this approach.

A third approach to measuring transference has emerged in recent years; it involves having outside experts make judgments based on audio or video tapes of sessions, usually transformed into written session transcripts. This approach first showed up in Luborsky's work on the core conflictual relationship theme (Luborsky, 1977) and has increased to the point that Luborsky and Barber (1994) were able to list 15 such measures currently in use. Seven of these are described in an issue of *Psychotherapy Research* (1994, Vol. 4, Numbers 3 and 4 combined). Typically, these systems are used to educe a central conflictual relationship theme evidenced in narratives excerpted from sessions or from transcripts of entire sessions. Most

of the systems have demonstrated reasonably good reliability, and beginning validity. They have the advantage of providing a systematic way in
which an expert observer can detect key transference-linked themes in a
client's life. On the other hand, several of the systems are unwieldy, do
not provide transference scores, and cannot be clearly identified as measures of transference per se. (Luborsky and Barber refer to them as
"transference-related measures.") It should be noted, though, that
Luborsky and his colleagues have provided strong evidence that the core
conflictual relationship theme method is a measure of transference
(Luborsky & Crits-Christoph, 1990; Luborsky et al., 1994). The expert-
rating-system approach has gained momentum over the past decade, and
we expect it to yield valuable results about transference.

In sum, three basic approaches to measuring transference have emerged,
each with its own set of advantages and drawbacks. After years of neglect,
research has increased in recent years, and all indications are that this
trend will continue.

THEORETICAL PROPOSITIONS
ABOUT TRANSFERENCE

In this section, we provide eight theoretical propositions about how transference operates in psychotherapy of varying theoretical orientations. As
noted when discussing working alliance, our propositions are based on
varied sources: experience in doing brief and long-term therapy, supervision of graduate students and experienced therapists, and existing theory
and research. Our aims in organizing these propositions are: to help guide
practitioners as they struggle to understand and make use of transference,
and to stimulate further theory and research. Whenever possible, we have
sought to connect our propositions to research findings.

1. *To varying degrees, transference occurs and affects process and outcome in
all psychotherapies, regardless of theoretical perspective.*

Transference, as we conceptualize it, occurs in all intimate and many
nonintimate relationships. (See Andersen & Berk, 1996, for a social psychology perspective on transference in everyday experience.) Displace-
ments from and repetitions of earlier relationships onto current ones are
especially sharp when the current relationships revolve around giving and
receiving, caring, and emotional problems and pain. The psychotherapy relationship is thus a natural for transference reactions; and the therapist's
theory of personality, health and psychopathology, and psychotherapy will

neither prevent nor require the occurrence of transference. As we shall clarify below, however, the therapist's theory, and certainly his or her actual behavior, will have something to do with how, and the extent to which, transference emerges.

Before addressing the relationship of therapist theoretical orientation and transference, we need to make a distinction between transference as an intrapsychic event and transference as an overt expression. Transference reactions occur within the client and may or may not become expressed directly in the therapy relationship. They occur intrapsychically in the form of affects and cognitions aimed at the therapist, either consciously or unconsciously. Regarding unconscious experience, the client may be unaware that the affects and cognitions are aimed at the therapist. Transference reactions, when expressed, are often manifested very indirectly—e.g., through clients' talking about other people, or through dreams in which the therapist appears in veiled form. Transference reactions are often not exhibited overtly, especially when therapists are attending to other events in the therapy. Even when expressed, however, the client is usually not aware that transference is occurring. Thus, for example, when the client experiences and expresses anger, hate, love, or dependency toward the therapist and/or anticipates (incorrectly) that the therapist holds certain affects toward him or her, the client is unaware or only dimly aware that at least a decisive portion of these affects and expectations is driven by transference, i.e., is rooted in another time and place, and in other object(s).

As we have noted, transference as both an intrapsychic event and an overt expression will occur and have an impact in all versions of psychotherapy. We expect its occurrence and impact, however, to be greatest in those therapies that seek to foster the development and expression of transference, and aim to help the client understand and work through transference difficulties (i.e., the psychoanalytic and psychodynamic therapies). Practitioners within these theoretical systems likely "see" more transference, because it is such a key part of their theory of therapy and change, but it also will actually occur more, both intrapsychically and overtly. One can observe this phenomenon of greater perceived (and perhaps actually expressed) transference in virtually any psychoanalytic study in which transference is tracked and rated. For example, in Graff and Luborsky's (1977) study of five cases of psychoanalysis, transference was typically moderate to high in sessions across the therapies; and in Patton et al's. (1997) study of brief psychoanalytic counseling, transference was at a moderate level initially, increased during therapy, and typically decreased during the final phase. These levels were higher than those found by Gelso et al. (1997) in brief eclectic therapy.

Although more transference occurs and is perceived by the therapist in analytic treatments, transference is still important in eclectic and nonanalytic treatments. As discussed below, this does not mean that transference must always be addressed directly for successful outcome. It does mean that how the client is experiencing the therapist, in both transferential and nontransferential ways, importantly colors what happens in therapy (as well as treatment outcomes). Although more research is surely needed, several studies do support the existence and importance of transference in nonanalytic therapies (Adelstein et al., 1983; Gelso et al., 1997; Rhoades & Feather, 1972; Ryan & Gizynski, 1971). The latter two studies are especially interesting in their documentation of the role of transference in successful (Ryan & Gizynski, 1971) and unsuccessful (Rhoades & Feather, 1972) behavior therapy.

2. *Transference need not be dealt with directly in order for therapy to be effective, except in cases in which transference becomes problematic.*

We consider transference, both as an intrapsychic event and an external reaction, important to the process and outcome of therapy. Unlike the psychoanalytic therapies, however, we propose that transference generally need not be dealt with directly, or as transference, for the therapy to proceed effectively. Nonanalytic therapists may follow their theoretical dictates, and, in most systems, these dictates do not involve transference interpretations. In many theories, transference is not even mentioned as a phenomenon to be addressed, interpretively or otherwise.

As shall be elaborated in our theory chapters (Part Two), person-centered therapists, for example, may concentrate on implementing the necessary and sufficient conditions; cognitive-behavioral therapists, on addressing cognitions and modifying behavior; and gestalt therapists, on fostering awareness. In doing so, the person-centered therapist will empathically understand direct expressions of transference (e.g., through reflections of feeling) and will likely not attend to subtler manifestations. Likewise, unless problematic feelings emerge in the relationship, the cognitive-behavioral therapist focuses on cognitions and behaviors in the client's life outside of therapy that are interfering with his or her well-being. Of the major theory clusters, the gestalt therapist is most likely to deal with transference, but in a way that actively dissuades it (e.g., "I am not your father") or deals with its overt expression as with any other feeling, seeking to enhance its experience in the moment.

After more than 40 years of controlled research, it is very clear that all of the major systems of therapy are effective (Lambert & Bergin, 1994). Thus, therapist operations within each system will help the client in ways promoted by that system. Also, as the therapist displays caring, concern, and competence (as he or she does or ought to do in any system), the client-therapist relationship will solidify and deepen. At times, this means that transference diminishes; at other times, the deepening relationship moves the transference in a positive direction (in terms of valence), which itself can aid the therapy, as clarified by Gelso and Carter (1994a).

Although we maintain that transference generally need not be dealt with directly, we also propose that whether and how it is dealt with will influence process and outcome. Not dealing with transference directly, for example, likely allows certain interpersonal problems to remain or at least not be worked through as fully as possible. The existence of transference in the therapy is a good indication that the client has certain conflicts outside the therapy that are related to that transference. Thus, if a male client's transference, which is rooted in unresolved issues with his mother, revolves around feeling uncared for by the therapist, and the client is consequently responding in a subtly angry manner, the chances are very good that these issues are occurring in the client's life outside of therapy. Ignoring these reactions within the transference impedes the client's working them through in his life, unless the therapy focuses directly on this pattern as an issue outside of therapy.

Other ways of responding to transference have their own effects. Actively dissuading it, for example, by insisting that the therapist is *not* the transference source ("I am not your father, so respond to me as me, not him") may drive transference underground, while at the same time usefully cultivating here-and-now relating. Maintaining the necessary and sufficient conditions, as in person-centered therapy, may both help the client resolve transference feelings indirectly and fixate the client on the positive side of the transference. It is hard to get angry at a therapist who is consistently empathic, unconditionally positively regarding, and fully genuine. In sum, not dealing with transference as such, or actively dissuading it, hinders outcomes in some ways but also allows for the positive outcomes dictated by the therapist's theory.

At other times, the transference does become problematic, and here it is important for therapists to be able to recognize and deal with transference (not necessarily interpretively, as in psychoanalysis). Such problematic transference is usually either very negative, or positive and eroticized.

Transference interpretations, confrontations, or empathic explorations in these cases are crucial. Not seeing or dealing with the transference can allow it to destroy the working alliance and thus the therapy, as suggested in research on impasses that bring therapy to a halt (Hill et al., 1996). At the same time, the therapist must be careful not to dismiss, for example, negative client reactions as purely distortion, because doing so may itself bring the working alliance to a halt (Rhodes et al., 1994). Thus, the therapist must walk a fine line between ignoring problematic transference, on the one hand, and interpreting it away as *purely* distortion, on the other. With empathic exploration, the client will usually come to understand how his or her reactions are rooted in another time and place, and, in the process, will feel understood and accepted by the therapist. Both client and therapist may also come to see how the therapist might have contributed to the transference, as well as to nontransference reactions.

There is some empirical evidence suggesting that therapists with a variety of theoretical orientations actually do deal with transference, especially negative transference, when it reaches problematic proportions. Gelso et al. (1991) found that, as therapists perceive more negative transference in a given hour, they increasingly aim to help the client explore issues in the client-therapist relationship and to uncover underlying or hidden feelings, dynamics, and unconscious motivation. Much more research is needed on how therapists with diverse theoretical orientations deal with problematic transference.

3. *The course of transference is predictable in psychoanalytic and nonanalytic therapy, and the course will differ for successful and unsuccessful cases.*

Based on empirical evidence that has emerged, it appears that the pattern of transference—its manner of unfolding—differs significantly for more, and less, successful cases. This picture, however, is further complicated by the theoretical orientation of the therapy. Thus, the type of transference pattern that contributes to more (or less) favorable outcomes depends on the theoretical base of the therapy. We shall disentangle this interaction below.

A number of years ago, Graff and Luborsky (1977) found that, in successful psychoanalysis, analyst-judged transference rose throughout the work. There was no evidence that it dissipated; instead, it appeared to increase (in ratings of amount) to the end of analysis. In contrast, in less successful cases, the level of transference remained stable. These findings make clinical sense because of the great emphasis on the analysis of transferences in psychoanalysis. This treatment seeks to create conditions in which transference may expand intrapsychically, emerge in the consulting room, and be interpreted and worked through. This process is more or less continuous during analysis.

What may be more surprising is the recent finding that, in brief psychoanalytic counseling, this pattern of rising transference (as rated by the therapist) is also associated with positive client outcomes. Patton et al. (1997) studied 16 clients who received up to 20 sessions of time-limited psychoanalytic counseling, and found that a pattern of increasing transference throughout the work was associated with positive outcomes in the form of reduced narcissistic vulnerability and fewer psychological and interpersonal symptoms and complaints. It may be that, in any treatment that is clearly psychoanalytic and in which the analysis of transference is central, a pattern of rising transference implies a positive process and good outcome.

In contrast to these studies, a recent study of theoretically heterogeneous brief therapy uncovered a very different pattern of transference and outcomes (Gelso et al., 1997). These researchers studied 33 cases of time-limited therapy at a university counseling center and found that the amount of overall and negative transference rose sharply during the fourth quarter of therapy for the less successful cases but declined for the more successful cases.

In seeking to integrate the research described above, a pattern of rising transference appears to be a positive sign in treatments that put transference at center stage in the helping process. In such treatments, change is often seen as arising most powerfully through the interpretation and working through of transference. However, in treatment that is not clearly psychoanalytic, rising transference in the latter part of therapy is a negative sign. In these treatments, the aim is to work through the client's inner and real-world issues, and transference is seen as an interference to be done away with so that the "real work" of therapy can be accomplished. Rising transference toward the end of treatment thus may be seen as a signal that something has gone awry.

4. *In the early stages of therapy, transferences toward the therapist are highly similar to the client's attitudes toward and perceptions of people in general and authority figures in particular.*

Earlier, we referred to transference as an organizing activity. All individuals unconsciously organize their early experiences into a template that they place over their interpersonal world. This template, formed by early experiences with significant caregivers, contains the expectations, conflicts, wishes, attitudes, affects, and perceptions that the individual experiences with and toward others, especially those with whom he or she is intimate, and those in authority positions. As part of this template, each person has one or more primary relationship themes. For the client seeking psychotherapy, we can nearly always see a conflictual theme similar to Luborsky and Crits-Christoph's (1990) core conflictual relationship theme.

In the earliest stages of psychotherapy, transference reflects these core themes in a certain manner. To the client, mostly unconsciously but also partly consciously, the therapist is the embodiment of a relationship figure and an authority who is responsible for helping, nurturing, and accepting the client. As part of this embodiment, transference is almost synonymous with generalized expectations of others, especially in intimate relationships where giving and receiving are issues. The therapist's idiosyncratic features are almost irrelevant.

Actually, the early transference often begins prior to therapy in the form of what Langs (1974) has called "preformed transferences." Langs tell us that:

> ... the therapist can detect transference manifestations in many initial telephone calls and first sessions, and these are relatively uncontaminated, non-therapist-evoked transferences .... These preformed transferences may be based on earlier experiences with parents and siblings, and are often colored by past experiences with other physicians and therapists. They may be the basis for the initial mistrust or trust .... An especially powerful source of such transferences is constituted by early childhood experiences in which a family member died; the negative images of the therapist that this provokes are often quite primitive and difficult to elicit and resolve. Similar difficulties in analyzing apply to experiences with a previous therapist, especially when this has been largely traumatic (e.g., seduction, much hostility, or termination because therapist died) and when there is an unsatisfactory outcome. These anticipatory transferences are also a reflection of the patient's pretherapy character structure, attitudes, and means of relation, whatever their earlier roots. (p. 206)

As therapy progresses, the individuality of the therapist continually and increasingly impinges on the relationship and the particular transference that is manifested. Every therapist pulls for certain transference manifestations, even though there would just as surely be a common thread if one client were to be seen by several therapists. This thread is represented by the client's core relationship theme(s) or transference template. In sum, this theme or template interacts with the person and behavior of the therapist, who simply cannot be a blank screen (see Gill, 1982), to determine the specific transferences that develop and emerge.

Preformed and early transferences do indeed reflect the deeper core relationship themes, in the same way that generalized expectancies in relationships reflect core issues. However, these early transferences seem more generalized, and less connected to the person and actual behavior of the therapist. As the client comes to an awareness of the deeper issues and themes, and as the unique ingredients of the therapist get played out, the transference both reflects more directly these deep themes and is colored more specifically by the uniqueness of the therapist.

A case example of the changing nature of transference was provided by a colleague of ours:

At the beginning of treatment, the client was a 21-year-old white female college student. She was referred for long-term therapy following brief supportive treatment at her college counseling center. A strong preformed transference was immediately evident as she responded to the therapist's question of "What brings you here now?" with an angry "You're supposed to know that, but I know you wouldn't even care. You're just a bitch—a cold, mean, icy bitch." Attempts to explore this reaction continued to run into the same response, and it became clear that it was a generalized reaction to authority figures. Transferentially, it was largely a displacement of her relationship with her mother, and she experienced interventions by the therapist as evidence of the validity of her reaction. Thus, for example, a question of "What are you feeling now?" was experienced as an intrusive assault with an attempt to control and undermine her. This was the case with the therapist, as well as in other relationships.

As treatment progressed (over a number of years, as this was an extremely troubled young woman with multiple hospitalizations), the generalized negative transference diminished, and the transferential reactions became more specific to both person and situation. An example that occurred late in the treatment was when the client began talking about a decision she had made to take a different job; she was asserting herself both in the external world and in the therapy. She was taking risks by making decisions based on her own assessment of herself and the situation. While the therapist listened with interest (and, in fact, approval), the client became anxious about the expected control, undermining, and assault. When the therapist did not enact these, the client accused the therapist (with mock anger) of *not* acting according to her expected role, saying, "What's the matter with you? Don't you know you're supposed to be angry with me for making my own decision?" At this point, the client was recognizing what was no longer an undifferentiated expectation, but was now a specific transferential response—when she was making an independent decision with which her therapist (a woman authority figure with the power of both judgment and caring for her) might not agree, her expectation of assault, intrusion, and undermining re-emerged. Her experience of the actual therapist (interested and approving, with a history of being understanding and concerned) surfaced at the same time as her expectations. The contrast between expectation and experience revealed both transference and accompanying insight.

This example also displays the role that insight plays in helping the client and the therapist come to grips with emerging transferences. It should be underscored that, in brief therapy, the early transference expectations or generalized transferences will likely be all that occurs. There simply is not the time needed for more specific issues to emerge.

5. *In brief therapy, the early transference that occurs must be largely positive if the work is to be successful.*

Given the time limitations inherent in brief therapies (i.e., duration of six months or less), there simply is not enough time to work through very negative client reactions, including negative transferences. Thus, if the treatment is to be effective, it is important that the transference that does occur early in the work is largely positive. Evidence for the existence of positive transference in brief, time-limited therapy has been documented in at least one small-sample qualitative study (Adelstein et al., 1983).

This is not to say that there should be no negative transference. As we shall discuss below, some negative transference can be very useful, provided that there is enough time for it to be at least partially understood and worked through. However, transferences that are largely negative (as in the case example above) can and often do poison the therapeutic relationship and damage the therapy.

How therapists should deal with initial negative transferences is a vexing question that deserves serious research efforts, especially in brief therapies. Our experience suggests that it is important for the therapist to understand empathically the client's reaction, demonstrate that understanding, and, at the same time, help the client come to understand that the negative transference expectations are from another time, place, and relationship(s). If this is not at least partially understood fairly early in the work, it is hard to see how brief therapy can proceed successfully.

In contrast, negative transference in the initial stages of long-term work are not as injurious. But here, too, the therapist needs to help the client understand where the reactions are coming from—that they are not befitting of the therapist. The delicate clinical task is to help the client understand these negative reactions without feeling dismissed and diminished to a point where the working alliance is damaged. Again, how to deal effectively with very negative transference that emerges early in the work is a topic that requires our best clinical and research efforts.

6. *Although the amount of transference need not be large at any point for brief therapy to be effective, the pattern of transference will differ for brief and longer-term work.*

Regardless of the absolute amount of transference, evidence suggests that, in brief therapy, transference displays a curvilinear pattern, the classic inverted U, in which it rises to a certain point and then diminishes in the latter part of treatment (Gelso et al., 1997; Patton et al., 1997). As transference rises, so does resistance (Graff & Luborsky, 1977; Patton et al., 1997), which makes sense because transference itself is often seen as at least partly a resistance (to recollection of earlier painful experiences, to awareness, and so on). Evidence suggests that the rise in transference and resistance is accompanied by a declining working alliance in brief therapy, as documented in Chapter 2. In successful brief work, however, the resistances and the problematic aspects of the transference become at least partially resolved, and the ruptures in the working alliance become healed. These processes go hand in hand. In long-term therapy, we would not expect a simple inverted-U pattern. Instead, there may be a series of inverted Us throughout the work.

As noted in our Proposition 3, this inverted-U pattern for transference may well be moderated by the theoretical basis of the therapy. If the therapy is explicitly and clearly psychoanalytic, the inverted-U pattern may not lead to positive outcomes. Instead, a pattern of increasing transference may yield the most positive results (Patton et al., 1997). In successful psychoanalysis and analytically based therapy, it appears that transference steadily (with, of course, many peaks and valleys) increases throughout the work, and resistance decreases.

7. *The effect of transference (both positive and negative) on process and outcome will depend on the amount of insight that accompanies the transference.*

It is a fact of life in psychotherapy that the process and its outcomes are influenced by complex interactions among variables. This concept of variables operating together in complex ways surely applies to the workings of transference.

When considering the effects of the client's transference reactions on the treatment, a variable that seems especially important in conjunction with transference is variously labeled "client insight," "awareness," and "self-understanding." In explicitly psychoanalytic treatments, "cure" is not seen as coming from the emergence of transference alone. Rather, successful outcomes result from both transference and the client's insight into his or her transference-based feelings, attitudes, and behaviors. For example, one client comes to see that his fearful feelings toward the therapist reflect fears he chronically experienced with a punitive father; another client becomes aware, over time, that her experience of her therapist as "icy" represents a projection of experiences with a mother who withheld a great deal emotionally while giving a great deal materially; a third client gradually grasps that his idealization of his therapist is tied to chronic disappointments with his father, who emotionally abandoned his family during the client's very early years. In each of these examples, the expression of the transference reactions—bringing them into the open—as well as the client's understanding of the needs and deprivations inform the transference and create positive movement in the therapy. High amounts of transference are beneficial if accompanied by understanding. On the other hand, transference in the context of little or no understanding may be very deleterious. Clients' experience of a lot of transference-based feelings, without insight into what they are about and where they come from, can and often does create serious obstacles to progress.

The value of transference and insight in psychoanalysis was underscored by Graff and Luborsky (1977), who tracked both of these elements over the course of more, and less, successful analyses. In the successful cases, transference rose over the course of treatment and was accompanied by rising insight. A likely interpretation of these findings is that transference, rather than going away, continues to build throughout successful psychoanalysis, but increasingly comes under the control of client insight. The client experiences more transference but is better able, as treatment progresses, to grasp transference reactions as such.

Is this transference-insight pairing important only in psychoanalytic work? We maintain that, although it is likely to be most prominent in psychoanalytic treatments, the value of transference and insight, in combination, will be high in any interventions, even those that do not focus on transference as such. This idea has been supported in two empirical studies of the transference-insight interaction in theoretically heterogeneous therapies. It has been found, for example, that the outcomes of a single session are best when both transference (overall, positive, and negative amounts) and insight are high. Conversely, the outcomes are worst when transference is high and insight is low (Gelso et al., 1991); the client is then experiencing much transference but little understanding. It has also been found that the early emergence of these patterns (in the first session and first quarter) in brief therapy is predictive of outcome (Gelso et al., 1997). Thus, the high transference-high insight pattern, as rated by the therapist early in treatment, predicted the most positive outcomes, whereas the appearance of the high transference-low insight pattern predicted the poorest outcomes.

We need to underscore that the kind of insight we refer to might best be labeled "emotional insight" rather than "intellectual insight." The latter is something one experiences cognitively, without a connection to affect. Because it can help give the client a cognitive sense of what is causing what, it does have at least limited benefit. We believe that emotional insight, however, can have a far-reaching impact in the client's life. Emotional insight connects cognition and affect. It embodies the kind of understanding that is accompanied by affect and reflects what is often referred to as "client experiencing" in therapy literature. When the client has emotional insight, he or she invariably experiences feelings at the moment of understanding, and the connection of intellect and affect is often a powerful experience for the client.

8. *Client transference and therapist countertransference reciprocally influence one another, and this interaction has a significant impact on process and treatment.*

This proposition is discussed in detail in our examination of countertransference (Chapter 4). We simply say now that transference and countertransference relate synergistically to one another to form what Stolorow (1994) refers to as the intersubjective context of therapy. Each is deeply wedded to and affects the other and, in turn, the treatment as a whole.

CONCLUSION

Transference is a fundamental component of all therapy relationships. As we conceptualize it, transference must always affect the process and outcome, regardless of the therapist's theory of personality and psychotherapy. Although effective therapy surely can and often does occur in the absence of attention to transference, it is important to recognize transference; at times, it is critical to work with it in therapy. Although there has been an abundance of theoretical and clinical writing about transference over the decades, research on it has been conducted at an exceedingly slow pace, probably because of the enormous complexity of the concept and the presence of some inherent ambiguity. Currently, approaches to measurement and study of transference are developing, and the years ahead should witness a vigorous increase in empirical efforts. Continued theoretical efforts are also needed to help therapists understand and work with transference from a variety of theoretical positions.

CHAPTER 4

Countertransference:
The Therapist's Contribution to
the "Unrealistic" Relationship

No psycho-analyst goes further than his own complexes and internal resistances permit. S. Freud, *The Future Prospects of Psychoanalytic Therapy*
(1910/1959)

Why do you look at the speck in your brother's eye, but pay no attention to
the log in your own eye? How can you say to your brother, "Please,
brother, let me take that speck out of your eye," yet cannot even see the log
in your own eye? . . . First take the log out of your own eye, and then you
will be able to see clearly to take the speck out of your brother's eye.
Luke 6:41–44

I N THIS chapter, we will cover a number of different aspects of countertransference, including thorny debate about the very definition of
countertransference, its relation to other psychological constructs,
how to measure it, and its clinical vices and virtues. The chapter also offers theoretical propositions designed to be clinically relevant and to promote much needed research in this domain. Along the way, we hope to
deepen current understanding of countertransference and its influential
role in psychotherapy.

Akin to the topic of transference, covered in Chapter 3, countertransference is often associated with a psychoanalytic approach to therapy, in part
because Freud pioneered the term and also because the bulk of the literature on countertransference has been generated by psychoanalytic authors.

The psychoanalytic jargon that laces much of the writing on countertransference frequently produces a polarizing effect on readers, intellectually invigorating some (those inclined toward Freudian thought) and disheartening others. Consequently, we think it is imperative to make clear at the outset our stance regarding countertransference. In this chapter, we take the perspective that countertransference is pervasive and pantheoretical, and need not be considered solely, or even most profitably, from a psychoanalytic perspective. Although the field is indebted to many psychoanalytic thinkers for their contributions to our current knowledge of countertransference, we do not believe that it is necessary to restrict oneself to a single theoretical orientation in addressing this phenomenon.

COMPETING DEFINITIONS OF COUNTERTRANSFERENCE

The term *countertransference* was coined by Freud in 1910. In *The Future Prospects of Psychoanalytic Therapy,* Freud wrote:

> We have begun to consider the "counter-transference," which arises in the physician as a result of the patient's influence on his unconscious feelings, and have nearly come to the point of requiring the physician to recognize and overcome this countertransference in himself.

Freud's initial use of the term, and his subsequent writing on the topic, spawned what has come to be known as the "classical" view of countertransference, namely the analyst's transference to the analysand's transference. The analyst's "countering transference" was, by definition, unconscious, neurotic, and to be surmounted at all costs. Regarding the adverse effects of countertransference, S. Freud (1910/1959) wrote that he was "almost inclined to insist that [the analyst] shall recognize this counter-transference in himself and overcome it" (pp. 144–145).

In Orr's (1954/1988) comprehensive review of various definitions of countertransference, he cites a paper that elaborates on the classical position that likens countertransference to transference (Stern, 1924). Stern wrote that countertransference "has the same origin as the transferences on the part of the patient" and "may manifest itself in any form that the transference does" (Orr, 1954/1988, p. 168). However, Stern took the position that, as opposed to the pervasive influence that transference has on analysis, the analyst's "theoretical knowledge and his actual clinical experience reduce considerably the field of activity of the countertransference" (p. 168).

One additional point with regard to the classical position on countertransference merits attention here. Reich (1951) made a valuable distinction between the therapist's "chronic" and "acute" countertransference. Chronic countertransference reactions are displayed with a wide variety, if not a majority, of one's clients. In this vein, chronic countertransference may be thought of as characteristic of a particular clinician. For example, the therapist who has a strong need for approval may react to many different clients, and many different client transferences, with something of a predictable response in which the therapist seeks to please or gratify the client to gain the client's approval. Acute countertransference, on the other hand, is manifested "under specific circumstances and with specific patients" (Reich, 1951, p. 26). While still rooted in a therapist's neuroses, acute countertransference is more heavily determined than is chronic countertransference by the unique interaction among client, therapist, and relationship variables. Thus, acute countertransference is more situational and less typical of a therapist than is chronic countertransference, though it is viewed from the classical perspective as no less perilous.

The classical view of countertransference held prominence until the 1950s, when a number of scholars began to take issue with the restrictive nature of the prevailing definition. These writers regarded it useful to consider the influence on psychotherapy of not merely the clinician's unconscious, neurotic reactions to the client's transference but rather the entirety of the clinician's reactions, conscious and unconscious, neurotic and reality-based, whether in response to the client's transference or to other phenomena. All such reactions were considered to be countertransference. This position came to be known as the "totalistic" view of countertransference. In one of the original expressions of this revised notion of countertransference, Heimann (1950, p. 81) wrote: "I am using the term 'counter-transference' to cover all the feelings which the analyst experiences toward his patient." Little (1951), another early proponent of the totalistic view, used the term countertransference to refer to "the whole of the analyst's attitudes and behaviour towards his patient" (p. 32).

Accompanying this expanded notion of countertransference was the belief that countertransference reactions were not uniformly detrimental to therapy. To the contrary, when reflected on, countertransference reactions were seen as possible sources of insight into the client and the therapy relationship (Fromm-Reichman, 1950; Heimann, 1960; Little, 1951, 1960). Little (1951) expressed this view in wondering, "If we can make the right use of counter-transference may we not find that we have yet another extremely valuable, if not indispensable, tool?" (p. 33).

Among the "right uses" of countertransference recommended by Little was therapist self-disclosure to the client about countertransference reactions. Although some clinicians oppose "burdening" the client with countertransference revelations (e.g., Kiesler, 1996, p. 306), and while Little herself did not advocate disclosing such reactions "injudiciously," Little advised that "Not only should the [therapist's] mistake be admitted . . . but its origin in unconscious counter-transference may be explained, unless there is some definite contra-indication for so doing, in which case it should be postponed until a suitable time comes, as it surely will. . . . Only harm can come from the withholding of such an interpretation" (1951, p. 37).

Although we agree that countertransference may be utilized productively, including through the use of carefully considered and prudently timed disclosures about one's countertransference, we nonetheless harbor concerns about the totalistic use of the term. It seems problematic that a term other than countertransference was not chosen to refer to the sum total of the therapist's reactions to a client. In using the word countertransference, proponents of the totalistic view retained a linguistic, but not conceptual, focus on the clinical phenomenon of transference. Freud was interested in the therapist's unconscious reactions to the client's transference; subsequent use of the term countertransference to refer to therapist reactions that are not "counter" to "transference" has created an array of competing definitions. Clinicians, theoreticians, and researchers alike have been plagued by a perpetual controversy about the "correct" meaning of the term and by confusion about one's intended meaning when using the term (see B. Singer & Luborsky, 1977).

Consistent with the totalistic version of countertransference, although not derived directly from it, is the perspective taken by interpersonal theorists and therapists. "Interpersonal theory redefines countertransference to include . . . *all* the therapist's emotional, cognitive, and fantasy engagements experienced from the client" (Kiesler, 1982, p. 17). These "engagements" or reactions are subdivided into objective and subjective countertransference, a distinction first proposed by Winnicott (1949). Objective countertransference is defined as those predictable therapist reactions that are evoked by the client's interpersonal dynamics. Such reactions are presumed to be universal, rational responses or "pulls" experienced as a function of the client's neurotic style. An example of an objective countertransference reaction would be a therapist's responding to a domineering client with submissiveness. Deviations from the predictable response would be indicative of subjective countertransference.

Subjective countertransference responses are posited to be unique to the particular therapist in question rather than universal to all therapists. Instead of responding to a dominant client with submissiveness, for example, a therapist who vied for dominance with the client would be exhibiting subjective countertransference.

Our concerns regarding the interpersonal theorists' definition of countertransference parallel our reservations about the totalist position. Countertransference, to our way of thinking, should no more consist of the whole of a therapist's reactions than transference should refer to all of a client's reactions. Furthermore, if all therapist reactions can be classified as countertransference, either subjective or objective, then the terms *reaction* and *countertransference* are redundant, and one might just as well theorize about objective and subjective therapist reactions. Of what additional utility is the term countertransference?

Not surprisingly, just as advocates of the totalistic view rejected the classical definition of countertransference because it was too constricting, problems with the overinclusiveness of the totalistic view led to yet another conceptualization of countertransference. This alternative position recognizes that "the totality of the analyst's emotional reactions, as in all interpersonal relationships, represents a blending, to a varying degree, of appropriate, defensive, and transference responses to the patient" (Berman, 1949, cited in Orr, 1988, p. 159). Inherent in this view is the idea that it is clinically valuable to distinguish various types of therapist reactions, particularly those grounded more or less in the shared reality of the therapy relationship, from reactions originating primarily in the therapist's unresolved conflicts (Blanck & Blanck, 1979). Along these lines, Langs (1974, p. 298) defined countertransference as "one aspect of those responses to the patient which, while prompted by some event within the therapy or the therapist's real life, are primarily based on his past significant relationships." We favor this more recent conceptualization of countertransference. It seems to us less narrow and limiting than the classical view, and more meaningful and useful than the totalist position. Consequently, we define countertransference as *the therapist's transference to the client's material, both the transference and nontransference communications presented by the client* (cf. Gelso & Carter, 1994a, p. 297).

Countertransference, then, from our perspective, is one among many important types of therapist reactions. For instance, we consider therapist reactions due to inexperience to be an important area of study, though one that is qualitatively different from countertransference. To further elaborate our position, we view countertransference, akin to our stance on transference, as stemming from unresolved intrapsychic conflicts. Moreover, we consider countertransference, like transference, to be fundamentally an error; that is, it involves perceptual distortion on the part of the therapist. At the same time, we recognize that no meaningful communication is ever free from distortion. Spence (1982) makes this point convincingly:

> In response to most utterances, some kind of internal picture will begin to form in the analyst's mind which only partly corresponds to what is being said, and once this happens, the listener has shifted from registration to interpretation. . . . [Yet] sensitive, empathic listening can probably take place *only* if the words spoken by one speaker are invested with private meanings by the other. Unless some kind of internal elaboration takes place, the listener hears only words—we can imagine our response to a long monologue in a completely foreign tongue—and communication fails. To listen with understanding and involvement requires the listener to be constantly forming hypotheses about the next word, the next sentence, the reference for a recent pronoun, or the color of the bride's eyes, because it is only in the midst of this kind of activity that words take on some kind of meaning. (pp. 115–117)

Spence (1987) provides further insight about the inevitability of distorted communication in a chapter called "The myth of the innocent analyst." Spence writes:

> Truly respectful listening acknowledges from the outset that our context of understanding is significantly different from the patient's and therefore to use our associations as a guide to understanding is the worst kind of naivete. . . . Truly respectful listening falls somewhere between the Scylla of evenly suspended attention and the Charybdis of unwitting projection. A certain amount of projection is a necessary part of enhanced listening, but the analyst must identify his assumptions as they come into play, label them as tentative, and by all means, avoid giving them the dignity of empathy. (pp. 66–68)

Finally, speaking directly to the issue of countertransference, Spence (1987) eloquently states:

> . . . unwitting projection is a constant ingredient in successful listening but extraordinarily hard to identify or pin down. Partly because of its invisible nature, we have found it easy to buy into the notion of the neutral observer and the protected model of evenly suspended attention. Indeed, the tradition is so persuasive that the only exceptions to this model are treated as gross errors—instances of countertransference intrusions—which is to say

that, aside from these mistakes, the rest of us hear only what the patient is saying. . . . We very likely *never* hear what the patient is saying in a form that is untouched by our own private accompaniment. . . . Thus, it could be argued that countertransference is a commonplace and needs to be seen as a necessary part of any therapeutic conversation. (p. 43)

We would agree with Spence that distortion is inevitable in virtually all interactions, including those in therapy. When distortion stems from a therapist's infusing the client's words with personal meaning that is colored by the therapist's unresolved conflicts, we would suggest that countertransference is at work and requires the therapist's attention.

Before concluding this discussion of historical and definitional debate about countertransference, we would like to comment on contemporary perspectives on the construct. Perhaps most notable is the recent work of Bouchard, Normandin, and colleagues (Bouchard, Normandin, & Seguin, 1995; Lecours, Bouchard, & Normandin, 1995; Normandin & Bouchard, 1993). These scholars have described three types of countertransference:

1. Objective-rational countertransference leads to a distant, observing, nonparticipatory stance on the therapist's part.
2. Reactive countertransference is a defensive type of regression on the part of the therapist and is considered a hindrance to the therapy process.
3. Reflective countertransference is considered an aid to psychotherapy in that it serves as a source of information and possible insight into the client.

In essence, then, objective-rational, reactive, and reflective countertransference may be construed as having, respectively, neutral, negative, and positive influences on psychotherapy process and outcome. We think Bouchard and Normandin's work holds promise for stimulating research that may help therapists recognize and understand factors involved in helpful versus hindering types of countertransference responses.

PSYCHOLOGICAL CONCEPTS RELATED TO COUNTERTRANSFERENCE

In this section, we explore the relationships between countertransference and three constructs from disparate areas of psychology: (a) schema, (b) Carl Rogers' proposed "facilitative conditions," and (c) attachment.

COUNTERTRANSFERENCE AS THE THERAPIST'S SCHEMA

The concept of schema has been studied in cognitive psychology for decades. Originally defined by Bartlett (1932) as "an active organization of past reactions or past experiences" (cited in D. Howard, 1983, p. 186), the construct of schema has been used to explain how individuals organize information retrieved from long-term memory, incorporate new information into their knowledge bases, and interpret information in a biased manner (A. Beck, 1967; Segal, 1988; Young, 1990). Schema theory also may be used to understand countertransference as a way in which clinical information is processed so that it becomes associated cognitively with the therapist's unresolved conflicts and gets distorted (J. Singer, Sincoff, & Kolligan, 1989). For example, a therapist might frequently employ a schema resulting from his or her "savior complex"; many clients are then inaccurately perceived as helpless and in need of rescuing. When such a schema is used repeatedly with a wide variety of clients, one may suspect the presence of chronic countertransference. As another possibility, countertransference may take the form of a therapist's avoiding certain schemas, especially negative schemas about self. The therapist with unresolved issues around dependency, for instance, may change the topic when the client begins to talk about needing others. On a more complex level, the therapist may avoid conflictual material by assimilating, into a more "neutral" category, novel client information that is related to conflict in the therapist; the therapist then assumes that she or he understands the client more fully than is the case. This false assumption that one understands the client thereby "justifies" lack of exploration of client material that is conflictual for the therapist. Regardless of how schemas are enacted pertaining to countertransference, we believe that the strategies that have been employed to empirically measure schemas might be fruitfully applied to countertransference research to advance our understanding of the manner in which conflictual clinical information is processed.

COUNTERTRANSFERENCE AND ROGERS'S FACILITATIVE CONDITIONS

Countertransference is likely to affect not only the extent to which unconditional positive regard, congruence, and empathy are present in the therapist, but also the manner in which they are communicated to the client. We discuss the relationship between countertransference and each of the facilitative conditions below.

Countertransference is most likely to interfere with unconditional positive regard for a client when a client stirs, in the therapist, unacceptable aspects of self, or reminds the therapist of significant others from the therapist's past with whom the therapist has unresolved conflicts. When the client's presenting issues, physical features, or relational style remind the therapist, consciously or unconsciously, of some repressed, painful aspect of self (or significant other), the therapist may avoid, distort, regress, punish, distance, and so on (Hayes et al., 1998). Unconditional regard itself can be a form of countertransference. Therapists who have personal difficulties with anger, for instance, may be so uncomfortable with their feelings of hostility toward clients that they deny or repress these emotions and instead communicate a sense of acceptance of the client and the client's enraging behavior. (For an extended discussion of therapist anger, see Sharkin & Gelso, 1993.)

The situation in which the therapist is unaware of or hides feelings of hostility, and conveys an attitude of acceptance to the client, highlights one manner in which countertransference may interfere with congruence. More generally, therapists may buy into the myth that they don't (or shouldn't) have countertransference, and when such reactions are present, the therapist consciously or unconsciously disavows them and is thus disingenuous. Congruence demands that therapists allow themselves to be human, accept their personal flaws and foibles, and permit themselves to experience unpleasant, awkward reactions when their conflictual issues are touched on or even intentionally sought out by clients.

With regard to the third of Rogers' facilitative conditions, we view the relationship between empathy and countertransference as bidirectional. Countertransference can certainly interfere with empathic relating, because countertransference entails some type of defensive response that, at least temporarily, lessens attunement to the client. For example, one of the authors had a positive, long-term relationship with a client who, unexpectedly, began a session by talking about material that the author was unprepared to hear—in part, because of his own issues in a similar area. The author quickly launched into a detached, intellectual monologue about how these issues seemed very important and would have to be examined from a number of different perspectives that would certainly be of therapeutic value, blah, blah, blah. After several minutes, the client interrupted him by asking bluntly, "What are you doing?" Only then did it occur to the author that he had abandoned his normal empathic stance toward the client and had distanced himself from the client, her material, and his anxiety. If such countertransference reactions come to be understood, they can serve to deepen empathy for the client (Hayes et al., 1998).

(The author ultimately was able to use his countertransference experience to come to an understanding of and develop a sensitivity toward the deep anxiety the client was experiencing regarding the issue she raised.)

Just as countertransference can affect empathy, empathy can either enhance or diminish countertransference. The therapist who is prone to deep empathy, considered by some as a trial identification with the client (e.g., Beres & Arlow, 1974; Kernberg, 1965), will occasionally experience an overidentification with the client, especially around issues that involve intrapsychic conflict for the therapist. On the other hand, strong empathic abilities within the therapist can help him or her to maintain a focus on and a resonance with the client when countertransference is experienced. Toward this end, Peabody and Gelso (1982), in a laboratory analog study, found a positive correlation between (a) empathic ability and awareness of countertransference feelings and (b) a trend toward a negative relationship between empathic ability and actual countertransference behavior. This inverse relationship, hinted at by Peabody and Gelso, was detected in a field study by Hayes et al. (1997), who found a negative correlation between empathic ability and displays of countertransference behavior.

ATTACHMENT THEORY AND COUNTERTRANSFERENCE

In Chapters 2 and 3, we explored the relationships between Bowlby's (1973, 1980, 1988) attachment theory and the constructs of working alliance and transference. Here, we discuss ways in which attachment theory may shed light on current understanding of countertransference.

Recent research has profitably examined client attachment to therapists (e.g., Fonaghy et al., 1996; Mallinckrodt, Gantt, & Coble, 1995), and we propose that knowledge about therapist attachment to clients ought to yield similarly beneficial information. In particular, we see as a fruitful area of inquiry the influence of countertransference on therapists' attachments, and vice versa. It seems plausible that countertransference that is not managed in some way will interfere with both the therapist's development of a healthy attachment to clients, and the process of allowing clients to develop secure attachments to the therapist. Conversely, in terms of the influence of therapist attachment on countertransference, therapists who have a personal history of avoidant or resistant-ambivalent attachments, or who currently lack attachment figures outside their work, might be prone to developing unhealthy attachments to clients, either by becoming preoccupied with or dismissive of clients (see Main, 1996). Research that examines countertransference as a function of therapist attachment styles would be extremely valuable. Therapist attachment styles could be assessed effectively via the Adult Attachment Interview (George, Kaplan, & Main, 1996) or the Adult Attachment Scale (Collins & Read, 1990), and then related to countertransference behaviors, such as therapist avoidance or overinvolvement. Alternatively, one could examine the effect of different pairings of therapist and client attachment styles on countertransference, working alliance, and outcome.

MEASURING COUNTERTRANSFERENCE

> How does one systematically study the core unconscious conflicts of the therapist and the extent to which they are aroused and influence his behavior in psychotherapy? Taken to an extreme, it would almost have to require an investigator lying hidden under the couch of the patient and the analyst (under the analyst's couch during his own treatment) in order to attempt to analyze the phenomenon in systematic detail. (B. Singer & Luborsky, 1977, p. 449)

The passage from Singer and Luborsky makes clear that countertransference is extraordinarily difficult to measure. We know this to be true from our own research experience, and we have become familiar with several factors that contribute to the enormous complexity of accurately assessing this construct. First, one of the obstacles to measuring countertransference is the unconscious nature of much that fuels countertransference. Because one cannot readily study the unconscious, "countertransference is something which cannot be observed directly as such, but only in its effects" (Little, 1951, p. 33). However, it is very difficult to be certain that the effects one is observing, whether in research or supervision or therapy, are actually due to countertransference and not to some other factors, such as lack of sleep, or skill deficits in the therapist.

Second, countertransference almost defies being captured fully because it can be manifested in so many varied forms. Whereas two therapists might both experience countertransference reactions to a narcissistic client, one therapist might react with boredom and the other with frustration. If a researcher conducted a study in which the two therapists were participating and countertransference was operationalized a priori as therapist boredom (see Flannery, 1995), one therapist's reaction would be classified as countertransference whereas the other's would not. If countertransference was operationalized a priori as therapist anxiety, neither therapist's countertransference reactions would be captured.

As testimony to the exceptional difficulty of measuring countertransference, we would like to share a humbling anecdote. Some years ago, we assembled a research team with the intention of conducting studies pertaining to the effects of countertransference on psychotherapy. Four of us gathered, each familiar with the literature on countertransference. One of our initial tasks, of course, was to decide how to operationalize countertransference. After meeting weekly for nearly two months, we agreed that we could not agree on how to operationally define or measure the construct. With equal parts resignation and determination, we decided to set about studying the slightly less prickly topic of countertransference management (see Hayes, Gelso, Van Wagoner, & Diemer, 1991; Van Wagoner, Gelso, Hayes, & Diemer, 1991).

Despite the obstacles inherent to measuring countertransference, researchers for nearly the past half century have attempted to devise methods for assessing this nebulous construct. Researchers' methods have been diverse, but two predominant operationalizations of countertransference have emerged from the empirical literature: (a) countertransference as distorted perception and (b) countertransference as avoidance behavior.

The first theme, countertransference as distorted perception, has its roots in two studies from the 1950s. In the first of these studies, Fiedler (1951) asked therapists and their clients to perform Q-sorts based on their self-perceptions, their perceptions of one another, and the therapist's perceived ideal self. Countertransference, defined in terms of the therapist's "unwarranted assumed similarities" between therapist and client, was found to be less common among therapists who had been rated highly competent than among those judged to be less competent. In a second study, Cutler (1958) found that when clients presented material that was related to areas of unresolved conflict in therapists, the therapists tended to under- or overreport the frequency with which clients actually discussed the countertransferential material.

Building on the work of Fiedler (1951) and Cutler (1958), Snyder and Snyder (1961) studied self-ratings of a therapist's and client's affect, as well as the therapist's ratings of the client's affect, over the course of 20 sessions. Countertransference, defined as the therapist's misperceptions of the client's affect, was found to increase across sessions. More recently, McClure and Hodge (1987) conducted a study in which countertransference was operationalized as the difference between measured aspects of the client's personality and the therapist's perceptions of these aspects of the client's personality. Results indicated that therapists' judgments of clients' personalities were more distorted when therapists felt strongly about their clients. Specifically, therapists tended to misperceive clients as overly similar to themselves when they liked their clients a great deal, and as overly dissimilar to themselves when they strongly disliked their clients. A similar approach to measuring countertransference in terms of cognitive distortion was employed in studies by Hayes and Gelso (1993) and Gelso, Fassinger, Gomez, and Latts (1995). Results did not support hypotheses related to distorted perceptions of client material in the study by Hayes and Gelso, although the lack of significant findings was due largely to the presence of a single statistical outlier. Gelso et al., on the other hand, found that, when working with a lesbian client, female therapists had more distorted recall of client material than male therapists; however, female and male therapists exhibited equally accurate recall of material when the client was heterosexual. Gelso et al.'s findings suggest that therapist gender may play a particularly important role in countertransference reactions to lesbian clients.

The other common operationalization of countertransference—therapists' avoidance behavior—also has its roots in the 1950s and was first evidenced in the Cutler (1958) study mentioned previously. Cutler found that (a) therapists had distorted perceptions of the frequency with which clients discussed countertransferential material; and (b) when clients discussed topics related to therapists' areas of unresolved conflict, therapists tended to respond defensively by avoiding further exploration of the conflictual subject. Cutler described these defensive, avoidant responses as "ego-oriented behaviors"; they seemed designed to meet the therapist's needs, as opposed to "task-oriented behaviors" that facilitate the therapy process. In a similar vein, Bandura, Lipsher, and Miller (1960) found that clinicians with a high need for approval tended to display more avoidant behavior in response to client hostility than did clinicians with a low need for approval.

Several years later, Yulis and Kiesler (1968) initiated a series of analog studies in which countertransference was operationalized as a particular type of avoidance behavior—namely, therapists' withdrawal of personal involvement in responding to clients. To elaborate, if a therapist were to choose between two equally accurate responses to a client by saying, "You seem angry" rather than "You seem angry at me," the former would be indicative of countertransference because of the lack of personal involvement in the therapist's statement. Yulis and Kiesler asked clinicians to listen to an audiotaped client-actress and, at predetermined pauses in the client's speech, to choose between two prepared, written responses to the client. The response that was less personally involving for the therapist was scored as evidence of countertransference behavior. This same procedure was employed in studies by Peabody and Gelso (1982), Robbins and Jolkovski (1987), and Hayes and Gelso (1991). Dissatisfaction with the high degree of artificiality involved in using an audiotape of a client and in studying therapists' choices among prepared, written statements led Hayes and Gelso (1993) to revise the analog methodology. They utilized videotapes, rather than audiotapes, of clients for stimulus material, and had therapists generate verbal responses, rather than choose a response from among written statements, at predetermined stopping points in the clients' speech. Therapists' responses were taped, transcribed, and then rated for evidence of avoidance behavior, using categories and definitions generated by Bandura et al. (1960). Hayes and Gelso (1993) found that therapists' verbal avoidance of gay clients' material was predicted by therapists' homophobia. Similar methodology for studying countertransference has been utilized in countertransference studies by Latts and Gelso (1995) and Gelso et al. (1995).

In an effort to offset the limited external validity of laboratory analog research, Hayes et al. (1997) and Rosenberger and Hayes (1998) conducted field research on countertransference. In both studies, countertransference was operationalized as avoidance behavior, using the categories originally identified by Bandura et al. (1960). In the study by Hayes et al., supervisors observed therapists' ongoing sessions and provided ratings of therapist avoidance behavior. In the Rosenberger and Hayes study, a team of graduate students watched videotapes of sessions from a case study, and rated the therapist's avoidance behavior. Both rating methods proved to be effective in measuring countertransference, and they hold promise for future research efforts.

Whereas most studies have measured countertransference in terms of its manifestations as distorted perception or avoidance behavior, recent research efforts feature new ways of assessing countertransference. Gelso et al. (1995), for instance, operationalized countertransference in terms of both underinvolvement *and* overinvolvement in therapists' responses to clients. Relatedly, Friedman and Gelso (1997) developed an instrument designed to allow raters to evaluate therapist over- and underinvolvement with clients. Along a different dimension, Lecours et al.'s (1995) tripartite classification of countertransference as reflective, reactive, and objective-rational may lead to new understanding of the construct. When Hayes et al. (1998) conducted a qualitative analysis of countertransference data gathered from postsession interviews with therapists, four categories of countertransference manifestations were discovered: (a) approach, (b) avoidance, (c) negative feelings, and (d) treatment planning. Approach reactions drew the therapist and client closer together, whereas avoidance reactions increased the distance between them. Negative feelings could either increase or decrease the distance between the therapist and client, and treatment planning involved therapist decisions, evaluations, and other thoughts about the course of therapy.

One additional piece of research, the case study conducted by Rosenberger and Hayes (1998), may shed light on how to measure countertransference. Rosenberger and Hayes compared a therapist's self-ratings of his needs to ratings from three close cohorts: his wife, his most recent therapist, and a longtime friend. Therapist conflict areas, or possible sources of countertransference, were identified as those specific needs where the therapist's self-rating differed significantly from the average rating of the cohorts. Three areas in which the therapist seemed unaware of his needs were classified as personal "blind spots" likely to engender countertransference reactions. In a pretreatment interview conducted with the therapist, he was asked to identify areas of unresolved conflict of which he was aware. These topics were labeled "conscious" origins of countertransference. Raters then classified every client speaking turn across 12 sessions of therapy according to whether it fit any of the categories identified as possible countertransference origins (blind spots or conscious origins). A separate team of raters classified each therapist speaking turn for evidence of avoidance behavior. Sequential analyses were conducted to determine whether there was a greater-than-chance probability that client speaking turns touching on conflictual material for the therapist were followed by therapist avoidance behavior. Although results were equivocal, this type of methodology may prove beneficial to future studies of countertransference not only in individual therapy but in groups as well (see Hayes, 1995).

One last possible manifestation of countertransference that has been identified in the clinical and theoretical literature but has yet to be explored empirically is therapist nonverbal behavior (Sherman, 1965). The underlying assumption here is that the therapist's unconscious conflicts may be manifested peripherally, through voice tone and pitch, facial expressions, and body movements. Though reliability and validity issues are likely to prove problematic in studying nonverbal behavior, this nonetheless seems a rich area to pursue empirically.

THEORETICAL PROPOSITIONS ABOUT COUNTERTRANSFERENCE

In this section, we present one general and six specific propositions about countertransference. As in the previous two chapters, our propositions are intended to stimulate both clinical thinking and research. Furthermore, we offer some propositions that generalize across different approaches to psychotherapy and one proposition that is specific to the various systems of therapy. Numerous sources of information serve as the basis for our propositions, including theoretical writings, our own clinical and supervisory experiences, laboratory and field research, and our personal reflections.

We start by offering our general proposition: *All therapists, by virtue of their humanity, have unresolved personal issues that stimulate countertransference reactions at least occasionally.*

We believe it to be a myth that some therapists are "above" or "beyond" having their personal issues interfere with therapy—or, even worse, that some clinicians have no unresolved personal issues. Nonetheless, the appealing and even seductive nature of these myths has provided them with a certain sustained power over the years. Perhaps, as Chesler (1972, p. 61) proposed in *Women and Madness,* some "clinicians . . . do not study themselves or publicize their own motives, personalities, and values" because they are "too busy, too unwilling, or too 'important'" to undergo intense personal scrutiny. Whatever the reason, the myth that "good" therapists do not experience or struggle with countertransference issues is dangerous in that it contributes to the denial and avoidance of countertransference, increasing the likelihood that countertransference will creep into one's work and adversely affect treatment. Of course, not all therapists avoid or deny their countertransference reactions. Many therapists take preventive or remedial action in subjecting themselves to honest and sometimes painful personal examination regarding their countertransference issues. In our own clinical work and supervision, we have found the willingness to engage in introspection to be both necessary for and directly related to the provision of effective psychotherapy.

To facilitate our presentation of subsequent propositions related to countertransference, we would first like to introduce a working model. We generated this model to detail, step by step, pantheoretical mechanisms thought to be involved in the process by which countertransference behavior is enacted in psychotherapy. Our reasons for presenting the model are threefold. First, the model will serve as a reference point for many of the propositions that follow. Second, we hope that the model itself, as well as the subsequent propositions, might stimulate research on countertransference. Third, by exposing our tentatively offered model on how countertransference is generated and played out, we provide an opportunity for others to expand on, refine, or simply correct the model. Here, then, is our model outlining five sequential steps in the enactment of countertransference behavior:

Model of Countertransference

1. Unresolved issues reside within the therapist.
2. A therapy-related event occurs; the event may occur within or outside of therapy (e.g., reading case notes).
3. The therapist associates the event, often unconsciously, with his or her unresolved issue(s).
4. An internal countertransference reaction is provoked in the form of the therapist's affect, cognition, imagery, visceral sensation, or some combination thereof; the reaction is associated with and rightfully belongs to the therapist's unresolved issue(s).
5. The internal countertransference reaction stimulates countertransference behavior.

A clinical example might serve to make the model clearer. One of the authors formerly possessed unexamined issues related to homosexuality, and these issues were raised, quite naturally, in his work with a gay client. Step 1, the existence of unresolved issues, is evident immediately. The therapist had had very little contact with people whom he knew to be gay, had subscribed to societal stereotypes about gay men and lesbians, and was fairly homophobic, in part because of some discomfort with his own feelings of attraction for men. Step 2, the occurrence of a therapy-related event, took the following form. In the first session, the client, whom the therapist knew to be gay, remarked that he expected therapy to be fairly emotional at times, and during those times, he wanted to be able to hold or be held by the therapist. Step 3, the perception of the event as related to the therapist's unresolved issue(s), unfolded in this fashion: the therapist instantaneously, though not consciously, associated the possibility of such an event with his conflicted attitudes and feelings about homosexuality. Step 4, the stimulation of an internal reaction, occurred immediately on the heels of Step 3. Having related the imagined event to his unresolved conflicts around homosexuality, the therapist formed a mental picture of himself holding the client in his lap. This mental image was accompanied by a considerable amount of anxiety that took the form of a rush of adrenaline, an increased heart rate, and shallow breathing. It is important to note that Steps 3 and 4 occurred almost instantly after Step 2 and, combined, transpired in less than a fraction of a second. Step 5, the therapist's countertransference behavior stemming from the internal reaction, in this case highlights the potential danger of countertransference. With only a partial awareness of his internal reactions, the therapist used a reprimanding tone in telling the client that there would be no physical contact between them at any time during their work together. Departing from his usual approach, the therapist went no further in exploring the meaning behind the client's request or the client's reaction to the therapist's prohibition against physical contact.

We have chosen what we hope is a fairly clear example of countertransference for the purposes of illustrating the various steps involved in our model. We would note, however, that most instances of countertransference are subtler and more difficult to detect. In fact, we think it is sometimes exceedingly difficult to determine the extent to which one's reactions are grounded in unresolved intrapsychic issues as opposed to some other phenomenon, like inexperience or fatigue. With these caveats in mind, we will present and elaborate our six specific propositions about countertransference.

1. *Countertransference that is not managed or attended to in some way will have a negative influence on therapy process and outcome.* Fundamentally, psychotherapy is a process designed to meet clients' needs, whether developmental, emotional, or otherwise. Countertransference behavior, on the other hand, can be conceived of as the therapist's attempt to meet his or her own needs. Except in those rare instances when behavior that is primarily aimed toward meeting the therapist's needs also fulfills the client's needs, countertransference behavior will negatively affect psychotherapy, at least temporarily. Cutler's (1958) description of countertransference behavior as "ego-oriented" rather than "task-oriented" is relevant here. In the clinical example above, the therapist's reprimanding of the client met the therapist's needs, not the client's. The reprimand served to minimize the therapist's anxiety and cut off further exploration of the client's wishes for physical contact between the two. In retrospect, with a less "ego-oriented" response, the therapist would have explored the client's desire for physical contact, empathized with the client's fear of intense emotionality, and engaged in a dialogue with the client about therapeutic boundaries. As it turned out, the therapist and client never established a strong alliance, and therapy was moderately successful at best.

What does empirical research tell us about the negative effects of countertransference on psychotherapy process and outcome? In reviewing research on countertransference that had been conducted through the mid 1970s, B. Singer and Luborsky (1977, p. 449) concluded that "uncontrolled countertransference has an adverse effect on therapy outcome. Not only does it have a markedly detrimental influence on the therapist's techniques and interventions, but it also interferes with the optimal understanding of the patient." (See, for example, Hill et al., 1996, for a description of how countertransference contributes to impasses in therapy.) There is widespread agreement about the validity of Singer and Luborsky's conclusion, but it is striking that, to date, not a single study has been published in which the primary focus is the relationship between countertransference and outcome. Most countertransference studies have been conducted in the laboratory using mock clients with whom it is nearly impossible to directly measure psychotherapy outcome. Instead, analog researchers have tended to operationalize countertransference along certain dimensions (e.g., avoidance behavior or distorted perception) and then speculate about the relationships between these constructs and psychotherapy outcome. In fairness to those who have conducted studies on countertransference, many researchers have been interested in countertransference as a dependent variable—that is, they have examined factors that predict countertransference reactions, rather than studying countertransference as a predictor of outcome.

Of the variables that have been found to predict countertransference, client type has been the most commonly investigated. For example, several studies have examined differential countertransference reactions to seductive, hostile, and passive/insecure clients (Hayes & Gelso, 1991; Peabody & Gelso, 1982; Robbins & Jolkovski, 1987; Yulis & Kiesler, 1968). However, hypotheses related to client type have not been generally supported, and no clear findings regarding client type have emerged from studies to date (Hayes, 1992). Perhaps such a state of affairs should not be surprising. Although some authors tend to advocate the importance of client dynamics that induce countertransference, there is growing consensus about recognizing countertransference as a coconstructed phenomenon to which client and therapist both contribute, as is true in contemporary thinking about transference (Gabbard, 1995).

Along these lines, and returning to the model we presented earlier, countertransference originates with some unresolved issue within the therapist. Thus, we would argue, countertransference can never be solely client-induced (unless one is referring, as interpersonal theorists do, to "objective" countertransference; we previously presented our objections to this term). On the other hand, we do not favor a conceptualization of countertransference as purely therapist-induced (see Springmann, 1986, for additional discussion of client- and therapist-induced countertransference). Although many therapists do exhibit "chronic" countertransference reactions to a wide variety of clients, some feature of the client or some activity involving the client usually triggers countertransference. Step 2 in our model, the occurrence of a therapy-related event, almost inevitably involves the client. Thus, we would agree with the emerging viewpoint that countertransference is the result of an interaction between therapist and client factors. In two of our studies (Gelso et al., 1995; Hayes & Gelso, 1993), for example, we were interested in countertransference reactions to lesbian and gay clients, respectively. In neither study did we find a main effect for client type; that is, client sexual orientation (homosexual versus heterosexual) did not affect countertransference. However, when a therapist factor was examined in conjunction with client type, significant findings emerged. Specifically, therapist homophobia was highly predictive of countertransference reactions to homosexual clients in both studies. In terms of our model, the existence of homophobia in the therapist (Step 1) and the disclosure to the therapist of the client's sexual orientation (Step 2) interacted to activate the therapist's conflicts regarding homosexuality (Step 3). Countertransference reactions (anxiety) were generated (Step 4), and countertransference behavior (in the form of avoidance of client material) was exhibited (Step 5).

Whereas most countertransference research is of an analog nature, from which the effects on psychotherapy outcome must be inferred, the limited field research that has been conducted on countertransference bears somewhat more directly on outcome. Strupp (1980a, 1980b, 1980c, 1980d) conducted a series of studies that examined data from one successful and one unsuccessful case for each of four therapists. In one of the unsuccessful cases, Strupp (1980d) observed that countertransference reactions had hindered the therapist's ability to confront the client, who terminated prematurely after seven sessions and demonstrated little gain from therapy. In generalizing from another of the cases, Strupp (1980b, p. 716) concluded that "the therapist's ability to . . . curb countertransference reactions undoubtedly plays an important part" in determining outcome. More recently, Hayes et al. (1997) examined the relationship between countertransference behavior and treatment impact in 20 therapy dyads. The study did not include a direct assessment of outcome per se (e.g., measured changes in client symptomatology or functioning), but findings indicated that countertransference behavior was unrelated to treatment impact (e.g., satisfaction) in successful cases, but showed a strong inverse relation to treatment impact in less successful cases. Hayes et al. speculated that, in successful therapy, countertransference is managed in such a way that it does not interfere with outcome. If countertransference is not managed effectively, however, it is likely to affect outcome powerfully and adversely. Hayes et al. concluded that "relationships predicated and sustained on illusory perceptions are not likely to succeed in helping clients attain their goals" (p. 151).

In sum, it might be said that countertransference negatively influences psychotherapy process and outcome by limiting the therapist's "instrumentality of the self." When countertransference reactions occur, part or all of the therapist's self becomes preoccupied. Whether consciously or otherwise, the therapist's attention becomes directed to some degree toward the therapist's own issues rather than the client's. More than is usually the case, the therapist's energy is devoted to private internal reactions: wondering about them, defending against them, or providing them an outlet in nontherapeutic behavior. We would argue, however, that countertransference reactions do not necessarily lead to irreparable harm, and that the triggering of one's own issues might reveal something helpful about the client and the therapy relationship itself. We pursue this point further in our next proposition.

2. *Countertransference may positively influence the process and outcome of psychotherapy.* Using the five-step model on page 96 as a reference, we consider two possibilities for how positive consequences might result from countertransference reactions. First, after an internal reaction is provoked in the therapist but before any display of overt countertransference behavior (i.e., between Steps 4 and 5), the therapist may develop an awareness of his or her internal reactions. By noticing and reflecting on his or her own thoughts, feelings, urges, fantasies, and bodily sensations, it is possible, though by no means easy, for the therapist to recognize that what is going on internally has more to do with his or her own unresolved issues than with the client. This awareness may be enough to prevent the therapist from acting out inappropriately with the client. Perhaps more importantly, however, the therapist also has the opportunity to capitalize on such a situation by contemplating what has transpired with the client to stimulate such reactions. What is it about this particular situation with the client that stirs up these specific reactions? How does the current configuration of the therapy relationship resemble other relationships in which the therapist has experienced similar reactions? The answers to these questions can provide pivotal insight into the client, the therapy relationship, and the work itself.

Given that all therapists experience countertransference on occasion, when countertransference reactions do occur, we view the above set of circumstances as an ideal. That is, it would be preferable if a therapist could derive insight from her or his internal reactions before they became manifested in adverse behavior. Nonetheless, as a second possibility, therapists can make use of countertransference even after it has been exhibited outwardly. Therapists can reflect on their behavior, searching for and examining underlying motives and intentions, and this deliberation may provide insight into countertransferential dynamics in the therapy relationship. Whether any such retrospective understanding can overcome the damage that may have been caused by overt countertransference behavior depends largely on how damaging the countertransference behavior was to begin with, the strength of the existing working alliance, and what the therapist chooses to do with his or her newfound awareness. The therapist may decide to disclose to the client some aspects of the countertransference, seeking to deepen the therapy relationship in the process. Or, the therapist might opt not to disclose such matters to the client, trusting instead that the insight gleaned from the countertransference eventually will profit the relationship in other ways, such as through greater empathy. We do not seek to offer prescriptions here; clinical judgment guided by empathy must, and often does, suffice in such circumstances.

One might profitably wonder how to take steps to increase the likelihood that countertransference reactions will lead to constructive rather than destructive consequences. Our working model provides different choice points about where therapists might focus their preventive energies. Attention to Step 1 highlights an obvious intervention: therapists ought to work to resolve their unresolved issues. What does this actually mean? We are not insinuating that therapists ought to be perfectly free of conflict or that really good therapists have somehow transcended the human condition, nor would we even suggest that one's conflictual issues are ever fully resolved. Instead, we take the position that one's issues need to be resolved *enough* that they serve to facilitate, rather than hinder, an understanding of the client—or, at a minimum, they don't get in the way of the work.

In addition to resolving their conflictual issues, therapists might benefit from countertransference by staying attuned to their internal reactions to clients in session (Step 4 in the model). In Chapter 2, we discussed the therapist's observing ego—the ability to stand apart from and take note of oneself—and its crucial role in fostering the working alliance. We would emphasize its importance in managing countertransference as well. *Awareness* seems to be the key in distinguishing whether countertransference will prove to be a therapeutic virtue or vice. As Robertiello and Schoenewolf (1987) advise, "We should be the constant objects of our own observation, looking for any intense feelings about patients, and being vigilant about what the next instant will be in which our unconscious mind may betray us" (p. 290). In the next proposition, we pursue further the importance of self-awareness and other factors in managing countertransference.

3. *There are several therapist qualities and activities that facilitate the management of countertransference.* In previous work (Hayes et al., 1991; Van Wagoner et al., 1991), we postulated the existence of five therapist factors believed to be constituents of countertransference management: (a) self-integration, (b) anxiety management, (c) conceptualizing skills, (d) empathy, and (e) self-insight. Each will be explored briefly here, followed by a review of pertinent research findings.

Self-integration, as we have used the term, refers to the therapist's possession of a unified, basically intact character structure. Self-integration is seen as necessary to the process of appropriately identifying with clients, without over- or underidentifying. Relatedly, we view self-integration as critical to effectively maintaining therapeutic boundaries, to "merging with and separating from the patient, participating with him and then standing back and observing his participation" (Gorkin, 1987, p. 80). We agree with Gorkin that "the kind of therapist who is most gifted in using his countertransference is apt to be a person who is able—and in fact predisposed—to engage in this merging-separating process" (p. 80).

Anxiety management refers to the ability to recognize, tolerate, and even learn from one's anxiety. Sullivan (1954, p. 100) stated, "Anxiety is a sign that something ought to be different at once." Cohen (1952) held a similar perspective, suggesting that anxiety in the therapist is strongly predictive of countertransference. Cohen's belief has received empirical support in studies investigating the relationship between countertransference and both state and trait anxiety (Gelso et al., 1995; Hayes & Gelso, 1991, 1993; Sharkin & Gelso, 1993; Yulis & Kiesler, 1968).

Conceptualizing skills allow for the cognitive processing of affect-laden material, thus increasing the chances that countertransference reactions will be understood when they do occur (Latts & Gelso, 1995; Robbins & Jolkovski, 1987).

Empathy, as discussed earlier in the chapter, permits the therapist to maintain a focus on the client when the therapist is feeling absorbed or overwhelmed by countertransference reactions. By remaining attuned to clients' feelings, therapists may be less likely to act out in accordance with their own needs.

Self-insight is considered crucial to managing countertransference, especially in terms of minimizing the number of therapist "blind spots" that might be touched on in therapy. We are reminded here of the prudence of Plato's simple maxim: "Know thyself." Stated more elaborately, "A knowledge of my propensities will hopefully keep me from falling too deeply into countertransference reactions or at least help me to deal with them more swiftly, before they have done any major harm" (Robertiello & Schoenewolf, 1987, p. 289).

Van Wagoner et al. (1991) examined whether reputedly excellent therapists differed from therapists in general on the above five factors theorized to be important to managing countertransference. Secondarily, Van Wagoner et al. sought to determine whether reputedly excellent therapists possessed the five factors to varying degrees as a function of their different theoretical orientations. The researchers constructed an instrument known as the Countertransference Factors Inventory (CFI) and used it to survey 122 experienced psychotherapists. Findings indicated that all five CFI factors distinguished reputedly excellent from average therapists, and psychodynamic therapists were judged to possess higher levels of conceptualizing skills than humanistic therapists. No other differences among the factors were found to be a function of therapist theoretical orientation.

The relationship between countertransference management factors and actual countertransference behavior has been examined in several studies. Robbins and Jolkovski (1987) found that therapists' awareness of their feelings was inversely related to countertransference behavior, and countertransference behavior was exhibited least often when therapists possessed high awareness of their feelings in conjunction with strong adherence to a theoretical framework. This latter finding was replicated by Latts and Gelso (1995) and, taken together, these studies underscore the importance of self-insight and conceptual skills in managing countertransference. In another study (Hayes et al., 1997), the relationship between countertransference behavior and four of the five CFI factors was explored (conceptualizing skills was not included due to measurement difficulties). Anxiety management and self-insight were found to be unrelated to countertransference behavior, but the remaining two factors, empathy and self-integration, each accounted for significant variance in supervisors' ratings of therapists' countertransference behavior. In an analog study, Gelso et al. (1995) found the CFI factors to be generally unrelated to countertransference, with two exceptions. When therapists responded to a client who was thought to be lesbian, self-integration and anxiety management were inversely related to countertransference feelings, operationalized as state anxiety. These data lend credence to the notion that the possession of certain therapist qualities might facilitate countertransference management in such a way that countertransference is less likely to occur. However, this is an area that clearly is in need of more research.

In addition to possessing certain innate or acquired characteristics that assist in countertransference management, therapists may manage their countertransference by engaging in particular activities. Among the activities described in the clinical and theoretical literature as facilitating countertransference management are: reviewing tapes of sessions, undergoing psychotherapy, seeking consultation or supervision, and gratifying oneself outside of work (Hayes, 1995). To date, none of these activities has been linked empirically to the management of countertransference behavior, although this is a potentially fertile area for future research.

4. *The degree to which countertransference affects outcome is directly related to the importance of the psychotherapy relationship within the therapist's theoretical approach.* As we discuss in Chapters 7 through 10, different theoretical approaches to psychotherapy place varying degrees of emphasis on the psychotherapy relationship. At one extreme of the continuum would be the radical behaviorists who stress heavily the use of certain techniques and virtually neglect the relationship between client and therapist. At the other end of the continuum would be the humanistic therapists who view the therapy relationship itself as the source of change, downplaying the importance of techniques. In between would be the various other systems of therapy that give relatively greater weight to techniques (e.g., cognitive-behavioral therapy) or the psychotherapy relationship (e.g., feminist therapy) without disregarding either.

We believe that countertransference will have less impact on the outcome of therapy when change is affected less directly by the relationship. Countertransference, to our way of thinking, primarily affects psychotherapy outcome via changes within the therapist, and ultimately, within the psychotherapy relationship. If the therapist relies heavily on using herself or himself as a "therapeutic tool," countertransference is likely to influence the work by aiding or hindering the use of that tool, in ways discussed in the first two propositions (e.g., by deepening insight or clouding understanding). On the other hand, if the therapist's orientation is such that the therapist does not rely heavily on the instrumentality of the self but utilizes instead more external and perhaps objective means of promoting change, countertransference is not as likely to affect outcome because the therapist is not as central to the change process itself.

This is not to say that countertransference will have no influence on the more technique-oriented (e.g., behavioral) therapies. In these approaches, for example, countertransference can affect the selection and delivery of interventions, as well as the client-therapist relationship. Our reflections in this area await empirical validation.

5. *The effect of countertransference on outcome will depend to some degree on the phase of therapy in which countertransference reactions occur.* We take the position that countertransference reactions are less likely to be damaging if they arise in the middle stages of therapy rather than early or late. Countertransference that occurs toward the beginning of therapy and persists can color all of one's work with a client, in ways discussed earlier (see Proposition 1). Furthermore, if countertransference behavior gets played out before a sound working alliance has been established, the relationship may not be able to withstand the ensuing strain (e.g., of avoidance behavior or overinvolvement), and the client may terminate prematurely. However, when countertransference occurs in the middle stages of therapy, the therapist has two advantages. First, there has been time to develop a working alliance that may be strong enough to enable the therapist and client to persevere through whatever difficulties might accompany the countertransference. Second, there is still time remaining for the therapist to acquire an understanding of his or her countertransference reactions and use the resulting insight in the service of the work. In the later stages of therapy, and particularly in the termination phase, however, time is less available for cultivating insight from one's countertransference. When single instances of countertransference occur late in the work, their effect may be minimal due to the overriding strength of the working alliance in a long-standing relationship. However, when countertransference arises and persists, and especially if it accelerates toward the end of therapy, it can conceivably undo the work that has transpired previously, or at least limit its effectiveness. This possibility is particularly troublesome because many therapists seem to have unresolved issues pertaining to the ending of relationships generally, or to termination specifically (Boyer & Hoffman, 1993; Hayes et al., 1998).

Scant research has been conducted on the evolution of countertransference across stages of therapy, and how the unfolding of countertransference might be predictive of outcome. Kivlighan, Gelso, Wine, and Jones-Cady (1987) found that differential patterns of countertransference development characterized successful and less successful cases of therapy. The amount of countertransference early in therapy did not distinguish successful from unsuccessful outcomes, but, in less successful cases, countertransference increased or remained high in the latter stages of therapy. In cases with positive outcome, therapists seemed able to get "unhooked" from or manage their countertransference such that it was present in lower amounts than were found in less successful cases. Snyder and Snyder (1961) reported a similar trend, although the operational definition and measurement of countertransference in both studies invites further refinement.

6. *Client transference and therapist countertransference reciprocally influence one another, and this interaction has a significant impact on process and outcome.* Transference and countertransference relate synergistically to one another: each is deeply wedded to and affects the other. The client's transference affects the therapist to some degree. Transference stirs a reaction in the therapist, and because the therapist is human, that reaction will consist of countertransference at least some of the time. Similarly, the therapist's countertransference is sure to have an effect on the client, occasionally stimulating transference reactions. This exchange of countertransference and transference between the therapist and client makes the therapist's role profoundly complex. The therapist must grasp how the client experiences him or her; how the client's experience of the therapist relates to the client's internal structure, template, and organizing activity; how these are related to what the therapist feels and does; how the client affects the therapist; and how this effect itself influences the therapist's reactions to the client. As therapists, we can only partially succeed at all of these concerns. But our aim ought to be in this direction, rather than in thinking about countertransference and transference in pure form, as if they did not affect one another. Exploration of this synergism represents a cutting edge of psychotherapy research in the years ahead.

CONCLUSION

Countertransference, with its many competing definitions, is generally agreed on as playing a consequential role in the process and outcome of psychotherapy. Although the impact of countertransference may vary in accordance with the therapist's theoretical approach and the various phases of therapy, countertransference has the potential to severely hinder or greatly facilitate treatment. Certain therapist qualities, such as self-awareness, seem to be central to determining whether countertransference will be an aid or an obstacle to effective psychotherapy. Significant strides have been made in measuring and studying countertransference, allowing for the possibility of continued research efforts that might deepen our understanding of this construct.

CHAPTER 5

The Real Relationship: Beyond Transference and Alliance

W HEN ONE uses a commonsense conception of a real relationship, it seems obvious that such a relationship exists between psychotherapist and client, and that this relationship is an important part of the therapy. After all, despite their "unnatural" roles, the therapist and the client are real people involved in real interactions about the client's very real problems. Despite this apparent obviousness, it seems to us that the real relationship has been the most neglected and least understood component of the therapy relationship. The real relationship construct, as originally described by Greenson (1967, 1978), contained considerable ambiguity, and Gelso and Carter's (1985, 1994a) attempts to clarify and elaborate this construct have been fraught with similar difficulties (Beutler & Sandowicz, 1994; L. Greenberg, 1994; Hill, 1994; Patton, 1994). Indeed, there has been controversy about whether the very idea of a real relationship is even scientifically promising. The first author (CJG) recalls a meeting, several years ago, at a psychotherapy research conference. A group of prominent therapy researchers congregated to discuss the scientific status of the working alliance. During the meeting, a question was raised about how the real relationship ought to enter into our equations. At that point, a leading psychodynamic theoretician who was holding the floor wrote the term "real relationship" on the chalkboard and proceeded to cross it out. He believed that the concept, real relationship, added nothing to our thinking about the therapy relationship. There was little argument among the conferees on this point.

In contrast to the sentiments expressed during that meeting, but in keeping with Gelso and Carter's (1985, 1994a) formulations, we maintain that the real relationship is a fundamentally important component of the overall therapy relationship. In this chapter, we attempt to clarify the real relationship, and its role in therapy, to a greater extent than has been done in the past. At the same time, it is important to recognize that a certain amount of ambiguity must exist when we theorize about a construct as general and complex as the real relationship. Furthermore, as we shall clarify, because there is inherent overlap between real relationship and both transference and working alliance, the distinctions among the three components cannot be too sharply drawn. Variables that overlap and interact in the real world ought not to be theorized as fully distinctive entities simply so we may have a clear theory. In such a case, theoretical clarity would be attained at the expense of validity.

Part of the problem with the concept of real relationship has been the term itself, and we have struggled with whether it is best to maintain that term. Uneasiness with the term stems partly from the fact that the word "real" implies a certain "reality out there," apart from the experience and perception of the observer. A fundamental question about such a reality revolves around who is its arbiter. Who determines what is real? Also, if there is a real relationship component, does this imply that there is also an "unreal" component, i.e., the transference-countertransference component? Is the transference thus unreal in some sense? Perhaps the term *realistic* would be a better choice. And yet there seemed to us to be something more to this third component of the therapy relationship than realistic (i.e., nontransferential) perception. Would the term *genuine, I-thou relationship* better capture the construct? Again, the real relationship seemed to us to be more than genuineness.

In the end, we decided to settle for the term *real relationship.* By using this term, however, we do not imply that the therapist (or the client, for that matter) is the arbiter of what is real—or, in fact, that there is a simple, objective reality outside of the reality created by the participants. At the same time, we hold to the view that there does exist a complex and often nonlinear reality, and, as discussed in Chapters 3 and 4, one's experience and perception of the therapy relationship can represent a distortion of that reality. Furthermore, as discussed below, some elements of the relationship that are outside of what we call a real relationship (i.e., transference) are "unreal" only in a certain sense. In another sense, they are fully and irrevocably real.

DEFINITION, HISTORICAL BACKGROUND, AND CONTROVERSIES

Our conception and definition of the real relationship come from Gelso and Carter (1994a), who in turn extrapolated from the writing of Greenson (1967, 1978), who proposed that there were essentially two defining features to the real relationship. The first may be termed *realistic perception and reaction.* Part of the client's and/or therapist's experience and perception of the other, and reaction to the other, is realistic—that is, more or less uncontaminated by the distortions emanating from transference and countertransference. "More or less" is an important element of this conception, for we would maintain that all experience contains elements of transference, and the main question pertains to how much transference, how much nontransference. Within the real relationship, perceptions of and experiencing with the other are largely realistic or nontransferential.

The second defining feature of the real relationship is *genuineness,* which Gelso and Carter (1994a) viewed as "the ability and willingness to be what one truly is in the relationship . . ." (p. 297). Other terms that come to mind related to genuineness are: authenticity, openness, honesty, nonphoniness, or Carl Rogers' (1957) concept, congruence. L. Greenberg (1985) gets at the operation of this concept nicely when he describes it as "the process of two human beings in the counseling situation stubbornly attempting to dispense with appearances and genuinely reveal themselves as they truly are in the moment" (p. 254).

In discussing the real relationship, Greenson (1978) noted:

> Like all object relations, it also consists of repetitions from the past; however, it differs from transference in being selective and discriminating in terms of what is repeated. Furthermore, a real relationship is modifiable by internal and external reality. In a real relationship between a husband and wife, for example, the wife may resemble the husband's mother in some bodily feature, but the resemblance does not bring with it all the instinctual and emotional components which were originally bound up with the mother. In addition the wife will have traits that resemble other people in the past, both remote and recent. Consequently, such a wife becomes a unique entity, free from the fearful and guilt-laden infantile connections to the past. Finally, the real relationship to the wife will be influenceable

and modifiable by changes occurring in each individual and the world they live in. (p. 429)

When considering the real relationship in relation to the transference configuration and the working alliance, it is worth noting that transference experiences are most often very genuine—the client expresses what he or she truly feels and believes. But the client's feelings and perceptions are not realistic. The working alliance, on the other hand, is generally composed of realistic perceptions, but it is an artifact of the work—it exists only to further the work. The real relationship is both realistic and genuine, and it is fundamental to any relationship, not just the relationship in which a client and therapist are involved. This conception of the real relationship, however, has been controversial, and we shall soon explore the controversy. First, though, we shall take a look at the historical background of the concept of real relationship.

HISTORICAL BACKGROUND

The humanistic/existential perspective, often referred to as the "third force" in psychology, has deeply rooted within it the idea that the client-therapist relationship is vital to successful therapy. The humanistic concept of relationship, as Gelso and Fretz (1992) underscore, is that of a real relationship (rather than a transference one) in which genuineness is a fundamental element. Thus, both client-centered (or now, person-centered) therapy and gestalt therapy view the therapist's genuineness as a key factor in successful therapy. The person-centered approach historically has paid particular attention to the therapist's genuineness, conceptualizing it as part of the three therapist-offered conditions that were critically important to successful therapy (being originally considered both necessary and sufficient; Rogers, 1957). The gestalt approach, to a greater degree than person-centered therapy, has tended to put the client into the equation, emphasizing both client and therapist genuineness.

We believe there has been a tendency in the psychotherapy field to consider the real relationship, especially as defined in terms of genuineness, to emanate only from humanistic/existential theories. This is not entirely accurate. Witness, for example, Sigmund Freud's (1937) comment when writing about the treatment of a colleague: "Not every good relation between an analyst and his subject during and after analysis was to be regarded as a transference; there were also friendly relations which were based on reality and which proved to be viable" (p. 222).

Anna Freud (1954) added the following viewpoint:

> . . . We see the patient enter into analysis with a reality attitude to the analyst; then the transference gains momentum until it reaches its peak in the full-blown transference neurosis, which has to be worked off analytically until the figure of the analyst emerges again, reduced to its true status. But—and this seems important to me—to the extent to which the patient has a healthy part of his personality, his real relationship to the analyst is never wholly submerged. With due respect for the necessary strictest handling and interpretation of the transference, I still feel that somewhere we should leave room for the realization that analyst and patient are also two real people, of equal adult status, in a real personal relationship to each other. I wonder whether our—at times complete—neglect of this side of the matter is not responsible for some of the hostile reactions which we get from our patients and which we are apt to ascribe to "true transferences" only. (p. 372f)

Then, in a personal communication to Greenson, Anna Freud commented: "I have always learned to consider transference in light of a distortion of the real relationship of the patient to the analyst. . . . If there were no real relationship, this idea of the distorting influence would make no sense" (cited by Greenson, 1978, p. 362, as a "recent personal communication").

As early as 1942, psychoanalyst Esther Menaker wrote very clearly on the subject of real relationship:

> It seems to us, however, important to distinguish between that part of the analytic experience which is relived *as* "real" (not to question the genuineness of this experience) and that part which *is* real, that is, which constitutes a direct human relationship between patient and analyst, which has an existence independent of the transference, and which is the medium in which the transference reactions take place. . . . In general, it is important that the real relationship between patient and analyst have some content and substance other than that created by the analytic situation itself. (p. 172)

It should be underscored that, in all of these quotes, the authors are going beyond what Sigmund Freud referred to as friendly and unobjectionable transferences, and what others have called rational transference (Fenichel, 1945) or the mature transferences (Stone, 1961). In the above quotes, the authors are alluding to nontransference reactions—experiences, reactions, and perceptions that belong in a different albeit overlapping realm from transference.

Despite these observations from the likes of Sigmund Freud, Anna Freud, and Esther Menaker, it is also clear that, as a group, psycho-analysts over the decades have neglected the real relationship, focusing instead on the transferences. Analysts have acted as if nothing of signifi-cance is realistic about the client's perceptions, and the therapist's real or actual behavior is of minimal significance in the relationship (see Gill, 1982, pp. 92–106). At the same time, analytic theoreticians have expected the therapist to perceive realistically (and, until recently, have ignored therapist countertransference; see Pulver, 1991). The role of the analyst was so muted that genuineness was irrelevant. The analyst was of course not expected to be phony or artificial, yet his or her personhood was con-ceptualized as so blurred or "gray" that it was hard to see a full and gen-uine person within that role.

THE CURRENT SCENE

With respect to concepts relevant to the real relationship, the scene has been shifting in recent years within psychoanalytic thought (e.g., Gill, 1982, 1985; Meissner, 1991; Pulver, 1991). Greenson's work was probably the major catalyst for such change. For him, it was impossible to conceive of an analytic relationship without a real relationship element, and ignor-ing that element resulted in damage to analytic treatment (Greenson, 1967, 1978). More recently, in discussing analytic interventions when dealing with developmentally primitive issues, Meissner (1991) noted that something beyond transference is at play in the patient's interac-tions, *even as* transference derivatives are detectable. He stated: "The pa-tient's interactive response to the analyst may reflect real aspects of the intersection of their personalities and style of relating, or may involve components of the here-and-now interaction that have nothing to do with transference" (p. 37). Likewise, Gill (1982) was very clear that realistic perceptions and a realistic relationship between patient and analyst are always a part of their interaction. Unlike some analysts, Gill claimed that the realistic relationship need not be deliberately fostered in order for it to exist: "The realistic relation is present whether the analyst wills it or not" (Gill, 1982, p. 105).

It is interesting to note that, for psychoanalyts such as Gill, the element of the real relationship that seems most important is realistic behavior and perception. The element of genuineness is not seen as a part of real relationship, presumably because genuine aspects of the relationship may be unrealistic, i.e., transferential (Gill, 1982, pp. 95–96).

As noted above, we believe there is another reason for analysts' downplaying the importance of genuineness in the real relationship. Historically, the analyst's role has been seen as so muted, and his or her figure so "gray," that genuineness was not a particularly meaningful concept. Yet times have been changing in psychoanalysis (see Meissner, 1991; Pulver, 1991). There has been a greater receptivity to a range of behavior on the part of the analyst, beyond the traditional technique of interpretation. As this wider range becomes a fully accepted part of analytic work, the concept of therapist genuineness will likely become a more accepted element of the real relationship.

In contrast to psychoanalysts, humanists have always placed something akin to a real relationship at the center of psychotherapy. The flavor of a real relationship is very clear in foundational writings of major humanistic figures such as Carl Rogers and Eugene Gendlin in the client-centered area, as well as Fritz Perls and Irv and Miriam Polster in the gestalt area.

It seems significant that, whereas psychoanalysts resonate to the realistic element of the real relationship rather than the genuineness element, humanists have the opposite tendency. Hill (1994), for example, believes that the realistic element should be dropped from the definition of real relationship, because it is at the opposite end of the continuum of transference (or unrealistic relationship). If "realistic" is the opposite of "unrealistic," then Hill rightly reasons that the two are redundant. She also dislikes the realistic element because she believes that we all distort and there is no "reality"; there are only subjective perceptions or constructions of reality.

Humanistic theoreticians such as Hill (1994) and L. Greenberg (1994), instead, resonate to the genuineness element of the real relationship. This fits with the great emphasis all varieties of humanists have placed historically on the therapist's being authentic, truly himself or herself, and congruent. If participants are genuine, the door is open for an I-thou relationship, which is seen as so vital to virtually all humanistic therapies.

In sum, then, both psychoanalysts and humanists have attended to and accepted different elements of the real relationship. Analysts, to the extent that they have addressed the real relationship at all, focus on the realistic element. Humanists, who have made the real relationship the centerpiece of therapy, emphasize the genuineness aspect. Our contention is that both genuineness and realistic perception are key elements of the real relationship. We recognize that this combination of genuineness and realistic perception makes for a much more complex construct, but believe that the two elements are both so vital to the real relationship component that the added complexity must be lived with.

THE OPERATION OF THE
REAL RELATIONSHIP

What does the real relationship look like in therapy? Greenson (1967) used the following example:

> A young man, in the terminal phase of his five-year analysis, hesitates after I have made an interpretation and then tells me that he has something to say which is very difficult for him. He was about to skip over it when he realized he had been doing just that for years. He takes a deep breath and says: "You always talk a little bit too much. You tend to exaggerate. It would be much easier for me to get mad at you and say you're cockeyed or wrong or off the point or just not answer. It's terribly hard to say what I mean because I know it will hurt your feelings."
>
> I believe the patient has correctly perceived some traits of mine and it was somewhat painful for me to have them pointed out. I told him he was right, but I wanted to know why it was harder for him to tell it to me simply and directly as he had just done than to become enraged. He answered that he knew from experience that I would not get upset by his temper, that was obviously his neurosis and I wouldn't be touched by it. Telling me about my talking too much and exaggerating was a personal criticism and that would be hurtful. He knew I took pride in my skill as a therapist. In the past he would have been worried that I might retaliate, but he now knew it was not likely. Besides, it wouldn't kill him. (pp. 217–218)

In this example, we see that the patient both perceived accurately *and* predicted the therapist's reactions without distortions. There is nothing special about this example, except that it is given by a classical analyst who is sensitively attuned to transference and has written what many consider one of the most comprehensive treatments of transference.

Although Greenson's case exemplifies the real relationship in terms of both the client's realistic perception/reaction and genuineness, it would be wrong to assume that any relationship (in therapy or otherwise) can be all transference or all realistic. Greenson (1967) captured this inevitable admixture nicely when he said "There is no transference reaction, no matter how fantastic, without a germ of truth, and there is no realistic relationship without some trace of transference fantasy" (p. 219). Thus, those who criticize the concept of real relationship on the basis that transference infuses all relationships are technically correct. At the same time, the extent to which transference or real relationship is operative in a given relationship or relationship episode is the major issue, for this is truly a question of degree as well as a matter of figure and ground. The therapist needs to pay attention to the degree to which transference and real relationship are operative, along with which component is in the foreground and which is the background of the client's material.

KEY FEATURES OF THE REAL RELATIONSHIP

In addition to the fact that all relationships consist of both transference and real relationship components, these two parts often exist side by side during the psychotherapy hour, and, as we shall discuss in the next chapter, each affects the other. Even though, as Hill (1994) notes, realistic perceptions and reactions are the flip side of transference, the fact that both exist in a given hour, and that both may exist powerfully, argues for not viewing the realistic perception element of the real relationship as merely low transference. High degrees of real relationship and transference, or low degrees of both, may and very often do exist during a given psychotherapy hour. For example, a client wrongly feels that her therapist will be angry with her because the client behaved in a way the client felt to be irresponsible. This expectation is a carryover from the many battles the client had with her overresponsible and critical mother. Even as the client experiences this fear/expectation of her therapist, she also experiences and accurately perceives her therapist's concern and acceptance. Transference and real relationship in this session are both at a high level.

Relationships vary over time and between one another in terms of both the strength and valence of the real relationship. Thus, the strength of the realistic/genuine relationship may vary from high to low for a given hour and for any period of treatment; and different therapist/client pairs will vary greatly on how genuine they are with each other and how realistically they perceive/react to one another. Generally, the more genuine and realistic the participants are with one another, the better we expect the work to go, and the more positive the outcomes. But this is not unequivocally so. An example of realistic perception/reaction serving a negative role occurs with the client who strives to keep the therapy at a realistic and rational level, but whose so-called realism serves a defensive function. Such a client may consciously or unconsciously seek to keep all irrational and/or unrealistic reactions out of the work, thus creating a sterile experience and preventing the therapy from progressing. We would maintain that, in such cases, transference expectations may serve to create such defensive "realism." The client, for example, may irrationally fear the therapist's reactions, should the client's irrational side emerge.

Degree of real relationship, in fact, is difficult to interpret without reference to valence. Just as transference may be positive, negative, or a mixture of the two, so may real relationship vary in this way. Generally, the more positive the real relationship, the better the process and outcome. In the positive real relationship, the participants have favorable realistic reactions to one another. Gelso and Carter (1985) singled out liking as the primary positive affect that therapist and client might have toward one another, but while liking is a key affect, it is not the only one. This is not to say that all of the client's realistic reactions are positive; some degree of ambivalence exists in all relationships, including good ones. But in the good therapy relationship, there is an essentially positive real relationship.

In the positive real relationship, the participants also share a sense of respect for one another that may approximate what is often referred to as an I-thou relationship (Buber, 1958). This concept is very close to what Orlinsky and Howard (1987) refer to as the "mutual affirmation" element of the therapeutic bond between participants. In such a relationship, as L. Greenberg (1985) points out, participants seek "to break down barriers between inside and outside, between image and experience, and to communicate intimately their moment-to-moment inner experience . . ." (p. 254). It must be noted, though, that the I-Thou relationship often referred to in psychotherapy is not as reciprocal as other relationships, in that the therapist is not equally acknowledged and confirmed. Instead, Buber (1958) refers to the kind of I-Thou relationship that exists in therapy as "one-sided inclusion," a relationship in which the therapist "willingly sets aside a personal investment to serve the learning of the other . . . " (Greenberg, 1985, p. 255).

The essentially negative real relationship, on the other hand, is likely to result in poor outcomes. It is hard to imagine good outcomes when the therapist and/or the client have unfavorable reactions to each other, no matter how realistic and genuine are those reactions.

THERAPIST AND CLIENT CONTRIBUTIONS TO THE REAL RELATIONSHIP

Just what the client and the therapist contribute to the real relationship and how they go about making that contribution are tied to a number of factors: their roles as therapist and as client, the therapist's theoretical inclinations, and the personal styles of each participant. The therapist's role, as Gelso and Carter (1985) discussed, is confusing and contradictory in certain ways. The therapist is expected to be genuine (although how open he or she is depends on several factors) and at the same time be "at work." Being at work implies, to varying extents, observing one's communications and behaviors, keeping them under some kind of rational control. The therapist is there for the client, and must keep what is best for the client at the forefront of consciousness. Because he or she cannot simply be open and honest, the therapist's role entails a kind of controlled genuineness. Thus, the therapist should not express feelings that he or she expects to be damaging to the client, even though the therapist may experience such feelings.

At the same time, the therapist's role regarding realistic perceptions/ reactions of himself or herself and of the client is more clear-cut. Although it is useful to allow oneself, as a therapist, to experience a range of feelings toward the client, the therapist is expected to work at perceiving realistically and reacting on the basis of such perceptions. This is essentially what countertransference management is about (see Chapter 4).

The client's role is far simpler regarding genuineness, but not as simple regarding realistic perception/reaction. The client is expected to at least try to be open and genuine at all times—to say what is on his or her mind, to share openly whatever is being felt and experienced, and not to hold back. Naturally, the client will not always succeed at this task and may not even approach success. But the role itself is clear. On the other hand, it is not expected that the client will perceive and react realistically. Although the aim of most therapies is to help clients work through and correct distortions or unrealistic perceptions of the therapist, it is expected that these unrealistic perceptions and reactions will occur. They are as inherent a part of the process as is the therapist's attempt to help the client understand them and work through them.

The therapist's theoretical orientation also plays a significant part in how he or she contributes to the real relationship. Despite changes in recent decades, analytic therapists are going to be less open about their feelings and experiencing than are humanistic therapists. Although psychoanalysts are more likely to recognize their actual contribution to clients' perceptions than in the past, there is still a major emphasis on not having one's own feelings and issues intrude on the client's process. There is, as a result, less acceptance of therapist self-disclosure than in either the humanistic or learning perspectives. Thus, in a very real sense, the client of an analytic therapist has fewer data to go on—less information about the therapist from which to form realistic perceptions/reactions. This makes the formation of a real relationship more difficult in analytic therapy, although the real relationship will surely exist, and in an important way, in this form of treatment.

We should note that therapists communicate aspects of themselves in myriad ways: the paintings on their walls, their attire and office decor, their sense of humor, the style as well as the content of their communication, the manner in which they greet the client, and so on. Even therapists who do not directly reveal a great deal about themselves are providing the client with information about who they are and what they are about.

Finally, just what therapists and clients contribute to the real relationship and how they go about making those contributions will partly depend on the individual personalities and styles of the participants. Therapists (apart from their theory) and clients vary widely in how expressive and revealing they are inclined to be, how effective they are at perceiving themselves and others realistically, and how directly they communicate.

Although therapists' and clients' variability in roles, theories (for the therapist), and personal styles will shape how they enact the real relationship, the constant is that both contribute crucially to its development. Gelso and Carter (1985) stated:

> Both parties in the interaction contribute to it [the real relationship] from the moment of their first exchange. The counselor does so through his or her attempt to see and understand the client realistically. The client contributes to the real relationship likewise through his or her struggle to be genuine and perceive realistically. We would also like to share the observations that clients will work to correct therapist errors in the relationship. Thus, we have experienced, firsthand and as supervisors, clients pointing out and puzzling over instances of therapists' distortions, closedness, and lack of authenticity. In such cases clients need to be listened to, and carefully. (p. 187)

THE REAL RELATIONSHIP AND OTHER RELATED CONCEPTS

As in prior chapters, we shall explore the connection of a key relationship component—in this case, the real relationship—to other concepts that seem to have a significant bearing on the psychotherapy relationship in its totality. The two concepts we explore here—the facilitative conditions and attachment theory—have also been examined in Chapters 2 through

4. Thus, these two concepts are explored in relation to each of the relationship components in our theory. We have done this because both the facilitative conditions and attachment theory are extremely important in understanding and fostering therapeutic relationships, and because we believe they are intimately connected to the therapy relationship and its components.

FACILITATIVE CONDITIONS AND THE REAL RELATIONSHIP

As discussed previously, Rogers' (1957) statement of the necessary and sufficient conditions for constructive change in therapy has had a deep and abiding effect on psychotherapy practice and research. Of the six conditions he examined, those given the greatest attention are the therapist-offered conditions of empathic understanding, unconditional positive regard (or simply, positive regard), and congruence (or genuineness). Although these facilitative conditions emanate from the therapist, we view them as synergistically related to each of the components of the therapy relationship: working alliance, transference configuration (transference and countertransference), and real relationship. Here, we briefly discuss how the facilitative conditions relate to the real relationship.

There are two primary ways in which the real relationship connects to the three facilitative conditions. First, we suggest that the conditions of therapist empathy, positive regard, and congruence reciprocally relate to the valence of the real relationship. The greater the therapist's ability to experience and express empathy, regard, and congruence, the more positive will be the real relationship—the greater the liking, caring, affection, and so on, each participant experiences toward the realistically perceived other. Likewise, the more positive this "liking bond," the easier it is for the therapist to experience and express the facilitative attitudes.

A second primary way in which the facilitative conditions are linked to the real relationship is through the concept of genuineness. Probably all psychotherapies place a value on therapist genuineness. The humanistic therapies, however, place this concept at the center of their theories. Congruent or genuine therapists are in tune with themselves and their organismic experiencing, and although they would not be expected to communicate all of their thoughts to their clients, these therapists display a synchrony between their inner experience and their outer behavior with clients. They *are* themselves; they do not act phony or disingenuous. Whereas person-centered therapists, following Rogers' lead, have focused on therapist genuineness, gestalt therapists have been more likely to include the client in the equation, stressing the importance of both therapist and client genuineness.

Genuineness (in both the client and the therapist) is of course one element of our two-pronged conception of the real relationship; and, as discussed earlier in this chapter, our conception of genuineness is essentially the same as that of the humanistic therapists, particularly when this genuineness occurs in the context of an essentially positive real relationship. Such a relationship approximates what is often referred to as "the good therapeutic relationship" or an I-Thou relationship, in which there is a deep respect for the other, and, on the therapist's side, a deep desire to facilitate the other's personhood and growth (see L. Greenberg, 1985, 1994). As noted earlier, however, in the good real relationship, one or both of the participants may experience and genuinely express realistically negative feelings toward the other. If understood and worked through, such experience and expression of feelings can ultimately benefit the work. At the same time, it would be hard to imagine therapy being successful in the face of ongoing and chronic negative feelings, however genuine and realistic.

In sum, the facilitative conditions relate to the real relationship through (a) their reciprocal influence on one another, and (b) the overlap in the concept of genuineness—a key element of both the facilitative conditions and the real relationship.

ATTACHMENT AND THE REAL RELATIONSHIP

In Chapter 2, we discussed some of the fundamental tenets of attachment theory and attachment phenomena as they bear on the working alliance. In Chapters 3 and 4, we also discussed attachment theory as it related to transference and countertransference, respectively. In the present chapter, we make some observations about attachment and the real relationship. The reader is referred to Chapter 2 for a review of the basics of attachment theory.

Attachment theory ought to relate to the real relationship in ways that are similar to how it relates to the working alliance, because much of the working alliance is infused with realistic perceptions (although transference is surely also present in the alliance). At the same time, the real relationship and working alliance are not the same thing, and the differences also should bear on how the two relate to attachment theory. The working alliance is an alliance or bond that exists solely for the purpose of the therapeutic work, to further the work of therapy. The real relationship, on the other hand, reflects another kind of bond. For example, to the extent that the real relationship is positive, the bond it involves might be seen as a bond of affection or liking that is based on realistic perceptions of the participants toward one another, and is fueled by their genuineness with each other.

How might the real relationship connect to attachment theory? In effective therapy, as noted by Farber et al. (1995), therapists usually become attachment figures who seek to provide their clients with a secure base from which clients can explore difficult issues and try out new behaviors. Bowlby (1988) likened this role to a mother's provision of a secure base from which her child could explore. A secure base comes not only from the therapist's presence, but from a host of actual behaviors and attitudes exhibited by the therapist. In discussing therapy based on attachment theory, Bowlby has underscored how the therapist takes the role of companion in the client's exploration of self and experience, rather than the role of interpreter, as in most psychoanalytic approaches. Bowlby summarizes the therapist's role as follows:

> This means, first and foremost, that he [the therapist] accepts and respects the patient, warts and all, as a fellow human being in trouble and that his overriding concern is to promote his patient's welfare by all means at his disposal. To this end the therapist strives to be reliable, attentive, empathic, and sympathetically responsive, and also to encourage his patient to explore the world of his thoughts, feelings, and actions not only in the present but also in the past. Whilst always encouraging his patient to take the initiative, the therapist is in no sense passive. On the one hand, he tries to be attentive and sensitively responsive. On the other, he recognizes that there are times when he himself must take the initiative. (p. 152)

In the ways so clearly described by Bowlby, the attachment-oriented therapist offers a strong reality stimulus. He or she presents a rather clear figure to the client. Thus, although Bowlby and other attachment therapists have an abiding concern for examining transference phenomena, they also do not seek to foster the development of transference through their own ambiguity. Instead, in their active caring and concern, as well as their active guiding at times, they foster a real relationship while also showing a sharp awareness that transference will emerge in the form of the client's carryover of working models of others from the past to the present.

Given the therapist's very active attempt to provide a secure base, the client quite naturally will tend to "take in" these positive behaviors and attitudes. The client, in other words, at least to some extent, realistically perceives and experiences these therapist actions. As Bowlby (1988) says, "[A] patient's way of construing his relationship with his therapist is not determined solely by the patient's history; it is determined no less by the way the therapist treats him" (p. 141). It is also clear from Bowlby's writing about attachment and therapy that the attachment therapist actively seeks to facilitate the client's realistic perception of him or her. The therapist works to help the client uncover old, and now problematic, working models of others; to understand how they are being extrapolated into the present (including the therapeutic relationship); and to take in the present for what it is. Part of this "taking in" of the present involves facilitating the client's perceptions of the therapist for who he or she is, and thus furthering the real relationship.

The client's taking in of the secure base offered by the therapist tends to enhance the positive real relationship. Thus, a liking or affectional bond is likely to develop based on the reality of the therapist's activity. This description is probably most likely to occur with clients who, in attachment theory terms, have secure attachment styles. For those with other styles (preoccupied, dismissing, fearful), however, things might not be so easy. As Farber et al. (1995) speculate, clients with insecure early attachments (and current attachment styles, we would add) are not likely to have strong positive feelings toward their therapist, and therapeutic work must focus on developing a strong, trusting, and stable relationship. These more troubled clients (e.g., borderline and schizoid individuals) may not be able to see the therapist as a real person for a long period of time, and may relate primarily through transference perceptions and feelings that are often negative. A positive real relationship will unfold very gradually and will require a great deal of patience, understanding, and tolerance from the therapist. As always, but to an even greater extent with a more profoundly disturbed person, the therapist must stay in close touch with his or her own issues and feelings, so that he or she is able to be genuine, to perceive realistically (and not defensively), and not to act out.

Just as with the working alliance and the transference configuration, the connection of real relationship to attachment styles is a fruitful area of future inquiry. How do different therapist and client attachment styles relate to elements of the real relationship (realistic perception, valence of these perceptions, genuineness)? Are there differences between clients with secure and insecure styles in the real relationships they develop? Do therapists with different styles offer real relationships of differing qualities? These are but a few of the myriad of questions that await scrutiny.

MEASURING THE REAL RELATIONSHIP

There has been considerable research on the role of therapist genuineness stemming from the person-centered therapy tradition. However, until very recently, no research had been conducted on the real relationship as it has been conceptualized here. This is not surprising, given the complexity and vagueness that have surrounded this construct.

By and large, the research on therapist genuineness has yielded favorable results. Clients' perceptions of their therapists' genuineness, on the whole, have been found to affect positively the process and outcomes of psychotherapy practiced from a range of theoretical perspectives (Orlinsky & Howard, 1986). Regarding the real relationship as conceptualized here, three very recent studies have yielded promising findings. Eugster and Wampold (1996), in the first study that we were able to locate on the real relationship, had 115 expert psychologists and 122 patients of these therapists rate a number of variables as they occurred during a given therapy session, as well as their overall evaluation of that session. One of the variables assessed was the real relationship, which was defined and operationalized in a way that was nearly identical to our conceptualization. Both therapists and patients rated the real relationship as engaged in by the therapist and by the client. Neither the patients' nor the therapists' ratings of the real relationship as engaged in by *the patient* were found to be related to their evaluations of the session. However, both the therapists' and the patients' ratings of the real relationship as engaged in by *the therapist* correlated significantly with session evaluation. Thus, the extent to which the therapist is genuinely himself or herself and perceives realistically during a session appears to be an important marker of a session that both participants view as effective.

Knox, Hess, Petersen, and Hill (1997) conducted a qualitative study of the role and effects of therapist self-disclosure as perceived by 13 clients in long-term psychotherapy (average of 5 years). One of the major research questions revolved around whether therapist self-disclosures could influence the real relationship in the sense that clients might see more of the humanness of the therapist. Using intensive semistructured interviews and rigorous qualitative methodology, Knox et al. concluded that therapist disclosure did affect the real relationship in the clients' eyes, by allowing the clients to experience their therapists as more real and human. The clients appeared to appreciate the realness of their therapists and did not experience this realness as a threat to the therapists' stature, as some theoreticians have feared.

In another qualitative study, Gelso, Hill, Mohr, Rochlen, and Zack (1998) conducted semistructured interviews with 11 psychodynamic therapists, each of whom discussed a case of successful long-term therapy in which transference played an important role. It was found that the real relationship, as conceived of by these therapists, played an important role in the therapy, often served to facilitate clients' expression of difficult transference feelings, and, consistent with Gelso and Carter's (1985) expectation, typically contained a strong element of mutual liking that was not strongly loaded with transference.

These three studies provide a hint of some of the ways in which the real relationship may be studied in the future. Probably a major impediment to date, however, has been the lack of a sound instrument that could efficiently assess the therapy participants' and observers' perceptions of the real relationship as defined here. The value of such an instrument has been readily apparent in the area of working alliance (see the discussion of the Working Alliance Inventory, in Chapter 2). Recent research on transference (Chapter 3) and countertransference (Chapter 4) has also yielded promising instruments. To date, however, no such instrument has been constructed in the area of real relationship, although Eugster and Wampold's (1996) efforts suggest what may be the beginning of development of such a measure.

As we would conceive it, a real relationship measure would include items assessing our two elements (genuineness and realistic perception) in the therapist, the client, and perhaps the relationship, as seen from a variety of vantage points: therapist, client, therapist's supervisor if the therapist is in training, and outside raters. The use of different rating sources or perspectives, as well as ratings of the client, the therapist, and perhaps the relationship, would allow for a number of valuable comparisons. With such an instrument, we could begin to address such questions as: What factors relate to the development of a good real relationship? How does the real relationship unfold over the course of therapy, and how does it interact with working alliance, transference, and countertransference as it unfolds? How does the real relationship affect the process and outcome of a given session as well as treatment as a whole? These are but a few of the general questions to be addressed; from them could evolve numerous questions of a more specific nature.

THEORETICAL PROPOSITIONS ABOUT
THE REAL RELATIONSHIP

In this section, we offer seven general propositions about the operation of the real relationship in psychotherapy. These general propositions are aimed at guiding practice and facilitating research. Given their general nature, the propositions are not capable of being empirically tested directly. Rather, our hope is that they can be readily translated into more specific and testable hypotheses. In contrast to propositions presented in the previous three chapters, the current ones are more provisional. There has been almost no research on the real relationship, and these propositions emanate from clinical experience and theoretical inference.

1. *The strength and valence of the real relationship, taken together, are significant factors in the effectiveness of psychotherapy.* We propose that as the therapist and the client are able to see each other more realistically, be more fully genuine with one another, and experience each other more positively within this realistic and genuine relationship, psychotherapy will be more effective. The positive real relationship, in which the therapy participants share a genuine I-thou relationship, and in which each experiences liking and affection for the realistically perceived other, promotes progress. It serves as a buffer against difficult transference feelings, and it provides a secure base from which the client is better able to explore and express transference reactions, and from which the therapist may more effectively examine countertransference. Quite apart from transference, however, the positive real relationship is profoundly helpful to both the therapist and the client. The positive feelings provide the client with security and confidence in his or her exploration of difficult issues. From the therapist's side, the real relationship fuels the therapist's deep investment in the process.

This proposition has been supported in an exploratory qualitative study by Hill et al. (1997), in which psychodynamically oriented therapists viewed the real relationship as important to the successful cases they described, and experienced mutual liking as a key element of the real relationship. The proposition was also partially supported by Eugster and Wampold's (1996) finding that therapists' and clients' perceptions of the therapist (but not of the client) offered real relationship during a given session were associated with their evaluations of the quality of that session.

Despite the fact that the real relationship has been minimized in some therapies (e.g., psychoanalytic approaches), our expectation is that this proposition applies equally to all theories. Even in therapies that do not emphasize it, the real relationship will exist and have its effects on the treatment. In addition, although the psychoanalytic theoreticians who have addressed the real relationship have tended to focus on the realistic perception part of it, whereas humanistic theoreticians have more likely explored the genuineness element, our proposition is that both elements of the real relationship are equally influential across theories.

We also expect that the real relationship is influential, in the ways we have described, in both brief and longer-term therapy. At the same time, our experience (as well as some research; see Gelso & Johnson, 1983) suggests that, in brief therapy, greater use is made of a real relationship, in tandem with the working alliance, and relatively less use is made of the transference (although transference is still important in brief work; see Chapter 3). Thus, the strength and valence of the real relationship, if anything, may be more important to the process and outcome of the brief therapies than to those of longer-term ones.

2. *Just as for the working alliance, it is important to have a positive real relationship exist from very early in therapy.* Much has been written about the value when a therapist and client "click." When clicking occurs, the participants share a sense that they can connect with each other emotionally and that, as human beings, they share similarities in important ways. Just as in any good relationship, there is a sense of "the right chemistry" in the relationship. This clicking phenomenon appears to be very important in the participants' formation of a solid human bond, and our contention is that clicking reflects a positive real relationship. The clicking process is likely to have a transference element as the participants unconsciously project into each other positive object parts that are carryovers from the past or projections of what the person wished for but did not have. Yet, we suspect that, in most cases, the clicking pertains largely to the real person of each of the participants.

One might ask how the real person of the therapist, in particular, can be communicated in a brief time, especially since the therapist is about the business of grasping the client's material rather than revealing himself or herself. Our answer is that the therapist reveals himself or herself in myriad ways from the first moment of contact—by the client's material that the therapist chooses to respond to and the *manner* of that response; by the therapist's sense of humor and nonverbal behavior; and by the seemingly less personal things such as the therapist's attire and office decor. All of these qualities communicate to the client, although the client may not be consciously processing any of them. Messages are also delivered in what and how the client communicates, although of course the client's role is to communicate directly about himself or herself.

The early appearance of a positive real relationship greatly fosters the hard work of therapy. The participants have a "liking bond" (as opposed to a "working bond" connected to the working alliance), and this helps carry the work through the difficult early stages. This liking bond is especially important in briefer therapies. If it is not there from the beginning, there is not a lot of time for a good relationship to develop. As with Proposition 1, we expect this "early effect" to be important in therapies of all theoretical persuasions.

3. *As the therapy relationship progresses, the real relationship deepens. Each participant holds a wider range of realistic perceptions of the other, and each is able to be more fully genuine.* As therapy moves forward, the participants come to know more and more about each other and are likely to feel safer in being themselves with each other. This is probably not a simple linear process; it occurs in spurts, just as each party's revelations of self occur in spurts. Evidence suggests that transference increases during the middle phase of therapy (see Chapter 3), but such an increase does not mean that real relationship decreases; real relationship is far more than only low transference. Actually, we expect that both increase. Note, however, that this does not mean that the real relationship is increasingly in the foreground of the work. (The issues of when the real relationship is foreground and background are discussed in the text accompanying Proposition 5.)

Although we expect the real relationship to deepen in all therapies as time progresses, it is also probably true that this deepening occurs more in successful therapy. In less successful cases, we might expect genuineness to increase at a slow rate, if at all. Likewise, in many less successful cases, realistic perception may not increase, but may become clouded by transference feelings that invade the work in the absence of accompanying client insight. This suggestion has been supported by research reported in Chapter 3, in which less successful therapy cases evidenced rising transference in the absence of rising insight during the latter phase of the work (Gelso et al., 1997). Therapist countertransference, too, may blunt the unfolding of the real relationship as therapy progresses, which is yet another reason why it is crucial that therapists work to manage their countertransference reactions, as explored in Chapter 4.

4. *The increasing emergence and depth of the real relationship parallels and reflects increasing client progress in psychotherapy.* Elements of this proposition have been discussed in earlier propositions. Suffice it to say here that we expect the progress of therapy to mirror the emergence of the real

relationship, with the two (progress and real relationship) reciprocally influencing one another. More precisely, as one part of this reciprocal impact, progress itself causes the deepening of the real relationship. Both the therapist and the client are spurred by the client's positive movement, and this positive movement itself fosters the softening of defenses, allows each to see the other more accurately, and facilitates mutual genuineness. Not only does client progress have an impact on the real relationship, but such progress actually reflects a deepening real relationship. For example, the client's ability to see the therapist more realistically, be more genuine with the therapist, and experience more positive feelings toward the therapist is indicative of the softening of defenses and of the client's emotional growth.

At the same time, the emergence and deepening of the real relationship itself fuels client progress. This side of the growth-real relationship synergy has been discussed in Proposition 1.

5. *During the initial and especially the latter stages of most therapies, the real relationship is most prominent, whereas the transference tends to recede.* Although the real relationship is ever present, our experience suggests that it is often in the background of the work—a silent companion, so to speak. The real relationship, however, comes to the foreground during certain periods, especially in the earliest and final stages of the work.

In the earliest sessions, although transference reactions are important, they are ordinarily low in quantity and intensity (see Gelso et al., 1997; Patton et al., 1997). Although the client does not have a lot of information about the therapist, the information is constantly coming forth. And the client initially experiences and perceives that information, to an important extent, realistically. The emerging transference creates certain filters through which the client interprets information, but we would call it a weak transference. Also, in this early stage, the client is struggling to present himself or herself genuinely, and, in this process, the genuineness is limited by the newness of the relationship and by the client's inevitable defenses. But the client struggles to tell his or her story in an honest and open manner.

From the therapist's side, there is naturally an attempt to understand the client and see the client realistically. Despite the ongoing nature of countertransference, just as is the case with transference, the therapist's countertransference is at a low point in the earliest stages of the work. Although the therapist's personal style and theoretical orientation create much variability in how open and revealing he or she will be, the therapist certainly seeks to present himself or herself in a nonphony manner.

In sum, the real relationship is in the foreground early in the work, and, as noted in Proposition 2, may be most responsible for the early "clicking" phenomenon that we see in psychotherapy and other relationships. The reality of each person to the other, and the reality of the relationship, are most salient. As Greenson (1967, 1978) suggests, this real relationship may be what underlies the early development of a working alliance between client and therapist. In any event, as the work progresses, the real relationship recedes into the background. The real relationship does not diminish in strength, for, as we have suggested earlier, the real relationship ought to deepen throughout. But other issues (the transference, the client's internal and real-world problems) come to the forefront and take precedence.

At this point, we must discuss some significant exceptions to the above suggestions. First, therapists may deliberately seek to magnify the real relationship at certain points in the work. For example, if a client mutes the personhood of the therapist, the therapist may formulate that it is important to keep his or her reality in the forefront at certain points. In such a situation, therapists may reveal more about themselves, be more active in the process, and seek to reduce ambiguity. Second, with some clients and in certain modes of therapy, the majority of the work may be done through the real relationship. For example, we suggest that with the most profoundly disturbed clients (e.g., borderline and psychotic clients), the therapist may make the judgment that the real relationship should be at the forefront throughout. Transference will surely emerge with such clients, but the therapist may seek to keep it at a minimum and keep the real relationship salient. This is done, as noted above, through therapist activity, direct guidance, expressiveness (reduced ambiguity), and the like. In brief therapy, the therapist may seek to work through the real relationship—keeping his or her reality in the forefront. Finally, the therapist's theoretical orientation may dictate that the real relationship be kept at the forefront throughout. Humanistic therapists may keep the relationship as the centerpiece of the work, and it is the real relationship with which they are most concerned.

The real relationship generally is also most salient in the final stages of therapy. Transference comes increasingly under the control of client insight, and against the backdrop of the real relationship, as Gelso and Carter (1994a) note, transference distortions become more delineated. Therapists tend to be more revealing as the work winds down; many analytic therapists seek essentially to dissolve the transference. The client, likewise, becomes more genuinely interested in the person of the therapist. Some clients seem to be constantly and intensely curious about their therapists, but such ongoing curiosity tends to have a voyeuristic flavor and seems tied to transference issues. It seems qualitatively different from the interest shown by the client toward the end of the work. In the latter instance, it is as if the client says, "We have spent all this time on me, and as my issues have gotten taken care of, and as we are coming to an end, I find I want to know more about this person who has been so central in my life— I find myself more interested in him or her as a person rather than only as my therapist."

6. *Whereas the importance of the real relationship depends on the therapist's theoretical orientation in the therapist's eyes, theoretical orientation is beside the point in the client's eyes.* As we have noted, the importance of the real relationship for therapists depends a great deal on their theoretical orientation. Generally, humanistic therapists focus a great deal on something like a real relationship in their emphasis on genuineness, the I-Thou relationship, and the experiential world of the client. These matter more than transference considerations. Cognitive-behavioral therapists attend less to the relationship than humanists do, but the relationship that is attended to seems to be the real rather than the transference relationship. Psychoanalytic therapists vary considerably in their attention to the real relationship. Many essentially ignore it, and many others believe that it is an inevitable part of the work. Still others, such as the intersubjectivists (e.g., Stolorow, 1991), are inclined to believe that the concept of "real" is unworkable. In their view, we cannot generally separate relationships into their realistic and unrealistic elements.

For the client, we contend that the therapist's theory is beside the point; the real relationship matters substantially to most clients. There are clients who need to mute the therapist's personhood. Their personal issues dictate turning the therapist into an impersonal, businesslike professional who is without feelings toward the client and has only technical expertise. But needs such as this are born of defenses and fear of relating.

By and large, clients wish for a therapist who realistically cares about them and likes them as the persons they are—their core, so to speak. They also want a therapist who relates to them without pretense and with genuineness and honesty. In essence, they want a positive real relationship. This suggestion is supported strongly by Eugster and Wampold's (1996) research, in which it was found that clients' perceptions of the therapist real relationship (defined similarly to our definition) during a given therapy session were a better predictor of the quality of the session than eight other therapist and patient variables that had been found to be solid predictors of success in therapy.

Although we have suggested that the real relationship is very important in clients' eyes, we are less clear about the importance of the client's contribution to the real relationship than the therapist's. Experience suggests that clients clearly and generally want to feel realistically positive about their therapists, and that they wish, themselves, to be genuine. Yet we also suspect that their own contribution to the real relationship is of uncertain value to them. Eugster and Wampold (1996), for example, found that client real relationship in a given session was not significantly related to session quality.

7. *Role differences between the therapist and the client create differences in how the two parties experience and enact the real relationship.* Although the therapist and the client are human beings of equal worth and dignity, the fact that one is the designated helper in the relationship and the other is the designated helpee creates wide differences in each participant's realities and expectations. Such differences show themselves in the real relationship as well as in many other elements of the therapy.

Regarding the therapist's role in the real relationship, he or she is expected to manage his or her countertransference and thus perceive the client realistically, unencumbered by his or her own issues. Although therapists naturally will slip from this standard occasionally, they are expected to strive to meet the standard and, by and large, to succeed at it.

The therapist's role regarding genuineness is more complex. The therapist surely is expected to be genuine, not disingenuous. This expectation is held by the client as well as the therapist, and is an underlying element of all theories. Yet, just what is meant by *genuineness* is not so clear. Therapists are to be themselves, but usually this does not mean they are to be constantly open about their feelings and experiencing. While "at work" in trying to understand and help the client, the therapist monitors his or her feelings, and chooses to express some and not others. What will benefit or hinder the client must be at the forefront of the therapist's consciousness at all times. At the same time, it is important that therapists do not deceive their clients, nor communicate feelings or thoughts that are contrary to their inner experiencing. Finally, the real relationship is affected by just how much therapists reveal of themselves, e.g., through direct self-disclosure and the use of techniques. Generally, the more active techniques (direct guidance, advice), more so than the uncovering techniques, tend to keep the relationship at a real relationship level.

In contrast to the therapist's role, the client's role in the real relationship has expectations around realistic perception that are more complex than expectations around genuineness. Although the aim is to help the client perceive others (including the therapist) more realistically, the client's role is to express whatever he or she does perceive, however inaccurately—distortions and all. The client cannot force realistic perceptions; they must come naturally, as defenses soften and esteem strengthens.

At the same time, the client is expected to work at being open, honest, and genuine—to say what is on his or her mind, and to express whatever he or she feels—at all times, even though he or she surely is not expected to succeed at this attempt in nearly all instances. The role expectation is clear, at least in theory, but is it agreeable to the client? This question merits study. One potentially fruitful area of inquiry regarding expectations in the real relationship is the extent to which therapist and client are in synchrony regarding genuineness and realistic perception of each other, and how this relates to process and outcome.

CONCLUSION

Every psychotherapy relationship contains a real relationship component. Although the therapist can facilitate the strength and valence of the real relationship, this component of the overall therapy relationship is going to exist even if the therapist does nothing to foster it. Despite its universal nature, and despite the fact that most therapists likely pay attention to something like a real relationship, this component has been ignored in theory and research. The complexity of the concept and the vagueness of its definition are the likely culprits for the lack of research. Postmodern philosophy, with its eschewal of the concept of an objectively defined reality, also is a part of inattention to the component. We have asserted that there is a reality to the therapy relationship beyond the perceptions of the participants, although that reality is certainly highly complex and surely often nonlinear. Despite impediments, beginning efforts to measure the role of the real relationship have occurred in recent years. Measurement devices are badly needed at this point in order to facilitate continued research. Continued theoretical efforts are also needed to further refine this component and its operation in diverse forms of psychotherapy.

CHAPTER 6

The Psychotherapy
Relationship in Operation

I N THE previous chapters, we discussed what we consider to be key
components of the client-therapist relationship and how these components individually operate during psychotherapy. Although each
component (working alliance, transference configuration, real relationship) had to be examined separately to permit an in-depth analysis, such
a separation inevitably leaves something out. It does not provide a picture
of how the client-therapist relationship actually operates as a whole—
how the components *together* become lived out in the ongoing process of
psychotherapy—and of how these components mutually influence one
another in that process. In the present chapter, we seek to capture this *living out* of the relationship and the interaction of its components.

There are many ways to divide the psychotherapy experience in order
to foster our understanding of it. One common division designates relationship factors and technical factors, where the latter pertains to the
techniques used by the therapist. Unfortunately, there has been a tendency to consider techniques and the client-therapist relationship as separate and independent entities. We believe this to be far from the truth of
psychotherapy (see S. Butler & Strupp, 1986). The therapy relationship
and therapist techniques, while surely not the same thing, are interrelated in the real world of therapy practice. A second aim of the present
chapter is to explore the interconnection of the relationship and therapist
technique.

In exploring how the therapy relationship and therapist technique mutually influence one another, we find it useful to consider the role of what we call relationship stances. Such stances suggest a certain view of the relationship and also represent techniques in a broad sense. These relationship stances will be discussed in the latter part of this chapter.

Throughout the chapter, we emphasize the role of theoretical orientation in understanding which components of the relationship are emphasized, as well as the connection of the relationship to technique. Although there surely is not a one-to-one connection among the theories adopted by practitioners, their views of the relationship, and the techniques they use, we believe that theory importantly, if not pervasively, influences what is emphasized in the relationship and the actual responses or techniques therapists employ (see Gelso, 1995; Poznanski & McLennan, 1995a, 1995b).

In the present chapter, we intend to map out how the client-therapist relationship and its three major components (a) operate during the living interaction between the therapist and the client; (b) mutually influence one another during treatment; and (c) interact with the therapist's use of techniques. In discussing the interplay of the client-therapist relationship and the therapist's use of techniques, we introduce the concept of relationship stances that at once reflect views of the relationship and represent general techniques.

THE RELATIONSHIP IN ACTION

In the lived and living experience of psychotherapy, the three components of the relationship do not often distinguish themselves sharply. An examination of what transpires during therapy may help clarify how the relationship components operate.

The client is about the business of carrying out his or her role. This usually involves exploring conflicts, contents, and feelings, and trying to arrive at solutions to problems. Some of the client's feelings may pertain to the therapist and the relationship, whether directly or indirectly. For some clients, the relationship is immediately central; for others, it takes on significance over time; for still others, it becomes only modestly significant.

In contrast to the client's role, the therapist is about the business of listening; empathically entering into the client's world; absorbing what the client expresses; reflecting on what the client's communications mean; and considering and making interventions aimed at facilitating the progression of the hour and positive change in the client. When therapists function as they ought to, they are also attending to their own internal processes, even as they involve themselves in the activities just noted. Effective therapists allow themselves to experience during the therapy hour, and they try to understand what those experiences mean in terms of the relationship. (Although attention to the therapist's inner experiences occurs more in theories emphasizing relationship, we suspect that the most effective therapists of any orientation are attentive to their feelings in the relationship.) Within the hour, things usually happen quickly. The therapist takes in a great deal of information, processes it, and responds—often in a matter of seconds.

In the midst of all this activity, the therapist and client develop attitudes and feelings toward one another. These attitudes and feelings, along with the manner in which they are expressed, constitute the psychotherapy relationship (Chapter 1; Gelso & Carter, 1985, 1994a, 1994b). Although some disagree with the need to make outward expression a necessary part of the definition of relationship (e.g., Hill, 1994), we believe that the manner of expressing feelings and attitudes must be part of any definition. The expression makes the relationship a reality. We do not necessarily mean explicit, direct expression. Relationship feelings and attitudes may be expressed in extremely subtle, almost unnoticeable ways—nonverbal expressions, allusions, metaphors. It is true that some feelings and thoughts are hidden, but we believe that these, too, manifest themselves in some way. In any event, the three components of the relationship (working alliance, transference configuration, real relationship) are a fundamental part of these feelings and attitudes and their expression.

The components of the therapy relationship unfold simultaneously during the hour. As stated earlier, the relationship usually is all of a piece; it is not separated into parts or components as it is lived out and experienced during the psychotherapy session. Even within a given expression by or experience of the client, for example, the components are all there, in different shadings and degrees. Consider the following example:

> The client is a 41-year-old woman in long-term psychoanalytically based therapy. During the hour, she is exploring her need to separate emotionally from her provocative father and her brother if she is to be able to truly enjoy sexual intimacy with her husband. But the thought of this necessary separation is frightening and saddening. She expresses the wish that her male therapist figuratively hold her hand in the process, and she realizes that one way of holding her hand that she wishes for maintains her disruptive connection to father—the therapist becomes the provocative and untrustworthy father. Another way allows the therapist, as a real person, to join with the client as the adult she has become in helping her cope with the loss involved in this necessary separation.

This therapy had occurred over several years, and the client and therapist (CJG) had a sound working alliance, which helped the client explore these threatening conflicts. The above vignette reflected both the client's transference wishes and the real relationship wishes she experienced. Both were present and both exerted their pull on the therapist at the level of countertransference, and of the therapist's wishes and needs in the real relationship. Thus, working alliance, transference configuration (transference and countertransference), and real relationship were all present in this brief sample of therapy. The working alliance in this instance was the ground, and the transference and real relationship were the figure.

As we discuss constructs such as working alliance, transference, and real relationship, it must be kept in mind that these so-called components are not concrete things. Rather, they are labels we place on processes—processes that flow through each other, parallel each other, and are exchanged to and from the therapy participants. The temptation to reify the constructs is great; as we theorize, it so easily seems like the processes we are labeling take on a substance and life of their own. But the temptation to reify must be avoided.

During the process of the therapy hour, the therapist is often unaware of the relationship components or of the relationship itself. His or her concentration is focused on the client's story, on empathically entering the client's world, on facilitating the client's experiencing, on constructing helpful suggestions, on conceptualizing the client's dynamics, and/or on analyzing disruptive cognitions and behaviors. This is as it should be, for even in the therapies that subscribe to the curative powers and central importance of the client-therapist relationship, a lot of what happens in the work does not and need not directly focus on the relationship. But the relationship is there, often in the background but at times moving to center stage. On occasions, it is so salient and relevant to the therapeutic interaction that only the therapist's defenses would allow him or her to avoid it.

Although theoretical orientation does play a key role in how therapists deal with the relationship, therapists are not as true to their theoretical orientations as one might think, based on their talk and theorizing (e.g., Rosso & Frey, 1973). Therapists holding just about any theoretical orientation try to grasp the client's feelings and thoughts, whether based on transference or real relationship, and perhaps do not even make distinctions between the two components unless some deviation from "normal flow" occurs. The aims during much of therapy, as we have observed, conducted, and studied it, are: to understand the client's feelings, cognitions, and behavior; to help the client understand them and their meanings; and ultimately to facilitate the client's modifying them in a way that improves his or her life.

During this process, the therapist is especially attentive to feelings and cognitions directed at him or her, but again not usually parceling them neatly into transference, nontransference, and working alliance—not saying to himself or herself, "Here is working alliance," or "This is real relationship"—unless something notable occurs and makes one stand out significantly above the others, or interferes with progress. At the same time, therapists from all theoretical persuasions do seek to foster a sound working alliance early in the work (Raue, Castonguay, & Goldfried, 1993; Salvio, Beutler, Wood, & Engle, 1992). How this is accomplished is examined in Chapter 2. For now, we shall only add that, from the therapist's side, efforts to understand the client deeply and empathically are probably the best way to further an alliance early in the work. In addition, the therapist's effectiveness in helping the client, in ways congruent with that therapist's theory of therapy and client change, also furthers the alliance in most cases (assuming this conception is reasonably congruent with the client's conception). For example, the analytic therapist's effectiveness in conducting analytic therapy, or the gestalt therapist's effectiveness in conducting gestalt therapy, will further the working alliance. Given a therapist who is empathic and skilled, evidence supports the idea that a "good enough alliance" is typically formed within the first few sessions; with more profoundly troubled clients, however, it may take many months for such an alliance to develop, if indeed it ever does (see Chapter 2).

THEORETICAL ORIENTATION AND THE RELATIONSHIP COMPONENTS

Therapists of all theoretical shades are about equally interested in facilitating a sound working alliance, but theories unsurprisingly differ in the extent to which they attend to transference and real relationship. This is so despite the previously mentioned observations that (a) during much of the process of therapy, the relationship is ground rather than figure, and (b) the relationship is most often experienced by therapists as all of a piece, rather than separated into parts as it is lived out.

The development and surfacing of transference (and its connection to countertransference) are very much linked to theoretical orientation. As the client's material emerges and the client-therapist relationship unfolds, with its inevitable mixture of the three components, the psychoanalytic therapist practicing psychoanalytic therapy or psychoanalysis pays particular attention to transference, seeks to foster its development, and facilitates its expression in the treatment hour. As the transference emerges in the hour, the analytic therapist works to understand and interpret it effectively, with the aim of creating insight and ultimately working through in the client. Experiential-humanistic and cognitive-behavioral therapists, on the other hand, are not on the lookout for transference, and they probably do not detect subtle signs of it. These therapists foster growth and change through means other than working with transference. Our stance is that this is not problematic; the evidence is overwhelming that effective therapy can occur in the absence of direct attention to the transferences. Some humanistic therapists, however, do pay attention to transference; most often, they seek to change transference distortions through direct confrontation when transference distortions show themselves (see Chapter 9 and Gelso & Carter's, 1985, discussion of certain versions of gestalt therapy).

At the same time, when transference problems interfere with progress, it is crucial that nonanalytic therapists recognize them for what they are. This especially can occur with negative transference early in the work, before a strong alliance has been developed. Clients' mistaken feelings that the therapist is bored, uncaring, hostile, critical, cold, and so on, are common transference-based feelings. Even though the therapist needs to understand what these are about, the therapist is not required to make transference interpretations for these distortions to be resolved. Person-centered therapists, for example, have found that empathic understanding of such transferences may foster their resolution (see Chapter 9). We agree that even when negative transference reactions threaten the early work, interpretations are not necessarily the best remedy. What *is* needed, though, is the therapist's recognition, understanding, and exploration of such feelings. At certain times, it is likely to be important to deal with the feelings *as transference*, which includes an exploration of what the feelings are about, with an eye to helping the client gain insight into the distortion and where it came from. As our understanding of psychotherapy becomes more and more refined, one of the goals of theory and research ought to be to understand the conditions under which it is important to deal with transference as transference, in nonanalytic as well as analytic therapies.

Just as psychoanalytic therapists attend a great deal to transference within the context of the total emerging relationship, varieties of humanistic therapies (person-centered, gestalt, process-experiential, existential) are more concerned with the development of the real relationship, especially the element that embodies genuineness. Humanistic therapists pay attention to and seek to cultivate a genuine I-thou relationship in which both participants relate to one another in an authentic manner. Learning-based therapists (e.g., the varieties of behavioral, cognitive, and cognitive-behavioral therapists) also pay attention to the relationship and are likely to deal with it as a real relationship (although they may not use that term), unless some clear indications of transference, especially negative transference or eroticized positive transference, surface and disrupt progress. Psychoanalytic practitioners, on the other hand, do not pay as much attention to the development of a real relationship characterized by genuine I-thou relating, although we believe that effective analytic therapists do establish such relationships.

At the same time, we suspect that just how the I-Thou relationship is enacted will vary for different theories. The features of a psychoanalytic I-Thou relationship, for example, may be quite different from those of a humanistic I-Thou relationship. The analytic I-Thou relationship may, to exemplify further, be marked by highly respectful interpretations, experienced and communicated empathy even as one seeks to understand transference, and a deep appreciation for the client as a human being, in the context of trying to understand the defenses the client uses to avoid anxiety and pain. By contrast, the humanistic I-Thou relationship is likely to witness more self-disclosure, openness, and spontaneity on the part of the therapist. In any event, it appears to us that, however it is enacted, the establishment of an I-Thou relationship characterized by authenticity, caring, and genuineness is vital to good therapy of any persuasion.

In summary, although the components are always there and are an important part of process and outcome, the processes they reflect operate simultaneously and interactively within the emerging and ongoing client-therapist relationship. Most therapists do pay attention to this relationship (the feelings and attitudes the participants have toward one another, and the manner in which these are expressed), although at most times in the treatment hour the relationship is all of a piece, and not neatly separated into segments. The segments (i.e., components), however, do become crystallized at times, and just which ones come to the fore, and how they come to the fore, is importantly influenced by therapists' theory of the relationship.

INTERACTION OF THE COMPONENTS IN THE THERAPY HOUR

As we have suggested, in the live world of psychotherapy, the three relationship components we have theorized about are constantly interacting with one another within the client-therapist relationship. As a step toward formally theorizing about this interaction, Gelso and Carter (1994a) offered nine theoretical propositions. In this section, we seek to refine those propositions further, combining some and deleting others. We discuss the resulting four general propositions about how the relationship components combine with one another in treatment.

The first two propositions are best presented in tandem:

1. *Transference and working alliance have a reciprocal impact on one another; each influences and is influenced by the other.*
2. *Countertransference and working alliance, too, have a reciprocal impact; each influences and is influenced by the other.*

In the literature on working alliance, there has been an implicit assumption that working alliance is synonymous with real relationship, and that working alliance is essentially free from transference and countertransference intrusions. To the contrary, our view is that both transference and countertransference influence, and at times invade, the working alliance, and the working alliance, in turn, affects these two processes in certain ways. Let us first examine the transference-working alliance link.

One primary way in which transference influences working alliance occurs when the transference is positive. Positive transference, especially when occurring early in treatment, may serve to strengthen the alliance. A brief summary of a case involving the first author (CJG) illustrates this effect:

> A 43-year-old male communication expert suffered from chronic depression tied to exceptionally stringent super ego/ego ideal demands, in turn stemming from a relationship with a physician father who was experienced by this man as highly demanding, critical, and insatiable, especially related to work performance. This client also experienced his father as cold. The client internalized the father's demands, and was never able to feel that he achieved enough in his work, although he was quite successful by ordinary standards. From within the first few sessions of therapy with this client, the therapist was responded to as the kind and accepting father that the client longed for but never had. Although the therapist in fact felt accepting, it also seemed to the therapist that the client's reactions went beyond what the therapist actually was offering, and this impression was confirmed as the relationship was explored later in the therapy. The transference distortion, however, served to strengthen the working alliance in the early phases of this two-year therapy. When negative paternal transference later emerged, the alliance was strong enough to buffer the relationship from those reactions.

If the therapist could count on this positive transference—if it were reliable—then all might be fine. But, as Greenson (1967) noted, transference is not a dependable ally; it is, in fact, a treacherous ally. Often, negative transference feelings that had been defended against will emerge and will take the place of positive transference; the portion of the alliance that was based on positive transference will then likely erode. Thus, although positive transference may give the relationship in general (and the alliance in particular) an early boost, it is important for at least much of the alliance to develop apart from transference. At the same time, evidence supports the idea that, in both brief therapy (Gelso et al., 1997; Patton et al., 1997) and long-term therapy (Gelso et al., 1998; Graff & Luborsky, 1977), transference occurs throughout the work, and we suggest that it will affect the alliance through the entire process.

The effect of negative transference and seemingly less desirable positive transferences (e.g., eroticized ones) on the working alliance may be clearer than the positive effects discussed above. Negative transferences, especially when occurring early in therapy, can seriously impede the development of the alliance, or can even destroy the fragile beginning alliance and thus the therapy itself. For example, when the intensity, duration, and frequency of angry feelings toward the therapist are too great, or when the client's belief that the therapist is experiencing certain negative feelings toward him or her is too pervasive, these reactions on the part of the client can essentially wipe out the beginning working alliance.

As therapists, we need to pay close attention to such transferences, and seek to empathically understand the experiences of the client that may underlie these transferences. (At times, the client's reactions are essentially realistic, and therapists ought not to be too ready to attribute clients' reactions to transference; see Chapters 3 and 5.) If the negative transference continues, it is probably vital that the therapist gently help the client see that the projections and distortions involved come from another time and place, and are not befitting the therapist. In the absence of such understanding, the client's transference-based negativity can profoundly injure the therapy relationship in a way that may be irreparable. On the other hand, the client's coming to understand these transference reactions will serve to strengthen the still fragile alliance.

Regarding the other side of the transference-alliance interaction, we suggest that the working alliance affects the transference in two primary ways. First, the alliance allows transference-based feelings to come into the client's awareness and gain direct expression. This is so because the alliance serves as a buffer—a secure base, in attachment theory terms—allowing difficult feelings the client may have, whether positive or negative, to come into the open with at least enough confidence on the client's part that these feelings will not destroy the therapy relationship. Thus, the stronger the alliance, the more it will spur the awareness and expression of transference. This seemed to be clearly the case from the therapists' perspective in a recent qualitative study of long-term, successful, dynamically based therapy (Hill et al., 1997).

The second primary way in which the working alliance affects transference is that strong alliances are likely to aid in the transference resolution process. Thus, the greater the working bond between participants, the more likely the client will become aware that transference-based reactions, especially negative transference, come from another time and place, and although they may be stirred up and colored by the actual therapy relationship, to an important degree they are not befitting of the therapist. The sound working alliance helps the client trust the therapist and become emotionally aware that the client's negative expectations and projections are not in accord with what the therapist actually feels, does, or will do with and to the client.

Regarding the countertransference-alliance interaction, the sound alliance helps the therapist feel safe with the client, an important feature of therapy that is rarely addressed in the psychotherapy literature. This sense of safety is likely to diminish, or help the therapist effectively manage, countertransference reactions (see Chapter 4). In addition, a strong alliance helps the relationship survive expressions of countertransference behavior that meet the therapist's needs rather than the client's. This, of course, assumes that the therapist is able to gain an understanding of and resolve the countertransference. On the other side of the ledger, if countertransference feelings and behaviors are not effectively understood and managed by the therapist, they will infiltrate and weaken the working alliance. When this happens, a number of bad outcomes may result. For example, such feelings may undercut the therapist's abiding commitment to the work. Or, the weakened alliance may result in less than effective use of techniques by the therapist. Finally, countertransference can, on occasion, be so pronounced that it can severely damage the alliance, and the client may discontinue treatment. Such countertransference may take numerous shapes and forms, for example, outright rejection of the client, seduction, or failure to empathically understand the client.

Although the interaction of alliance and countertransference is similar to that between alliance and client transference, there is an essential difference. It is the therapist's job to monitor, understand, and manage his or her countertransference reactions so that they may be used to further therapy and not injure it. The client's job, on the other hand, is to genuinely express what he or she thinks and feels, and to work toward problem resolution. In the process, when transference occurs, it is supposed to come into the open. Thus, the therapist manages countertransference to help the client; when the client expresses transference, it is with the aim of fostering his or her own growth. These profound differences in roles, of course, have major implications for the alliance and transference or countertransference connection.

Our third proposition pertains to the two parts of the relationship that are often seen as synonymous: the working alliance and real relationship. Although they surely overlap, we do not see these two processes as being the same.

3. *The working alliance and real relationship have a reciprocal impact; each influences and is influenced by the other.*

The sound working alliance, as discussed in Chapter 2, is marked by a spirit of collaboration and a mutual attachment. But the collaborativeness and attachment are work-based, and we might call the bond involved in the working alliance a working bond. The collaborativeness and attachment exist for the purpose of furthering therapy. The positive real relationship, on the other hand, is reflected in realistically based positive feelings and attitudes toward the other person (e.g., liking, caring, loving) and a genuine I-Thou connection between therapist and client. Thus, the positive real relationship is more of a caring or liking bond than a working bond. It is not work-based, but simply has to do with the participants' realistic and genuinely expressed feelings for one another. The real relationship simply *is,* and it exists for no practical reason, although it surely has practical effects. It is a significant element of all relationships, work-based or otherwise.

The positive real relationship helps each participant form and then strengthen the working bond. For example, the client's realistically based liking for the therapist, the therapist's liking of the client, and their genuine expression of this mutual liking help the client experience and trust the therapist's competence, positive intent, and motivation to help. In this way, the positive real relationship helps the working alliance develop.

The reciprocal is also importantly true. For example, the therapist's abiding concern for the client as a client, his or her patience as a therapist, and his or her motivation to help are all part of the working alliance and contribute to making the therapist more likable as a person to the client.

Likewise, the client's courage and motivation to do the difficult work of therapy make the client more personally appealing to the therapist. In these ways, the working alliance, and the qualities that go into that alliance, strengthen the real relationship.

There is another way in which the working alliance aids the real relationship. Stronger alliances will allow the client to express realistic feelings that otherwise might not come into the open. A case example from a therapy conducted by CJG will help illustrate this point:

> The client (a 35-year-old woman) and the therapist had worked together twice a week for 2 years in analytically oriented therapy. It was clear that they had a very sound working alliance. However, the client became increasingly troubled by a particular reaction of her therapist. Each time the client expressed her difficulties with her children, the therapist seemed to respond unempathically, often offering unneeded suggestions, and at times even appearing critical. The client perceived these reactions realistically and responded with realistic hurt and frustration. She expressed these feelings to the therapist, along with her impressions of his reaction during one session, and the therapist became aware that, in fact, his conflicts about his own parenting were impeding the empathic process with his client. Once his countertransference conflicts were grasped, the therapist was able to regain his empathic stance during the client's exploration of her parenting.

In this case, the strong working alliance that existed between the therapist and the client allowed the client to express realistic problems she was having with the therapist. She perceived him accurately and was able to communicate her problems with him directly. The alliance thus fostered the expression of realistically based feelings and observations.

Our last proposition involves the real relationship and the client's transference. Although transference and real relationship are often seen as mutually exclusive, we suggest that they inevitably relate to one another.

4. *Transference and the real relationship have a reciprocal impact on one another; each influences and is influenced by the other.*

Like the working alliance, the positive real relationship serves as a buffer against difficult transference reactions. In other words, the realistic positive feelings and attitudes the therapist and client experience toward one another, and their genuineness with each other, provide a strong and secure base for the relationship. Thus, when negative transference emerges, this base aids the client to at least sense that something is amiss with those reactions that are under the influence of transference. The good real relationship also allows the client to feel safe in exploring threatening transferences. This good relationship conveys a sense that the overall relationship can endure and will not be destroyed by negative feelings. This pattern of the real relationship—both facilitating the exploration of transference and helping the client gain insight into the transference as such—appeared over and over in the qualitative analysis of eleven cases of successful dynamic therapy to which we have referred (Hill et al., 1997). In fact, the helpful influence of real relationship on expression and resolution of transference was evident in therapists' reports in nine of the eleven cases studied.

Although less frequent, a reciprocal effect also occurs: resolution of transference enhances the positive real relationship. This is especially true as negative transference feelings get worked through. This pattern was apparent in therapists' assessments of three of the eleven cases in the aforementioned qualitative analysis (Hill et al., 1997).

Can the real relationship be too positive? For example, can one or both of the participants feel too caring toward the other, such that the understanding and resolution of transference are impeded? Although too much caring is, more likely than not, a reflection of transference and/or countertransference, our clinical and supervision experiences suggest that, at times, this is a real relationship problem. Either the therapist or the client can find the other so appealing that the examination of transference feelings, or even the awareness of such feelings, becomes less likely. This is a very complex issue because feelings such as liking, caring, enjoying, and even a kind of nonromantic loving (the term *agape* is apt here) are valuable and perhaps essential elements of the good real relationship. Thus, the question becomes: When are these feelings too much? When do they become an impediment? There are no easy answers, unfortunately; but the therapist's ongoing self-awareness (along with the therapist's keeping the client's best interests in the forefront) may be the most useful guide in seeking answers. The therapist who is in touch with his or her own feelings in an ongoing way, and who is alert to subtle client reactions, even in the form of allusions and metaphors, is more likely to prevent, or at least come to grips with, this problem.

In this section, we have focused on the positive real relationship and its connection to transference. What if the real relationship is more toward the negative side of the continuum? Do negative real relationships actually occur? Or is negativity always due to transference and countertransference? Our tentative impression is that, occasionally, there do exist negative real relationships in which the client and/or the therapist, for example, do not "take to" the other. It is difficult for us to envision successful therapy occurring in the context of a negative real relationship, and it seems likely that such real relationships would stimulate negative transferences. The question of how therapy proceeds when one (or both) of the participants simply does not take to the other in the context of a helping relationship deserves theoretical and empirical attention.

The reciprocal interaction of real relationship and transference (including countertransference) takes on a figure-ground quality. Thus, even though all therapist and client interactions contain a mixture of transference and real relationship, and despite the fact that both are present in virtually all expressions and feelings, one will usually predominate—will become figure—while the other shifts into the background. This interaction occurs throughout the work, regardless of the duration of therapy. Transference and real relationship are always there, from beginning to end; at any given time, however, one is likely to predominate over the other.

THE RELATIONSHIP AND THERAPIST TECHNIQUES

To understand the connection between technique and the therapy relationship, we need first to define the term *techniques*. Following Harper and Bruce-Sanford (1989), technique may be seen as "a defined tool or method that is employed by the counselor in order to facilitate effective counseling or positive behavior change in the client" (p. 42). Generally, techniques may be thought of in terms of verbal behavior, nonverbal behavior, and general strategies. *Verbal behavior* is often separated into classes, typically referred to as response modes. Although there are over 30 different systems for categorizing response modes (Hill, 1990), it appears that all systems include the verbal techniques or response modes of therapist questioning, information (giving and getting), advice, reflection, interpretation, and self-disclosure (Elliott et al., 1987). Therapist *nonverbal behavior*, too, may be used as technique, although therapists do not as often use their own nonverbals as deliberate technique. The third category of technique, *general strategies,* constitutes broader procedures that are ordinarily tied to theory, for example, empty chair technique, systematic desensitization (Gelso & Fretz, 1992).

The techniques used by therapists are intimately connected to the quality and kind of relationship these therapists develop with their clients. In fact, we suggest that there is a synergy between relationship and technique: each affects and is affected by the other in profound but often subtle ways. Thus, the quality of the relationship has an effect on what is said by the therapist, how it is said, and the broader strategies that are used in treatment. In turn, what is said, how it is said, and these broader strategies (including *how* they are used) surely impinge on, color, and alter the relationship. For example, the fact that a therapist decides to make an interpretation, in contrast to the myriad of other responses that could be made, is likely indicative of the quality of his or her relationship with this particular client. Furthermore, many aspects of the interpretation—its content, duration, tone, overall quality—are surely affected by the relationship. In this sense, ineffective (e.g., ill-timed, negatively toned, wordy, or inaccurate) interpretations may be more reflective of difficulties in the relationship than anything else. In turn, the fact that interpretation was selected and the nature of the interpretation itself, along the lines just noted, are going to have an effect on the developing relationship (including the components). The same may be said for the use of any other techniques.

One aspect of how techniques affect the relationship pertains to how certain techniques foster the development of particular components of the therapy relationship. For example, exploratory techniques revolving around interpretation (e.g., of defenses, of transference) will likely foster the unfolding and resolution of transference. Well-timed interpretations of transference help the client focus on feelings toward the therapist, which include transference. Because such techniques direct the client's attention to his or her feelings toward the therapist, such feelings are more likely to surface. At a more general level, a technique may also entail broader relationship stances (see below). A technique-based stance of ambiguity by the therapist would also foster greater transference. The fuzzier or "grayer" the therapist, the more likely that clients' perceptions of and feelings toward that therapist will entail projections of the clients' own issues.

On the other hand, more active, guiding, and self-revealing techniques on the part of the therapist are likely to foster the real relationship rather than the transference relationship. Such techniques show the client who the person of the therapist is, and, even more to the point, they communicate the therapist's intent of enacting a real relationship with the client. They say, in effect, "Here is who I am, and here is who I want you to see me as." Techniques such as self-disclosure leave less room for client distortions, although, as we have underscored throughout, distortions will inevitably occur. But they will occur less, and the real relationship will become relatively more central, when therapists use self-revealing and guiding techniques.

THEORETICAL VISIONS, RELATIONSHIP COMPONENTS, AND TECHNIQUE

Each theory of psychotherapy possesses a vision of the client-therapist relationship in terms of which components it focuses on and emphasizes. Theories then embrace techniques that are compatible with and foster their visions. We are not saying that practicing therapists solely or even consistently enact the techniques tied to their favorite theory. There are some major departures. For example, in one study (Hill et al., 1997), psychodynamic therapists conducting long-term therapy were found to use a wide range of techniques in dealing with transference in cases they deemed to be successful, including some clearly nonanalytic or even antianalytic ones, such as "teaching, advising, educating" techniques and self-disclosure. Generally, these "departures" from theory likely stem from the person of the therapist—his or her needs, wishes, and personality—as well as from what the therapist believes the client needs. Be that as it may, theories themselves do contain techniques that reflect their vision of the client-therapist relationship, and adherents *more or less* use those techniques in their practice.

The psychoanalytic vision of the therapy relationship centers squarely on the transference-countertransference component. As indicated above, this vision is fostered and ultimately validated by the use of the broad technique or relationship stance of ambiguity (see the next section for a discussion of relationship stances). The vision is also fostered and validated by the use of more specific exploratory techniques revolving around interpretation. Thus, the therapist's ambiguity in terms of his or her personhood fosters transference projections, and then his or her exploratory/interpretive activity serves to communicate to the client that transference is occurring, is important, and is worth the client's attention. Such therapist activity also aids in bringing the transference into the open and then resolving or working through the transference.

The humanistic vision, on the other hand, centers on the real relationship component, especially genuineness. In keeping with this vision, at the technique level, the therapist strives to be spontaneous, open, and authentic with the client. Humanistic therapists, in fact, often are repelled by the very concept of technique, because technique implies to many humanists a kind of nonspontaneity or artificiality. However, because response modes revolving around self-disclosure and fostering authenticity are a recommended mode of intervention for humanistic therapists, consideration of these techniques is useful.

Humanistic therapists' empathic and technical attention is surely focused on the client, but these therapists seek to be genuinely themselves in the relationship and to foster genuineness in their clients. The aim is to create an I-Thou relationship, which itself has crucial curative power.

The cognitive-behavioral therapies (including therapies that are more cognitive than behavioral, and vice versa) embrace a vision of the relationship that, like the humanistic therapies, focuses on the real relationship, even though these therapies do not make the relationship as central to their efficacy as do the humanistic approaches. The techniques used to further the real relationship are also similar to those in humanistic therapy, for example, therapist self-disclosure. In addition, the cognitive-behavioral therapies use active-directive techniques; such an active and directive stance also promotes a real relationship, though perhaps one that is less egalitarian. For example, when therapists make suggestions, direct the hour, and give homework assignments, they are displaying significant aspects of themselves; and to the extent that they do so, these therapists further and work through the real relationship.

Finally, the vision of the relationship held and promoted by every theory of therapy includes the working alliance, and a wide range of techniques within each theory can facilitate the alliance. Generally, techniques that are sensitively employed, are well timed, and fit the needs of the client will help the working alliance grow and develop.

THERAPEUTIC STANCES AND THE THERAPY RELATIONSHIP

When discussing techniques above, we proposed that techniques could also be considered in a broader way, in terms of therapist relationship stances. Such stances *are* techniques in a broad sense. In terms of the definition of techniques offered earlier, stances do represent defined tools or methods used by the therapist to bring about desired changes. Each of these stances suggests a view of the relationship, furthers certain kinds or elements of the relationship, and is also affected by the existing relationship. Such stances may be seen as existing on at least five interrelated therapist dimensions: (a) gratification-abstinence, (b) activity-permissiveness, (c) cognitive-affective, (d) uncovering-understanding, and (e) ambiguity-clarity. Each of these is briefly discussed below.

The *gratification-abstinence* dimension may be defined in terms of how "giving" the therapist is, where giving refers to the therapist's general tendency to support (vs. withhold) and gratify (vs. frustrate). A therapist who takes a gratifying stance tends to be supportive with clients, and this therapist gratifies the client's affectional and dependent demands or longings. A therapist who takes a more abstaining stance, in contrast, will tend to help the client analyze or experience rather than bolstering the client through support, suggestions, and explicit expression of caring. The more traditionally psychoanalytic therapist is the prototype of the low gratifier, following Freud's famous rule of abstinence: "Analytic treatment should be carried through, as far as is possible, under privation," and then "Cruel though it may sound, we must see to it that the patient's suffering, to a degree that is in some way or other effective, does not come to an end prematurely" (S. Freud, 1919, pp. 162–163). Freud believed that the client's underlying issues, which drove the client into therapy to begin with, would come out in the analysis and seek gratification from the analyst. For example, the needy, dependent client would seek to be taken care of in the analysis, or the affectionally hungry client would seek to be loved by the analyst. To the extent that these longings were given a kind of substitute gratification by the therapist, Freud worried, the client's need to understand and truly resolve his or her problems would be diminished. The client would substitute the need to be treated for the need to be cured, in Freud's terms. The frustration (nongratification) provided by the analyst was aimed at allowing the client to regress and the entire neurosis to be funneled into the transference—the vaunted transference neurosis, which was then understood and worked through by the client, with the help of the therapist's interpretive activity.

In recent decades, there has been a tendency for psychoanalytic therapists to be less frustrating and to gratify somewhat more. Some psychoanalytic therapists, often those espousing a self-psychology position (see Chapter 7), are now more concerned with the concept of "optimal provision" rather than that of abstinence. Linden (1994), for example, believes that the rule of abstinence ought to be done away with and replaced by that of optimal provision, which he defines as "any provision that, by meeting a mobilized developmental longing, facilitates the uncovering, illuminating, and transforming of the subjective experiences of the patient" (p. 559).

At the same time, much attention is still given within the psychoanalytic orientation to issues around abstinence. The analytic therapist is careful about how much to gratify, and generally favors helping clients to uncover and work through underlying issues rather than providing gratification/support. Other orientations are higher on the gratification side, and still others gratify some needs and are abstinent in response to others. Gestalt therapy, especially the kind promoted by Fritz Perls, appears to us to be highly abstinent in response to clients' dependency needs, but more gratifying around affectional needs. Perls seemed, for example, adamant about not satisfying clients' wishes to be taken care of and about the need for people to take care of themselves. Yet he and other gestaltists seem more willing to express direct affection to clients under circumstances in which these therapists see such expression as therapeutic.

The cognitive-behavioral therapies generally lean toward the gratifying stance, particularly in their willingness to offer therapeutic suggestions, provide positive reinforcement, and help clients structure their change efforts. Our impression is also that cognitive-behavioral therapists are more willing to express a range of feelings to clients if they believe this approach makes clients feel supported, bolstered, and more responsive to cognitive-behavioral techniques.

The *activity-permissiveness* dimension may be defined in terms of how "directing" the therapist is. It of course overlaps with the gratification-abstinence dimension just discussed, as does each dimension with every other one. From the beginnings of the psychotherapy enterprise, therapies have varied widely in terms of how much responsibility they take for directing the client and the treatment hour (active stance), as opposed to allowing the client to take whatever direction he or she chooses to in the work (permissive stance). The cognitive-behavioral therapies most obviously take the high-activity stance, whereas person-centered therapists take the most permissive stance in treatment. Other therapies reflect a complicated stance on this dimension. For example, whereas psychoanalysis is highly permissive in using free association techniques and allowing the client to say whatever comes to mind, the analyst or analytic therapist does lead the hour in a way through interpretations. The gestalt therapist, while being highly permissive in facilitating the client's expression of affect, takes a highly active stance when using gestalt experiments to direct the client's activity in the hour.

The *cognitive-affective* dimension is defined in accord with how experiential the therapist is and how much she or he seeks this "experientialness" from the client. The cognitive stance is a general technique that aims to help clients think through their problems and usually resolve the irrationality of their thinking. Cognitive-behavioral therapists naturally favor this stance, especially those cognitive-behavioral therapists who adhere to Ellis's rational-emotive therapy or Beck's cognitive therapy. Among the current major theories, gestalt and person-centered therapy are clearest in taking the affective stance on this dimension. These humanists place a premium on affective experiencing in the hour, and such experiencing is probably the key mechanism for client personality and behavior change. Intellect, especially in gestalt therapy, is often seen as getting in the way of growth. This is reflected most strikingly in Perls's admonition that we should "lose our minds and come to our senses."

Psychoanalysis and the various versions of analytic or dynamic therapy also lean strongly toward the affective stance. Although there is a popular caricature of analysis as involving a kind of obsessive and intellectualized preoccupation with "analyzing," good analytic work is very clearly affect- and experience-laden. At the same time, the client's observing/rational ego is usually seen as helpful if not essential to the process of understanding and integrating affect.

The fourth dimension is labeled the *uncovering-understanding* dimension. This dimension may be defined in terms of how "trusting" the therapist is of clients' capacity to take responsibility and resolve things for themselves. The uncovering stance, as embodied in psychoanalytic treatments, seeks to help the client look at wishes, needs, and fantasies that are not in the client's conscious mind and are defended against through the use of various defense mechanisms revolving around repression. In effect, the therapist does not trust that the client can or will work through fundamental issues by simply partaking of an understanding therapeutic environment. More is needed, and that need usually involves the therapist's helping the client, usually through interpretation, to make the unconscious conscious. Cognitive therapists also take an uncovering stance, but they focus on different client material than do analytic therapists. The aim of cognitivists is actively to uncover irrational and/or self-destructive cognitions that hinder the client. Like the analyst, the cognitive therapist believes something must be done to get the client to see the underlying problem. The therapist's understanding is not enough.

Therapists who lean toward a humanistic orientation, especially the person-centered approach, most often reflect the understanding stance. The understanding stance dictates that the therapist must create a deeply empathic therapeutic environment in which the client is accepted, indeed prized, for whoever he or she is, and is positively regarded in a way that approaches unconditionality. The fundamental belief is that, in such an environment, the client will be able to actualize his or her basic self and resolve the psychological issues and anxieties that are crippling him or her. Deep empathy (which really also connotes acceptance and positive regard) is sufficient to produce change. This kind of good therapeutic relationship is, in itself, curative. Nothing needs to be done *to* the client beyond this.

Like person-centered therapy, recent versions of psychoanalytic self psychology get close to this understanding stance (Stolorow, Atwood, & Brandchaft, 1994; Wolf, 1988). Therapists of this orientation suggest that a deep empathic understanding of the client is often sufficient to promote change. Unlike the person-centered therapist, however, the self psychologist usually also reflects the uncovering stance, in that interpretations are used to make unconscious material conscious, and this is viewed as mutative.

The final dimension, labeled the *ambiguity-clarity* dimension, may be defined in terms of how open and self-revealing the therapist is. The ambiguous stance is fundamental to the classical psychoanalyst, who reveals little of himself or herself, and in fact seeks to be "gray," for fear that self-revelation would contaminate the emerging transference to the point that helpful interpretation and working through would be impossible. Ambiguity is aimed at providing essentially a neutral stimulus figure to the client, so that the client's reactions to the therapist represent true transference projections, emanating from the client's issues and not the therapist's person. What might be labeled the high-clarity stance, on the other hand, aims at presenting the therapist as he or she truly is, and at providing a genuine human encounter. The gestalt therapist is probably the prototype of this posture. Within this stance, self-disclosure is relatively high, although the therapist naturally devotes much more time to the client's expression than to his or her own self-expression. The therapist taking the high-clarity stance is certainly not "gray," but instead presents a fairly clear stimulus picture to the client, with the underlying belief that it is ultimately helpful for the client to relate to a real person who is truly herself or himself in the relationship, and who also truly cares about the client.

A PERSPECTIVE ON RELATIONSHIP STANCES

We want to be clear in communicating our view that none of the relationship stances that have been described is superior to others in affecting client change. Each represents a general technique or approach that is tied to theoretical orientation and, in turn, dictates a set of more specific techniques. These relationship stances depict the interface between relationship and technique in that they indeed convey profound meaning about the kind of relationship that is to be developed; and, *at the same time,* relationship stances *are* techniques that themselves dictate more specific techniques.

Although no relationship stance is inherently superior to any other, it is probably true that certain clients will profit more from certain relationship stances than other stances—just as clients differ as to what theoretical approaches will help them most. Given the general finding that the major theoretical approaches are about equally effective (see the recent meta-analysis by Wampold et al., 1997), it is probably also true that most clients profit about equally from any stance and approach; yet we suggest that a certain unknown proportion of clients will profit differentially from different stances. The growing edge of outcome research is to un-cover which types of clients or problems profit most from which stances/ orientations offered by which therapists.

Finally, although we have focused on how the therapist's theoretical orientation determines his or her relationship stances, there is another, perhaps more fundamentally powerful, determinant of these stances. The person of the therapist—his or her personality, needs, wishes, and iden-tity—comes to play in the choices of both theoretical orientation and rela-tionship stances. This reality of the therapist—his or her essential being in the relationship—is a profoundly significant element of the real rela-tionship and of everything the therapist does in the work.

CONCLUSION

The components of the therapy relationship are often not clearly distin-guishable from one another in the lived and living experience of psy-chotherapy, although at times one component will come to the fore while the others move to the background. The therapist's theory of therapy and of the relationship importantly influences which component tends to be figure and which is ground. The major components, however, do interact substantially with one another during treatment; each affects and is af-fected by the others. The relationship (including its components) and therapist techniques, likewise, are constantly and reciprocally influenc-ing one another in ways that fundamentally affect process and outcome. At a broader level of technique, certain relationship stances exist that re-flect a general technique, dictate what specific techniques are used, and mutually affect the therapy relationship. While no stance is superior to the others, the growing edge of research involves the study of which stances and which therapists are best with particular clients.

Part Two

CHAPTER 7

Psychoanalytic Visions of the Psychotherapy Relationship: Beyond Transference

O F ALL the varied approaches to psychotherapy, the vision of the client-therapist relationship in psychoanalytic treatments may be subject to the greatest misunderstanding. From outside the psychoanalytic perspective, the common stereotype of the analytic relationship is that of the aloof psychoanalyst who makes minimal responses to his or her patient, and whose comments reflect interpretations that are at best far removed from the patient's experience, and at worst far-fetched. Part of this stereotype reflects the view that psychoanalysis is represented only by Freudian theory (often antiquated versions of Freudian drive theory), according to which the therapist or analyst's role is to maintain strict neutrality (often misunderstood as distance) so that the patient's transference (defined only by the analyst) may emerge in pure, uncontaminated form. All other "analytic-sounding" treatments are seen as not really psychoanalytic, but rather some version of vaguely described "psychodynamic" theory. Perhaps these misunderstandings about psychoanalytic theory and treatment are inevitable, given the extraordinary influence of Freud and the tendency of Freud and his followers to view any departure from established Freudian theory at once as something other than psychoanalysis and as misguided thinking due to the neurosis of the theoretician.

Putting such stereotypes aside, what actually is the nature of the client-therapist relationship in psychoanalytic theory? It is impossible to arrive at any simple, singular answer to this question, for essentially three reasons. First, as Gill (1954) long ago noted, there exist levels of psychoanalytic treatment (clarified below), and each has its own set of implications for what the relationship, and particularly the therapist's contributions to the relationship, ought to be.

Second, psychoanalytic theories are currently highly diverse and often conflicting. Four broad theoretical clusters, or what have been called "psychologies" (Mishne, 1993; Pine, 1990), are most prominent: (a) Freudian drive theory, (b) ego psychology, (c) object relations theory, and (d) psychoanalytic self psychology. Each of these psychologies has a different vision of the therapeutic relationship, and some of the variations are pronounced. In light of the differences among these psychologies, observers such as Mitchell (1988) maintain that "psychoanalysis appears to be more diffuse and divided than any comparable intellectual or professional discipline" (p. 5).

A final reason why we cannot offer a simple answer, when asked what constitutes the relationship in psychoanalytic treatment, pertains to changes occurring in this orientation. What at an earlier time seemed to be a monolith now appears to be spreading in several directions (often contradictory) at once. Gelso and Carter (1985) noted such changes over a decade ago. If anything, it appears to us that change has been even more accelerated during the past decade or so, has often seemed revolutionary in nature (Mitchell, 1993), and has possessed far-reaching implications for what the therapeutic relationship ought to be. These changes are related to developments in the four psychologies, as pointed to above, but they go beyond the four psychologies. In the present chapter, we take each of these three interrelated considerations into account. Thus, we shall discuss the relationship according to levels of treatment in analysis, the four psychologies of psychoanalysis, and the changing scene in analytic theory and practice.

As a preface to discussing the relationship in psychoanalytic approaches, we begin by examining what constitutes a psychoanalytic theory and what makes such a theory distinctive from other theories. This step back seems necessary, given the great ambiguity that exists regarding what is and is not "psychoanalytic." We then move to an examination of the client-therapist relationship as it is seen across diverse psychoanalytic perspectives and forms of treatment. Although we do so with some trepidation because of the three interrelated considerations noted above, we do believe it is possible to make at least some generalizations about the client-therapist relationship in what might be considered modal psychoanalytic treatment. Following a presentation of these generalizations, we explore how conceptions of the relationship are moderated by the considerations that have been noted: levels of treatment, diverse approaches within psychoanalysis, and the changing scene in analysis.

As in the next three chapters on humanistic, cognitive-behavioral, and feminist therapies, we also examine psychoanalytic treatments in terms of the four key themes or dimensions described in Chapter 1:

1. The centrality of the relationship in this persuasion.
2. The extent to which the relationship is an end in itself or a means to an end, i.e., curative in itself versus curative through something done to the relationship or because of it.
3. The extent to which the focus is on the real relationship versus the "unreal" relationship (transference and countertransference).
4. The use of power in the relationship—how much power the therapist assumes and how that power is used.

The chapter concludes with a discussion of the role of research in psychoanalytic treatment. We point to issues that surround research in psychoanalysis, and emerging areas of empirical inquiry regarding the analytic relationship.

WHAT CONSTITUTES A PSYCHOANALYTIC THEORY

Although there is no fully agreed-on conception of what constitutes a psychoanalytic theory, the elements offered by Robbins (1989) are persuasive. Robbins notes that common elements exist in contemporary psychoanalytic theories. First, all psychoanalytic theories posit the existence and importance of unconscious determinants or motivators of behavior. The theories vary somewhat in just how crucial these unconscious processes are, but all agree that such processes are central. A corollary of this concept of unconscious determinants is that of defense mechanisms. Thus, the idea that anxiety-provoking thoughts, feelings, impulses, and so on, are eliminated from consciousness through the use of defense mechanisms is a central part of all psychoanalytic theories (Gelso & Fretz, 1992). Second, psychoanalytic theories are all developmental in that they posit a sequencing to human learning and development, often in the form of stages that are either psychosexual (e.g., Freud) or psychosocial (e.g., Erikson). Third, all psychoanalytic theories attend to the interplay of instinctual, social, interpersonal, and biological determinants, although theories vary in the weight they give to these different factors.

Finally, all psychoanalytic theories subscribe to the primacy of mental functions and structures, which are constitutionally determined and/or acquired early in life. Once in place, they have an enormous impact on the person's life, including what environments and relationships are consciously or unconsciously sought out, as well as what behavior is enacted in those environments and relationships. The effect of internal functions and structures on the person's behavior is referred to as psychic determinism.

Inherent in these common elements is the notion that the person's early life is a crucial determinant of his or her personality and development. Although experiences throughout life are surely important, early life creates the blueprint of personality, the internal lenses or schemata through which we see, experience, and comprehend the world. Some analytic theories address the effects of periods as early as infancy (e.g., certain object relations theory), while others attend to early childhood (e.g., drive theory); but all subscribe to the notion that what occurs early critically affects what happens later.

THE RELATIONSHIP IN PSYCHOANALYTIC TREATMENTS: SOME GENERALIZATIONS ACROSS THEORIES

Despite the variations among psychoanalytic theories and among the levels of analytic treatment, as mentioned above, it is possible to detect some general trends and commonalities about the client-therapist relationship in contemporary psychoanalytic thought. First and perhaps foremost, it is safe to say that the therapeutic relationship is generally considered to be a vital factor in successful treatment. This was apparent in Freud's earliest writing and it is even more evident in writings of current object relations theorists (e.g., J. Greenberg & Mitchell, 1983; Mitchell, 1991) and psychoanalytic self psychologists (e.g., Wolf, 1988, 1991).

One might wonder whether the great importance placed on the relationship in psychoanalytic treatment is also evident in the brief analytic therapies that have blossomed in recent years. After all, in brief work, there is not a lot of time for a relationship to develop, and the focus on "getting the job done" may preclude careful attention to relationship.

Contrary to this view, examination of the brief psychoanalytic therapies suggests that virtually every one of them places a premium on the relationship (see Burlingame & Fuhriman, 1987). It is noteworthy, in this respect, that in one large-scale study of brief psychotherapy (Sloane, Staples, Cristol, Yorkston, & Whipple, 1975), the researchers pointed out that, for the psychoanalytic therapists they studied, the therapeutic relationship and psychoanalytic treatment were almost synonymous.

A second generalization that may be made about the relationship in psychoanalytic treatments is that the working alliance is increasingly accepted as a crucial part of effective treatment. In his review of changes in psychoanalysis during the 1980s, Pulver (1991) notes that objections among traditional analysts to the importance of working or therapeutic alliance (as apart from transference) have subsided, and "It now goes without saying that the analyst must pay attention to the way he and the patient are working together" (p. 75). Pervading the writings of psychoanalytic clinicians is the belief that the working alliance must be fostered and preserved in all versions of psychoanalytic work.

A third generalization about the relationship in contemporary analytic work is that transference (and, increasingly, countertransference) continues to be a pivotal element in treatment, or at least in the clinicians' conceptualizations about treatment. Because we shall explore this generalization in detail later in the chapter, let it suffice to say here that from the time of Freud's discovery of transference in the early part of the 20th century, this construct has been the center of analytic treatments of all kinds.

A fourth generalization is that, although what we have called the real relationship has always taken a back seat to transference in analytic treatments, it is increasingly viewed as important by many analytic clinicians. Greenson's (1967) treatise on classical analysis was probably the most influential work on the real relationship, promoting the view (actually long held by others, including both Sigmund and Anna Freud; see Chapter 5) that the real relationship was a legitimate element of psychoanalysis. For Greenson, the real relationship was of fundamental importance. Witness his comment: "For the analyst to work effectively and happily in the field of psychoanalysis it is important that his analytic and physicianly attitude be derived essentially from his real relationship to the patient" (1967, p. 222; see Chapter 5 for a detailed discussion of the real relationship).

Although it is unusual for contemporary psychoanalytic therapists to address the real relationship directly in their writing, the sense one gets from the perspective of current object relations theory (e.g., Mitchell,

1991), self psychology (e.g., Wolf, 1991), and intersubjective theory as a derivative of self psychology (e.g., Stolorow, 1991) is that the analytic relationship represents, at its best, a genuine I-Thou encounter between two meaning-making persons, in which the therapist seeks to grasp empathically the subjective experience of the client and, in the process, genuinely shares his or her (the therapist's) own personhood. Although transference is maintained as a central feature, the sense that there is a realistic element of this relationship (with both the client *and* the therapist being the arbiters of reality) seems to be implicit in every one of these contemporary theories.

A fifth generalization is that the concept of an analytic attitude (Schafer, 1983), a hallmark of psychoanalytic treatment from the inception of this theoretical approach, continues to be seen as a vital element of the analytic relationship, although some change has occurred in how an analytic attitude is to be enacted. The analytic attitude reflects an approach to treatment that places a premium on exploration and understanding, without judgment. At the core, this attitude represents an investigative approach to treatment. The therapist or analyst's mission is to understand deeply what is going on in the client, and by deeply we usually mean at a level that has not previously been in the client's conscious awareness. To foster this deep exploration, it has always been viewed as important that the analyst maintain his or her neutrality, as well as a spirit of abstinence, in the therapeutic relationship.

These two interconnected concepts, neutrality and abstinence, have been subject to great misunderstanding and controversy, both within and outside psychoanalytic circles. For example, S. Freud (1915/1959) first discussed neutrality as a safeguard against early analysts' overgratifying their patients, and in particular gratifying infantile erotic wishes. As Pulver (1991) notes, however, over the decades, the meaning of neutrality shifted toward a stance entailing objectivity rather than involvement. Pulver tells us:

> As more analysts began leaning toward the objective stance, the caricature of the rigid, withdrawn, and isolated analyst who made one interpretation per session and communicated in no other way with the patient became prevalent in the intellectual community. To the horror of most analysts, it also seemed to reflect to some degree the actual *modus operandi* of some of their colleagues. (pp. 69–70)

As Pulver and many others have noted, although the analytic attitude continues to be perhaps *the* central feature of analytic work, the move has been toward greater personal involvement in the relationship on the part of the therapist, while at the same time maintaining a neutral posture in the sense of not taking sides in the patient's intrapsychic struggles and external conflicts with significant others in his or her life. Regarding intrapsychic conflict, Schafer (1983) notes that "the analyst does not crusade for or against the so-called id, super ego, or defensive ego. The analyst has no favorites and so is not judgmental" (p. 5). We believe this quote applies across the different approaches to analytic work, even if the structural terms (id, ego, super ego) are not used. Also, part of the analytic attitude involves guarding against overgratifying the patient's demands, conscious or unconscious, to be taken care of and cared for directly in the therapy. Freud's rule of abstinence, as discussed in Chapter 6, aimed at guiding the analyst away from overgratifying, which would result in the client's experiencing a reduced need to grapple with his or her underlying issues, for example, because of feeling taken care of in the therapeutic relationship itself.

In sum, the modal, or perhaps ideal, analytic relationship has always been marked by an attitude of inquiry or exploration, and part of this attitude entailed maintaining a certain kind of neutrality and being careful to not gratify the client's neurotic wishes and wants. In past decades, the concepts of analytic attitude, neutrality, and abstinence were too often understood as embodying an objective, emotionally aloof, and unresponsive approach to treatment. The current scene, or at least the ideal, in psychoanalytic work seems to reflect the analytic therapist's goal of maintaining the spirit of nonjudgmental inquiry, as well as greater attention to neutrality and abstinence than other approaches, while also optimizing therapist involvement and engagement. In other words, although the contemporary analytic practitioner, as in the past, refrains from taking sides in the client's internal struggles (neutrality) and abstains from gratifying or supporting those client wishes that seem neurotically based (abstinence), the therapist does seek personal involvement and engagement in the therapeutic relationship and process.

Let us now examine the three factors that bear on the nature of the relationship in psychoanalytic treatment: (a) levels of treatment in psychoanalytic work, (b) widely different theories within psychoanalysis (the four psychologies), and (c) the changing scene in psychoanalysis.

LEVELS OF TREATMENT IN
PSYCHOANALYTIC APPROACHES

Any generalization about the relationship in psychoanalysis must take into account the notion of levels of treatment. The distinction between two such levels, psychoanalysis and psychoanalytic therapy, has long been recognized (Gill, 1954), but at least two other levels are important with respect to the relationship, how it is to develop, what aspects of it are to be attended to, and what effects it is expected to have.

In keeping with the first author's earlier writing (Gelso & Carter, 1985; Gelso & Fretz, 1992), four so-called levels of treatment seem most relevant to relationship issues: (a) psychoanalysis proper, (b) psychoanalytic psychotherapy, (c) supportive-analytic counseling or therapy, and (d) analytically informed counseling or therapy. Prior to a discussion of these four levels, it should be noted that, regardless of the level of treatment, a good relationship in any psychoanalytic work is seen by virtually all analytic therapists as involving caring, concern, respect, nonjudgmentalness, and sensitivity.

PSYCHOANALYSIS PROPER

What we are calling psychoanalysis proper largely conforms to the general conception of psychoanalysis. Treatment occurs three to five times a week; the analysand reclines on a couch and communicates largely through free association; the analysand's dream life is considered important material for the analysis; the analyst is positioned behind the analysand and uses primarily interpretive responses; the analyst is relatively (in comparison to other therapies) restrained in terms of sharing aspects of his or her feelings and life; the treatment is long-term, generally ranging from three to seven years in duration.

Within this treatment format, the analysand-analyst relationship is considered deeply significant. Although technical factors (i.e., techniques) are, too, seen as crucial, the relationship is the bedrock of analysis.

Although working alliance and, to an extent, real relationship are seen as important components of the relationship in psychoanalysis, the transferences and the transference-countertransference matrix are of greatest interest. In fact, psychoanalysis proper is often defined as *the systematic analysis of the transferences* (cf. Gill, 1982; Kernberg, 1975). In this treatment, attention is given to the creation of an analytic climate in which the transference relationship can flourish. That is, the analyst's aim is to facilitate the analysand's experience of transferential feelings and thoughts, verbalization of these in treatment, and then working through of the transferences aided by the therapist's steady interpretive activity. With respect to this last point, interpretation is clearly viewed as the primary, if not the sole, response mode used in analysis. As noted earlier, the analyst's analytic attitude is vital to the emergence and working through of the transferences. Thus, the analyst maintains neutrality as described above and is careful to refrain from gratifying the analysand's wishes and fantasies such that his or her need to self-explore would be abated.

Although it is not as prominent today as in earlier years, many analysts still view the transference neurosis as important. In the transference neurosis, the transference builds to a crescendo, at which point much of the analysand's energies get funneled into the analysis and into his or her feelings about and toward the analyst. Through steady and well-timed interpretation of the transference, these transference neuroses come to be understood and resolved in the analysand. This insight and the working through of the transferences (whether or not the concept of transference neurosis is employed) are usually seen as the essence of cure in psychoanalysis. In other words, the increased understanding and working through of the transferences—the many conflictual and problematic ways in which the analysand perceives, needs, and uses the analyst—are viewed as generalizable to the ways in which the analysand deals with significant others outside of the analysis. Transference resolution in this sense is part and parcel of the resolution of relationship problems in the client's life (as well as of the intrapsychic issues underlying those problems).

Much has been written about spontaneity in psychoanalysis, relative to other therapies, but this is a highly controlled spontaneity. Also, the premium placed on transference analysis through the use of interpretation creates a feeling tone to the relationship that seems quite different from, for example, the humanistic therapies. As shall be discussed later, this tone seems "softer" and warmer in the current analytic approaches that stress analyst empathy than in traditional approaches. The newer approaches, revolving around psychoanalytic self psychology, interestingly, bear some striking similarities to person-centered humanistic approaches (see E. Kahn, 1989, 1996).

PSYCHOANALYTIC PSYCHOTHERAPY

The differences between psychoanalysis proper and psychoanalytic or psychoanalytically oriented psychotherapy are very much matters of degree rather than kind. Structurally, this therapy ordinarily involves face-to-face interactions; sessions are usually once or twice a week; and the duration may be brief (a few sessions) or longer-term (over six months), but is usually the latter. Although the client or patient is encouraged to say whatever is on her or his mind, less use is made of free association. The therapist is usually restrained, as in psychoanalysis, but is somewhat more varied in technique—although interpretation is still the favored technique. Relatively greater attention is paid to helping the client solve problems in his or her "real life," as opposed to the nearly exclusive focus of analysis proper on understanding intrapsychic life (which is believed ultimately to affect "real life" conflicts).

The client-therapist relationship in this level of analytic intervention is similar to that in psychoanalysis proper, but is also different in ways that stem from the treatment differences noted in the preceding paragraph. Because the sessions are less frequent and the therapy is briefer, the relationship is likely to be less intense than in analysis (although it certainly may be quite intense). The transference relationship is still of major interest and concern, although extratransference conflicts are given more weight and air time. There is rarely an attempt to create conditions that allow transference to build to the point of a transference neurosis, and there may be more give-and-take to the client-therapist interaction, with the therapist being more active in the relationship. Overall, the relationship in psychoanalytic therapy is a key part of the treatment; and, as in psychoanalysis proper, the relationship is the subject matter of at least much of the interaction.

SUPPORTIVE-ANALYTIC COUNSELING

Supportive-analytic counseling is both similar to and different from the prior two levels of analytic work. This therapy usually is on a once-a-week basis (at times, it is less frequent), occurs in a face-to-face context, and is most often brief. In fact, we would classify most psychoanalytic brief and time-limited therapies as being of the supportive-analytic type. At the same time, some very long-term analytic work is of an essentially supportive nature. Such work often occurs with a more severely disturbed client who does not have the internal resources to do well in a strictly uncovering, insight-oriented therapy (as are psychoanalysis and psychoanalytic therapy).

Supportive-analytic counseling differs from the two prior therapies essentially in the therapist's use of a range of techniques and in providing suggestions, reassurance, advice, and reinforcement. These responses are part of the supportive element of the therapy. Relatedly, the therapist may take an educational posture, imparting information and even teaching when necessary or useful (e.g., Time-Limited Psychotherapy, Mann, 1973;

or Psychoanalytic Counseling, Patton & Meara, 1992). While still main-taining an important degree of analytic restraint, the therapist in supportive-analytic work is more "giving," more open, and more focused on the realities of the client's life and the realistic component of the therapy relationship. It is important to add, though, that the therapeutic relationship still does include the more analytic features: the analytic attitude (as discussed earlier), attention to transference and counter-transference, and the use of insight-rendering techniques such as insight. These elements get mixed with the more active, supportive features just noted.

It is often said that supportive therapy seeks to support defenses rather than uncover or work through them. Although this can be a confusing suggestion, the spirit of it, as evidenced in supportive-analytic counseling, is that improved functioning and problem resolution are brought about through more focused insight and support of appropriate patterns rather than uncovering and resolution of core unconscious conflicts and the working through of defenses, including those reflected in the transference relationship.

Helpful case examples of supportive-analytic counseling are provided by Horwitz (1974) in his discussion of the Menninger Foundation study of 42 cases treated by psychoanalysis, psychoanalytic therapy, and/or supportive-analytic counseling. Thus, in highly successful treatment of a woman hospitalized for marked agitated depression (and assessed as having weak ego resources, great depressive potential, and marked narcissism), the therapy "consisted largely of skillful counseling about the complex life circumstances she had to untangle" (p. 186). When the patient rejected interpretive efforts to link past to present and to bring transference into the open, "the therapist respected her rejection of transference interpretations and used the uninterpreted positive transference as a vehicle of the treatment . . ." (p. 186). In another highly successful case in which the client, a 27-year-old professional man, suffered from a long history of depression and an inability to apply himself to work, "The therapist focused upon day-to-day problems, offering himself as a benevolent, helpful authority figure, never insisting that the patient discuss matters that were too upsetting for him" (Horwitz, p. 187).

ANALYTICALLY INFORMED THERAPY

Analytically informed therapy is more heterogeneous than the above three levels. Its frequency may range from less than once a week to more than once a week, it occurs in a face-to-face context, and it ranges from very brief to very long term. The essential feature of analytically informed therapy is that the therapist uses analytic theory to conceptualize the client's dynamics and the therapy relationship. Such analytic understanding is also used to tailor the therapist's techniques and the treatment plan. However, the treatment itself is theoretically heterogeneous. In other words, the therapist may use a wide range of responses, and does not seek to implement an analytic attitude in terms of a baseline for treatment. Within this theoretical heterogeneity, the therapist may use non- or even antianalytic responses (e.g., in vivo desensitization, gestalt techniques). The bottom line, though, is that psychoanalytic theory is used to understand the client and to formulate treatments (analytic or otherwise) that are likely to work with the client.

Given the technical heterogeneity of this treatment, it is difficult to make a statement about what the therapeutic relationship will look like or even what it ought to look like, beyond the generalized qualities noted earlier: caring, concern, sensitivity, nonjudgmentalness, respect. Perhaps the most that can be said is that, in analytically informed therapy, the client-therapist relationship will be seen as very important, although the ways in which that importance is manifested will vary from treatment to treatment.

THE FOUR PSYCHOLOGIES OF PSYCHOANALYSIS

As we noted at the beginning of this chapter, generalizations about psychoanalysis and the relationship in analytic treatments are difficult to make and must be proposed with great caution, in part because there are many different theories within what, in its earlier years, seemed like a monolithic system. As a way of understanding the diverse theories or psychologies of psychoanalysis, some writers (e.g., Mishne, 1993; Pine, 1990) have divided the analytic pie into four major slices: (a) Freud's drive psychology, (b) the ego psychology that originated in Freud's later years and then became part of classical psychoanalytic theory, (c) object relations theory that has both British and American origins, and (d) psychoanalytic self psychology as pioneered by Heinz Kohut. There is definitely an overlap among them, but each of the four psychologies possesses importantly different visions of what makes people tick—about development, health, and psychopathology—as well as the psychotherapy relationship. In this section, we provide a brief summary of each psychology and examine what each has to say about the therapeutic relationship.

FREUD'S DRIVE PSYCHOLOGY

To Freud, drive was synonymous with instinct. Drive or instinct is part of human beings' biology and is a source of energy that produces psychic excitation or tension. Such excitation serves to motivate the organism to action. To the individual, drives may be represented as urges, leading to wishes and fantasies. The vision of human beings from the perspective of drive psychology is nicely summarized by Pine (1990) as follows:

> ... the individual is seen in terms of the vicissitudes of, and struggles with, lasting urges. These are initially forged in the crucible of early bodily and family experience, but of course undergo modifications as the person moves developmentally through oedipal, childhood, adolescent, and adult phases. From the perspective of drive psychology, then, the person is and carries the history of his or her encounter with such inner urges. These urges are seen as (1) ultimately biologically based but achieving psychological representation and form; (2) unfolding according to a preprogrammed epigenetic sequence, yet susceptible to profound disruption and alterations of this program in the complex organism that the human being is; and (3) subject to near endless varieties of transformation via delay, displacement, sublimation, and other defensive and expressive vicissitudes, such that their currently active forms and their presumed origins do not stand in any clear one-to-one relationship to each other. (p. 33)

The fundamental drives in Freud's dual instinct theory were sexuality and aggression, but Pine goes on to say that the positing of these two drives is, in a certain sense, "secondary to the core position of drive psychology—namely, that *some* lasting urges, undergoing modification and transformation, have lifelong effects and must be understood adequately to understand current behavior" (p. 33). These basically biological urges blend into psychological wishes, and the wishes in turn may be acted on or reflected in conscious or unconscious fantasies. Because certain wishes may be experienced as dangerous or unacceptable, psychic life is viewed as organized around conflict and its resolution, "signified by anxiety, guilt, aspects of shame, inhibition, symptom formation, and pathological character traits" (Pine, 1990, p. 33). It follows that much of drive psychology seeks to understand our wishes and urges, defenses against them, and conflict. To the extent that it is based on drive theory, much of psychoanalytic treatment, too, seeks to understand these phenomena.

It must be noted that relationships are certainly important to the person within the context of drive theory. Their importance, however, is in terms of their role in dealing with drives. Thus, for example, relationships with parents in early life are certainly of crucial significance in drive theory, but their significance lies in how these relationships support, negate, channel, and deal with the individual's biologically rooted drives.

What does this vision of the human being suggest about psychoanalytic treatment in general, and the client-therapist relationship in particular? Although it does not *inevitably* do so, drive theory permits, and perhaps fosters, the kind of psychoanalytic treatment often associated with classical analysis. The key to insight and working through is the analysand's urges and wishes, including the defenses and conflicts that surround them. The relationship with the analyst is important in that it helps illuminate these phenomena, primarily through the analysand's transference distortions of the analyst. The analyst needs to maintain neutrality and anonymity, and to adhere to Freud's rule of abstinence. If the therapist does so, the transference distortions will emerge into the treatment, and will ultimately be subject to confrontation, interpretation, and working through. The underlying assumption is that if the therapist or analyst creates a safe, accepting, nonjudgmental atmosphere in which he or she adheres to the qualities just noted, the transference will emerge in something close to pure form—uncontaminated by the analyst's personhood. This belief that the client's neurosis will get funneled into the treatment hour if the therapist only succeeds in not interfering (and, in the process, holds her or his own personhood back) underlies the view of orthodox Freudian analysis as a one-person psychology. In discussing drive psychology's view of analytic treatment, and the one-person psychology it embraces, Mitchell (1988) captures what the psychoanalytic relationship looks like from a drive theory format:

> If one views the analysand's experience of the analysis and the analyst as fundamentally monadic, the analyst is outside that experience and should *stay* outside it. Ultimately it has nothing to do with him. The analysand's free associations and transferential experiences unfold in his presence, and would do so (the same in all fundamental respects) with any analyst employing proper technique. Efforts to relate to the material himself would make the analyst an intruder, a contaminant, whether one regards the process as an unfolding of infantile wishes or of developmental needs. (p. 300)

Although Mitchell includes psychoanalytic self psychology in the above description of one-person theory, the description seems to us most fitting of drive theory. Regarding drive theory, Mitchell (1988, p. 299) goes on to say: "The analyst provides an 'objective' perspective; nothing in the patient's perception sticks to him. This is a model of the analytic situation composed of one subject and one observer, both studying the mind of the patient, and the analytic situation is structured in hierarchical fashion." Although Mitchell's views are from the standpoint of a critic of drive theory—from the outside, so to speak—we believe that they give an accurate flavor of the therapeutic relationship from a drive theory perspective.

Although Freud was certainly interested in developing therapeutic relationships, one does not sense that he promoted warm relationships in which he attempted to enter the client's world and understand it from the inside. Eagle and Wolitzky (1997) note, for example, that Freud did not attend to analyst empathy in a central or explicit way. [They point out that his 15 references to empathy in 23 volumes "hardly suggests an abiding interest in the issue" (p. 222).] Rather, Freud's advocacy of the "blank screen" and the "surgeon's role" suggested his interest in understanding the patient from an external or "outside" perspective. Witness his famous surgeon's analogy: "I cannot recommend my colleagues emphatically enough to take as a model in psycho-analytic treatment the surgeon who puts aside all of his own feelings, including that of human sympathy, and concentrates his mind on one single purpose, that of performing the operation as skillfully as possible" (1912/1959, p. 327).

Ego Psychology

Drive psychology occupied Freud in the earlier part of his career, but he eventually became vitally concerned with the role of ego (S. Freud, 1923/1953) and created his famous structural model of id, ego, and super ego—a model that gave ego a central place in his theorizing from that point on. For Freud, though, the ego was seen as the part of the psyche that emanated from, drew its energy from, and dealt with, drives—and then erected defense mechanisms against these drives when they threatened the organism's safety. These mechanisms came to be seen as having adaptive value in Anna Freud's (1936/1966) work, where they were theorized to play an important role in normal development.

Subsequent psychoanalytic ego psychology also focused on the ego as the *agency within* that enabled adaptation to the outside world (Hartmann, 1939/1964) and fostered reality testing on the part of the individual. In sum, whereas drive psychology underscores the taming, socialization, and gratification of drives, ego psychology "emphasizes the development of defenses with respect to the internal world, adaptation with respect to the external world, and reality testing with respect to both" (Pine, 1990, p. 50).

As early ego psychology was developed by Hartmann, a central tenet was that the ego, although it may have emerged from the id, developed autonomously in a sphere that could be free of conflict. In other words, the ego did much more than react to conflicts originating from the id (or super ego). It aided the person in adapting to the world and, through the process of perception, allowed the individual to perceive and test reality.

Just as the ego could foster development, ego defects or deficits are seen as playing a central role in psychopathology (Blanck & Blanck, 1979). The ego's strength is determined by constitutional factors and early family relationships, and once ego deficits emerge, they have major implications for further development. Mishne (1993) thus notes that developmental failures are caused by ego deficits (e.g., impaired reality testing, poor drive modulation, precarious self/other boundaries). In addition, a paucity of sound ego defenses underlies affect intolerance, impulsivity, and panic states. As part of this emphasis on early ego development and its role, psychoanalytic ego psychologists have tended to focus on very early (i.e., pre-Oedipal) development and deficits tied to this period of life.

Although Freudian drive psychology is often seen as *the* traditional theory of psychoanalysis, a more contemporary view states: "Currently within the national and international psychoanalytic community, amid increasing theoretical diversity and pluralism, the ego psychology paradigm and its structural theory predominate as the classic perspective in America" (Mishne, 1993, p. 191). What are the implications of a psychoanalytic ego psychology for psychoanalytic treatment and the therapeutic relationship?

Similar to our discussion of the therapeutic relationship in drive theory, ego psychology is also a one-person theory with all of the implications of a one-person psychology noted earlier. Treatment, including the relationship, would be similar to that fostered by drive psychology, although greater emphasis would be placed on the client's conscious experience and on ego functions such as adaptation to the world outside, reality testing, and effective and ineffective defense mechanisms. Although the client-therapist relationship would be similar to that in a drive-based therapy, as one moves away from psychoanalysis proper and toward psychoanalytically based therapies, the focus on ego and conscious adaptation to the outer world allows for greater activity on the part of the therapist and more of a give-and-take relationship. To the extent that early ego deficits are the focus, especially with clients with more profound psychopathology than is usually associated with psychoanalysis proper, the therapy would likely involve a more supportive, guiding, reality-oriented approach. Tied to this approach, less emphasis would be placed on the interpretation and working through of transference, and more emphasis would be placed on the real relationship between therapist and client. A therapy that is driven by attempts to strengthen the ego could even look behavioral in its enactment. Thus, a psychoanalytically informed therapy could use psychoanalytic understanding of the client's ego deficits and strengths to devise a treatment focused on effective functioning in the world outside of therapy. The real relationship, and perhaps the uninterpreted positive transference, could provide the therapist with leverage in his or her use of behavioral techniques in such a treatment.

OBJECT RELATIONS THEORY

The focus on ego processes is, in many ways, compatible with drive theory in the sense that a thoroughgoing ego psychology could also subscribe to the importance of drives and pay attention to the vicissitudes of those drives. Object relations theory, on the other hand, has developed in a way that is sharply divergent from drive theory. While object relations theory is itself quite diverse, containing many clashing viewpoints (see reviews by Greenberg & Mitchell, 1983; Mishne, 1993), there does seem to be a tie that binds widely divergent object relations conceptions. Probably the basic tenet of contemporary object relations theory is that people are fundamentally object seeking rather than drive or pleasure seeking. The need for others and for relatedness to others is wired into us as a basic part of human nature, with, as Bowlby (1969) so powerfully articulated, great species adaptation and preservation value. Eagle (1984) summarizes this position, and the empirical foundations favoring it, as follows:

> . . . all of the evidence taken together indicates that an interest in objects as well as the development of affectional bonds is not simply a derivative or outgrowth of libidinal energies and aims or a consequence of gratification of other needs, but is a critical independent aspect of development which expresses inborn propensities to establish cognitive and affective links to objects in the world. (pp. 15–16)

The leading figures in object relations theory are many and diverse: W. R. D. Fairbairn, Ian Suttie, Harry Guntrip, Melanie Klein, D. W. Winnicott, John Bowlby, Michael Balint, Otto Kernberg, Stephen Mitchell, Jay Greenberg, and others. Often included in the object relations group are interpersonalists, e.g., Harry Stack Sullivan, Erich Fromm, Karen Horney, Frieda Fromm-Reichman, Clara Thompson. The interpersonal perspective has been subject to wide criticism from traditionalists in psychoanalysis for its focus on culture and social relations rather than drives. The criticism has been that this cultural emphasis results in a superficial theory of personality, a theory lacking in the kind of depth that has been a trademark of psychoanalysis. Greenberg and Mitchell (1983), however, take a view that seems more current: "Sullivan, Fromm, and Horney all portray the human experience as fraught with deep, intense passions. The *content* of these passions and conflicts, however, is not understood to derive from drive pressure and regulation, but from shifting and competing configurations composed of relations between the self and others, real and imagined" (p. 80).

It would nonetheless be a mistake to view object relations theory as simply concerned with interpersonal relations. Just as important as relatedness is the concept of internal representations. These representations are of significant others, in part or whole, and are usually formed early in life. The representations are far from exact replicas of others. Rather, they are based on how the person has experienced the other, which itself is determined by a wide range of factors. Pine (1990) summarizes the object relations view as follows:

> . . . the individual is seen in terms of an internal drama, derived from early childhood, that is carried around within memory (conscious or unconscious) and in which the individual enacts one or more or all of the roles . . . . These internal images, loosely based on childhood experiences, also put their stamp on new experience, so that these in turn are assimilated to the old dramas rather than being experienced fully in their contemporary form. These internal dramas are understood to be formed out of experiences with the primary objects of childhood, but are not seen as veridical representations of those relationships. The object relation *as experienced* by the child is what is laid down in memory and repeated, and this experience is a function of the affect and wishes active in the child at the moment of the experience . . . . the same quietly pensive and inactive mother will be experienced as a depriver by the hungry child, but perhaps as comfortingly in tune by the child who is contentedly playing alone. Significant for the clinical relevance of the object relations psychology is the tendency to repeat these old family dramas, a repetition propelled by the efforts after attachment or after mastery or both. (pp. 34–35)

The object relations perspective on psychopathology is that the tendency for perceptions of and interactions in the present to be determined by these internally carried representations, rather than by current reality, including the reality of the other person, is a reflection of pathology. Also, the nature of the internal drama itself, which is carried around and lived out, reflects issues of psychological health and pathology. Put simply, some dramas are healthier than others. In sum:

> . . . Object relations theory focuses on the task of simultaneously carrying within us (through identification and internalized object relations) the record of the history of our significant relationships—which is essential to our humanness and is a basis for social living—and, on the other hand, of freeing ourselves from the absolute constraints of those relationships so that new experiences can be greeted, within limits, as new and responded to on their own, contemporary terms. (Pine, 1990, p. 50)

What are the implications of an object relations theory for psychotherapy and, specifically, for the client-therapist relationship in psychotherapy? First and foremost, the analyst or therapist as a person becomes more central to the process. If the client is inherently object and relationship seeking, even when defending against this basic urge, then the therapist becomes an important figure as a person to be related to (regardless of how much transference is enacted in that relating). In what now has shifted from the one-person psychology of drive and ego to a two-person psychology, the therapist, by his or her very presence, also contributes to the relationship in a way that far exceeds that of the neutral figure onto which drive- or ego-based needs are projected. Everything the therapist does, including maintaining neutrality, influences the relationship and colors the transference-countertransference matrix. Therapist and client interact with one another in creating the relationship, and while transference is still derived from the client's life and psyche, it is also shaped by the therapist's actions. The distinction between a one-person and two-person perspective in the psychoanalytic relationship is clarified by Mitchell (1988). Here we extend the quote presented earlier:

> If one views the analysand's experience of the analysis and the analyst as fundamentally monadic, the analyst is outside that experience and should *stay* outside it. Ultimately it has nothing to do with him. The analysand's free associations and transferential experiences unfold in his presence, and would do so (the same in all fundamental respects) with any analyst employing "proper" technique. Efforts to relate the material to himself would make the analyst an intruder, a contaminant . . . If one views the analysand's experience of the analysis as fundamentally interactive, as an encounter between two *persons,* the analysand is struggling to reach *this*

analyst. Familiar timeworn strategies are employed, to be sure, but as pathways to connect with what the analysand has experienced about this particular analyst as a person. The problem is no longer past significant others, but how to connect with, surrender to, dominate, fuse with, control, love, be loved by, use, be used by, *this* person. (p. 300)

As one reads current object relations theorists (e.g., Eagle, 1984; Mitchell, 1993) and contemporary views on object relations theory (e.g., Meissner, 1991), the clear impression is that the analysand-analyst and client-therapist relationships are seen as having curative elements in themselves. The good therapeutic relationship with the therapist allows one to rework internal object representations so that the images carried with the person are more constructive and more responsive to realities of current relationships, rather than distortions of them. Transference and countertransference are quite central in this process, but to the object relations therapist there is also a profound person-to-person relationship that coexists with the transference, gives it shape and form, and helps the client to experience the self and the therapist's self more fully and to move forward in developing healthier relationships. Also, transference is not understood as simply a reenactment or projection of earlier issues on an anonymous observer, but rather as a melding of those issues with the person of the therapist in a way that is both personally richer and more complicated than in classical one-person psychologies.

PSYCHOANALYTIC SELF PSYCHOLOGY

Stemming from the work of Heinz Kohut (1971, 1977, 1984), self psychology has had a powerful influence on psychoanalytic thought in the relatively short period of time since its original presentation (Kohut, 1971). The impact has been of such proportions that self psychology may legitimately be seen as a "fourth force" in psychoanalysis.

As the term implies, self psychology is primarily concerned with the development of the self, with the term *narcissism* being used liberally as a synonym for self, self-development, and self-esteem. It should be underscored that Kohut and the self psychologists do not use the term narcissism as a pejorative, but rather as a quality that exists in all human beings, a quality that may develop in psychologically healthy or unhealthy ways. Be that as it may, in Kohut's first major presentation (Kohut, 1971), the focus was on pathological narcissism—the development and analytic treatment of narcissistic personality disorders. He posited two lines of self or narcissistic development: that of the grandiose self and that of the omnipotent object. The former pertains to the young child's grandiose-exhibitionistic self and how its development depends on the parent's capacity to mirror empathically the child and his or her normal developmental needs. The second line of development (the omnipotent object) pertains to the child's need for all-powerful parental figures to idealize and to be a part of ("self-objects"). This self–self-object connection was seen as providing strength to the growing child's self. As the child gradually becomes ready to perceive the parent as imperfect, the strength of the parent could become internalized as part of the self. Narcissistic personality disorder was seen as resulting from major traumatizing failures of parents to provide the needed empathic mirroring and all-powerful self object experiences for the young child. Usually, the major disturbance resulted from self or narcissistic injury in one or the other of the two lines of development (that of the grandiose self or the omnipotent object).

Regarding analytic treatment, Kohut (1971) posited essentially two kinds of transferences tied to disturbances in the two lines of development: mirror transferences (tied to the grandiose self) and idealizing transferences (tied to the omnipotent object). The analyst's role involved empathically immersing herself or himself in the analysand's inner world, and using the empathy as a tool for understanding the client and providing helpful interpretations.

In Kohut's early work (Kohut, 1971), a clear link to Freudian drive theory was maintained. Kohut viewed drive theory as being valid for what he referred to as object-instinctual development (i.e., the development of relationships related to basic drives), and his own theory as valid for self or narcissistic development. Although empathy was seen as a major part of treatment—much more than had been the case in other analytic theories—empathy was not seen as curative in itself. Rather, it was a tool for analytic understanding, and it allowed for more effective interpretations.

As Kohut's theory developed over the remaining years of his life (Kohut, 1977, 1984), and as psychoanalytic self psychology has been furthered and expanded by others (e.g., Bacal & Newman, 1990; Goldberg, 1988; Lachmann & Beebe, 1992; Wolf, 1988), shifts have taken place that have major implications for the client-therapist relationship. Contemporary self psychology is now seen as not an extension of Freudian drive theory, but an alternative—and, in many ways, a competing—theory. While maintaining many of Kohut's essential features, the theory has transcended a narrow focus on narcissistic personality disorder and, instead, addresses the healthy and unhealthy development of the self more generally. Theory and treatment examine issues around the development of the self—self-esteem, self-cohesion, self-vulnerability, self-depletion—and explore how these self issues play themselves out in psychoanalytic work.

Regarding the relationship from a contemporary self psychology perspective, several theoretical directions are noteworthy. For one, therapist empathy continues to be seen as vital to effective treatment, both as a tool for understanding (as Kohut had originally conceptualized) and as a direct, healing ingredient. As a tool, what is often referred to as "prolonged empathic immersion" or "sustained empathic inquiry" (Kohut, 1959, 1971; Trop & Stolorow, 1997) is seen as the most powerful vehicle through which the therapist could deeply understand the client and his or her unconscious issues. As a healing ingredient, empathy is seen as providing the client with what he or she needed but only insufficiently had as a child. Wolf's (1991) observations reflect this aspect of the self psychological view of empathy:

> Such a reawakening of apparently lost potentials may occur when a person enters psychotherapy conducted by an empathically sensitive therapist who is careful to create an ambience of interested and attuned responsiveness . . . Regardless of whether we are talking about a normally incomplete self or about a more seriously defective self, in such an ambience the atrophied or arrested aspects of the self may find the psychological nourishment to resume their growth. . . . In these selfobject relationships the selfobject therapist is experienced as part of the self, thus making it more complete and less defective. These self-object experiences also create and strengthen self-selfobject bonds, with resulting increased cohesion and vigor of the self. (pp. 128–129)

A second major direction in self psychological conceptions of the client-therapist relationship is hinted at by Wolf's recommendation of an atmosphere of "interested and attuned responsiveness." That is, psychoanalytic self psychologists, perhaps more than any other psychoanalytic group, are concerned about the therapist's responsiveness to the client, and are uneasy with concepts such as neutrality and abstinence. Rather than think in terms of "optimal frustration" (a central element of the rule of abstinence), the self psychologist prefers to think in terms of optimal provision. Linden (1994), for example, believes that the rule of abstinence was never of value, and has been maintained for essentially defensive purposes. Citing Freud's own behavior with analysands, which was often tremendously gratifying by "orthodox Freudian standards" (e.g., feeding patients, showing patients his precious small statues, sending patients postcards, giving patients gifts), Linden offers case examples of optimal provision that go far beyond analytic orthodoxy. He defines optimal provision as "any provision that, by meeting a mobilized developmental longing, facilitates the uncovering, illuminating, and transforming of the subjective experiences of the patient" (p. 359).

It is important to underscore that, true to its psychoanalytic basis, optimal provision seeks to aid the processes of uncovering, illuminating, and transforming. In other words, it does not simply seek to support the patient, but rather to investigate, bring into the open, and change that which is hidden and disruptive. Furthermore, Linden makes very clear that, at times, being abstinent *is* optimally providing. Sometimes—or often—the client needs abstinence in order to engage in the uncovering process that Linden seeks to facilitate. At the same time, we believe that when the therapist conceptualizes in terms of optimal provision, she or he is more likely to provide a warm, caring, responsive, and, at times, supportive relationship.

A third major direction of thought regarding the relationship in self psychology also pertains to the role of the therapist. What has come to be called the intersubjective perspective (Stolorow, 1991; Stolorow et al., 1994; Stolorow, Brandchaft, & Atwood, 1987; Trop & Stolorow, 1997), a perspective that emerged from and seeks to extend self psychology, focuses on the cocreated relationship of therapist and client. According to intersubjectivists, even when we address the client's transference, and even as we conceptualize transference as the client's way of organizing his or her intimate interpersonal world, the role of the therapist is a vital part of the therapeutic process. The therapist or analyst's being and behavior, no matter how active or inactive he or she is, become a part of the transference, and must be considered in seeking to understand transference. Like many current object relations theories, the intersubjective approach to therapy reflects a two-person psychology, whereas earlier self psychology was a one-person psychology in that the client's transferences were fully determined by his or her own developmental needs (Richardson, in press).

Given this orientation to the role of the therapist in the client's transference, there is also a great deal of attention to countertransference in this perspective. Thus, Trop and Stolorow (1997) note:

> The attitude of sustained empathic inquiry, which informs the therapist's interpretations, must of necessity encompass the entire intersubjective field created by the interplay between the differently organized subjective

worlds of patient and therapist. Thus, a more accurate characterization of the investigatory stance would be empathic-*introspective* inquiry because it includes the therapist's ongoing reflection on the contribution of his or her own organizing principles [i.e., those principles that organize the therapist's own psyche]. (pp. 282–283)

THE CHANGING SCENE IN PSYCHOANALYSIS

The landscape of psychoanalysis is undergoing vast changes, to the point that some observers (e.g., Mitchell, 1993) consider the changes to be revolutionary. A full exploration of such change would require a book in itself. For the present chapter, however, the major issues revolve around the therapeutic relationship and the changes in analytic thought about the relationship. Most of these changes have been hinted at or noted earlier in this chapter, so the present section is more a consolidation than a presentation of new material.

First and perhaps foremost, in the past few decades there has been a major paradigm shift in psychoanalysis, a shift that has enormous implications for what is meant by an effective psychoanalytic relationship. The essence of this change has been movement away from classical drive theory and toward object relations theory (e.g. Mitchell, 1993), self psychology (Wolf, 1991), and an integration of the two (e.g., Bacal & Newman, 1990). Inherent in this shift is a loosening of rigid rules about abstinence and neutrality, and an attendant emphasis on therapists' active involvement; a postmodern view of transference that goes beyond viewing it as nothing but client distortion, and instead moves toward the idea of a reality coconstructed by client and therapist; and a movement away from seeing the transference relationship as the only important aspect of the analytic relationship, and toward viewing components such as working alliance and real relationship as also important. Each of these aspects of the changing landscape of psychoanalysis has been discussed earlier in this chapter.

As these changes have occurred, many theoreticians have reflected on ways of maintaining the best of the more traditional views, revising aspects that may be worth keeping in at least modified form, and perhaps integrating the old with the new. Pine's (1990) work is seminal in this way, for it proposes that all four psychologies of psychoanalysis have their place in analytic treatment, and each will enter into the work as the client's material warrants. Each can be useful at different points in time (cf. Mishne, 1993). What this shifting focus may mean for the analytic relationship, however, is not clear, and may represent a valuable area for future inquiry.

An aspect of the changing scene that has only been hinted at earlier, for example, pertains to the analytic therapist's countertransference reactions. The days of viewing countertransference simply as a neurotic expression that needed to be resolved are essentially in the past. Although there is an awareness that countertransference conflicts may have neurotic roots and surely should not be acted out in the treatment, the more contemporary view is that, as human beings, all therapists will encounter internal conflicts with perhaps every client, and, when properly understood and managed, these conflicts can be valuable in the treatment. Also, at times, the enactment of countertransference may be inevitable, and it, too, may be helpful if the therapist strives for understanding about herself or himself and for the light such enactments may shed on the therapeutic relationship (Weinshel & Renik, 1991). Whether countertransference issues should be disclosed to the client is another matter, and one of considerable complexity (Aron, 1996). But the movement toward the view that the internal conflicts that are part of countertransference are an inherent and potentially invaluable part of the analytic process is very clear.

As all of these changes are occurring in the vision of the analytic relationship, one topic that goes to the heart of controversy about how the analytic therapist ought to be has emerged much more fully than in earlier times—the topic of analyst or therapist self-disclosure. The opening up of this topic for consideration is pointed to by Aron (1996), as follows:

> A study of the accumulating analytic literature on self-disclosure should lead us to marvel at the incredible transformation that has taken place in the world of psychoanalysis in just a few short years. It is, indeed, only recently that the analyst's self-disclosure has appeared on the psychoanalytic scene as a topic of panels and symposia in our meetings and as a subject worthy of investigation in our journals. In the near future, textbooks on psychoanalysis will undoubtedly contain chapters on self-disclosure, and institutes will have courses and clinical case seminars devoted to this subject. (p. 221)

Current thinking, as reflected in Aron's (1996) thoughtful treatise, is quite mixed on the topic. Aron, for example, raises numerous vital questions of who, what, when, and where, regarding self-disclosure, and his suggestions seek to take into account this inherent complexity. At this point, it is safe to say that self-disclosure is no longer a dirty word in psychoanalysis, and is beginning to be examined openly. Analytic therapists, on the whole, are surely less disclosing than their humanistic and feminist cousins, but are just as surely more open to the possible benefits of "controlled disclosures" than they were in times past.

THE PSYCHOANALYTIC RELATIONSHIP AND THE FOUR DIMENSIONS

Now that we have examined the therapeutic relationship in analytic work from several perspectives, we are ready to address the status of the relationship in psychoanalytic treatment according to the four key dimensions that we employ to analyze each theory cluster: centrality, means-end, real-unreal, and the use of power.

THE CENTRALITY OF THE RELATIONSHIP

As should be clear by now, the relationship in virtually all shades of analytic treatment is seen as highly central. Even in the brief analytic therapies, where there is little time for the cultivation of a deep relationship, we have noted the importance of the relationship. So, too, is the relationship central in what we have called analytically informed therapy. Despite the technical eclecticism of this modality, the importance of the relationship is perhaps the one feature that treatments within this level have in common.

As the scene has changed in psychoanalysis, and as theories focusing on object relations and self psychology are coming to rule the theoretical roost, the therapeutic relationship is (if anything) becoming even more central. This is occurring because contemporary object relations theory, self psychology, and the intersubjective derivative of self psychology all are more relationship-centered than either classical drive theory or ego analytic theory. Concepts such as therapist empathy, attunement, personal involvement, and relatedness are vital elements in these approaches to treatment. And even the transferences are more likely to be viewed in terms of the client's and therapist's cocreation.

THE RELATIONSHIP AS A MEANS TO AN END OR AN END IN ITSELF

Is the relationship in analytic treatments an end in itself, in the sense that the relationship, in and of itself, is the mechanism through which change occurs? Alternatively, is the relationship a means to something else (e.g., technique) which is the major mediator of change? In other words, is it the relationship, or something done to or because of the relationship, that is the major catalyst for change? The answers to these questions in reference to analytic treatments are complex. On the whole, as noted in Chapter 1, we would suggest that the relationship is a means to an end in this theory cluster. Because the focus of so much analytic work is on the transference relationship, or the transference-countertransference matrix, and because transference reactions are viewed as phenomena that ultimately are to be worked through, it is a *change* in the relationship—through the process of interpretation, insight, and working through—that produces healing. In this sense, the transference relationship is, according to Prochaska (1979), a source of content to be processed by therapist and client. The processing—the interpretations and working through of the transference—is what is mutative, not the transference relationship in itself.

Some of the changes in psychoanalysis that we have discussed above, however, argue for a different vision. This vision is especially tied to the psychoanalytic self psychology movement, in which at least an important part of the client's change and growth emerges directly from an empathic, emotionally attuned relationship offered by the therapist. Eagle and Wolitzky (1997) capture this self psychological thrust, and the developmental basis for it, when they state:

> . . . according to Kohut, the need to experience empathic mirroring in infancy and childhood is universal. Its fulfillment facilitates the development of a cohesive self and the traumatic unfulfillment generates self defects. The experience of empathic understanding in treatment, then, constitutes the partial meeting of an earlier unmet need. The meeting of this need, in turn, facilitates the resumption of developmental growth and the "repair" of self defects. (p. 239)

THE REAL-UNREAL DIMENSION IN PSYCHOANALYTIC TREATMENT

To what extent do psychoanalytic theories focus on the real relationship versus the transference or unreal relationship? [We follow Gelso and Carter's (1985) use of the term "unreal" to connote the transference relationship, but underscore that transference is unreal only in the sense that it involves, to some extent, unrealistic perceptions of the therapist. The transference relationship, including countertransference, is certainly real in every other respect.]

It should be clear by now that the emphasis of psychoanalytic theories (in sharp contrast to humanistic, cognitive-behavioral, and feminist therapies explored in subsequent chapters) is on the unreal or transference relationship. Even when treatment involves what we have called "levels" of analytic interventions in which transference may not be dealt with directly (e.g., supportive-analytic counseling, analytically informed therapy), the unreal relationship is still a key part of the clinician's conceptualization of the work, and is taken into account as the therapist frames his or her responses to clients.

At the same time, we have pointed to the increasing emphasis in contemporary object relations and self psychological theories on what we would call the real relationship (although these theories do not use that term). The emphasis on an empathic, I-thou encounter between two human beings in the process of coconstructing their reality does have a very strong flavor of real relationship, as we have conceptualized it. So, in this sense, despite the continued emphasis on transference as the hallmark of analytic work, something of a greater balance has emerged in this theory cluster in recent years. The realistic and genuine aspect of the relationship is much more likely to be given credence, if not center stage.

POWER AND THE PSYCHOANALYTIC RELATIONSHIP

How power is conceptualized and used in any system of psychotherapy is tricky business. The use of power is a complex process that has more than its share of paradox. No theoretical system would claim to empower the therapist and disempower the client. At the same time, systems may differ in the extent to which the therapist is given both explicit power and subtler implicit power. Probably all systems of therapy and all therapists understand that there are inherent, inevitable power differences in the roles taken by the therapist and the client. The client is facing troubles that she or he has been unable to resolve, and seeks help from an expert in dealing with such troubles. Much of therapy involves the client's expressing these troubles in one way or another, and the therapist's listening and trying to figure out ways of helping the client understand and change. These vast role differences produce what we would consider irreversible power differences.

In psychoanalytic treatment, the issue of power is imbued with paradox. The major paradox is this: Psychoanalysis and the various forms of psychoanalytic therapy seek to provide the client, patient, or analysand with the greatest possible freedom of choice. These therapies seek to *not* intrude on the client, to *not* take sides even with different intrapsychic forces within personality (the concept of neutrality), and to be as free as possible from moral judgment by the therapist of the client. Partly because of these aims, analysts even argue against being "educative" with analysands. The analysand, and the analysand alone, must choose and direct his or her life. At the same time, especially within the confines of classical drive theory, classical ego analysis, and certain forms of object relations theory, one gets the sense that the implicit message is: "Therapist knows best" (in a way that goes beyond the legitimate knowledge that comes from extensive training in human behavior and psychotherapy). When neutrality translates into "objectivity," as opposed to involvement; when ambiguity translates into keeping personal distance from the client; when the relationship is seen as essentially all transference, which is defined solely as the client's distortion of the perfectly neutral and ambiguous analyst; and when it is this analyst who is the sole arbiter of what is transference and what is reality—then psychoanalytic treatment would appear to involve enormous, albeit very subtle, power on the part of the therapist, even as the conscious aims of treatment seem to entail providing the client with maximum freedom of choice (i.e., power). Even though the analyst or therapist who fits this mold may treat his or her clients in a humane and sensitive manner, the power differences would be seen by many as excessive.

Although power differences may be magnified in a theoretical system such as psychoanalysis, in which therapist and client both seek to penetrate the *client's* unconscious, and in which the therapist often does understand underlying issues better than the client (due to the client's inevitable defenses and resistances), we believe that changes in the psychoanalytic scene in recent years have served to at least reduce some of the unnecessary power differentials. As one reads self psychologists such as Wolf (1988, 1991) and object relations therapists such as Mitchell (1993)—as but two examples of an emerging pattern—one clearly senses the attenuation, if not the elimination, of unnecessary power differences. One perceives, as well, a great humility along with a respect for the client and her or his power. This emerging pattern is also evident in psychoanalytic therapy practiced from a feminist perspective, as discussed in Chapter 10.

RESEARCH AND THE
PSYCHOANALYTIC RELATIONSHIP

Historically, empirical research and psychoanalysis have had what might be described as, at best, a shaky relationship. From its inception, psychoanalysts have promoted the view that the proper and most effective way in which to conduct "research" was through the analyst's "observations" of his or her analysand. Controlled empirical research, it has been repeatedly contended, could not possibly capture the enormous complexities of the psychoanalytic process. Instead, the psychoanalytic case provided the data through which hypotheses could be confirmed or disconfirmed, and the case presentation provided the medium through which these data were made public. In fact, it is very hard, if not impossible, to find case material that disconfirms psychoanalytic authors' hypotheses. Instead, cases are used to support theoretical propositions, and it is unclear how— or in fact *if*—the propositions are put to any empirical test at any point in the process.

This tendency to use one's cases for "research" works just fine, we contend, at the theory construction level of science. It works poorly, however, at the theory testing or confirmation level, and here lies a major weakness in psychoanalysis as a science. Fortunately, however, things have been changing in recent decades. Empirical research is emerging on many key psychoanalytic constructs that bear on the therapeutic relationship. Examples of this work are presented on Chapters 2–4, on the working alliance, transference, and countertransference. [For research findings pertinent to the relationship in analytic therapy, see N. Miller, Luborsky, Barber, & Docherty (1993).]

Many topics pertinent to the therapeutic relationship are in need of empirical scrutiny; psychoanalysis appears to be just now discarding its shroud of antiempiricism. As empirical research is increasingly conducted, one methodological approach may be worth noting because of its easy fit with psychoanalysis. The *qualitative approach* (e.g., Hill, Thompson, & Williams, 1997; Hoshmand & Martin, 1994; Stiles, 1993), which is now gaining increasing respectability and prominence in psychotherapy research, may allow investigators to tap the rich complexities of the psychoanalytic process and the psychoanalytic client-therapist relationship in a way that traditional quantitative research has been unable to do. Examples of such research in which the authors have been involved are the qualitative study of (a) transference and related constructs in 11 cases of long-term, successful psychodynamic therapy, as discussed in Chapter 3 (Gelso et al., 1998) and (b) countertransference, using postsession interviews with therapists after 12 to 20 sessions of time-limited therapy (Hayes et al., 1998). Qualitative and quantitative research ought to supplement each other in the developing area of inquiry on the relationship in psychoanalytic treatment.

CONCLUSION

The relationship between therapist (or analyst) and client (or patient or analysand) in psychoanalytic treatments defies simple description. Although we have offered some generalizations about the relationship in "modal psychoanalytic treatment," a more precise statement requires attention to what we have called levels of analytic treatment, to variations among the four psychologies of psychoanalysis, and to the changing scene in psychoanalysis. As paradigm shifts have occurred within psychoanalysis, especially the movement away from drive theory and toward theories rooted in the psychology of self and object relations, the relationship in analytic treatments has appeared more and more "humanistic"—in its focus on therapist involvement, empathic attunement, and responsiveness in an I-Thou context. Transference is still the hallmark of this approach, but even the conception of transference fits this emerging focus, in that the therapist's role in the transference that developes is recognized, and the therapist is no longer seen as the sole arbiter of reality. Along with these major transformations, empirical research is increasingly accepted as an important part of the psychoanalytic study of the relationship, and such research, both qualitative and quantitative, is expected to be conducted at an increased pace in the years ahead.

CHAPTER 8

Cognitive and Behavioral Views of the Therapeutic Relationship: Beyond Techniques

THE COGNITIVE-BEHAVIORAL tradition can be characterized by its commitment to incorporating and applying to therapy empirical knowledge about human behavior. Early in the behavior therapy movement, this commitment took the form of a strict reliance on certain principles of learning (e.g., modeling; classical and operant conditioning). As the cognitive revolution emerged in the late 1960s, behavior theory expanded to include principles related to cognitive processes such as perception and reasoning. More recently, as research has elucidated the significance of biology, emotions, and interpersonal relations in human behavior, cognitive-behavioral theory and practice have begun to incorporate these aspects of human functioning as well. Thus, although some scholars both within and outside the cognitive-behavioral camp continue to associate this approach to therapy solely with principles of learning, such a stance now seems overly limiting and dated. In fact, cognitive-behavioral theorists have even started to consider the role of unconscious processes in cognitive processing, which is a far cry from behavior therapy's traditional insistence on restricting attention to observable phenomena (Mahoney, 1995; Safran & Greenberg, 1987; Safran & Segal, 1990). Because cognitive-behavioral theory now embraces so many different components of human functioning, a leading spokesperson for this approach has even argued that cognitive-behavioral therapy should be considered the prototypical integrative psychotherapy (A. Beck, 1991).

A host of individual theories exists under the cognitive-behavioral umbrella, but it is neither useful nor perhaps even possible to accurately differentiate them based on their treatment of the psychotherapy relationship. In fact, one of the commonalities among the various cognitive-behavioral theories is their view of the therapy relationship as important, though insufficient to bring about therapeutic change (Gelso & Fretz, 1992). Other common themes among theories that are primarily cognitive and/or behavioral include: taking clients' presenting problems seriously, rather than considering presenting problems to be merely symptoms of some underlying cause; attending to the present more than the past; viewing behavior as learned and capable of being unlearned and relearned; clearly specifying and defining therapy goals; paying attention to overt behavior and related cognitive processes; and valuing an active, directive, and prescriptive therapist role (Gelso & Fretz, 1992).

Because of the many commonalities among the cognitive and behavioral theories, and particularly given the similarity in their treatment of the therapy relationship, we shall deal with the various cognitive-behavioral theories collectively, noting individual differences where they seem salient and nontrivial. As in the previous chapter on the therapy relationship in psychoanalytic approaches, the material in this chapter will address, and in fact be organized around, four major themes: (a) the centrality of the psychotherapy relationship, (b) the extent to which the relationship is viewed as a means or an end, (c) whether real or unreal components of the relationship are emphasized, and (d) the nature of power dynamics within the relationship.

THE CENTRALITY OF THE
PSYCHOTHERAPY RELATIONSHIP

HISTORICAL PERSPECTIVES

The characteristics and role of the therapy relationship historically have been of minimal importance in behavioral and early cognitive theories (Bandura, 1969; Eysenck, 1960; Lang, 1969; Mowrer, 1964). Techniques were considered to be the primary, if not the only, agents of client change. For instance, Ayllon and Michael (1959) espoused the view that the therapy relationship is of virtually no significance and described behavior therapists as "behavioral engineers." Similarly, London (1972) referred to the behavior therapist as a "technician," and Eysenck (1975) stated that behavior therapists could be trained to perform therapy simply by following a set of instructions about how to carry out techniques.

By way of contrast, the therapy relationship was attributed at least some significance in other behaviorists' writings. For example, Lazarus and Abramowitz (1962) noted that behavior therapists should demonstrate warmth and try to establish rapport with clients. Kanfer and Phillips (1966) commented on the importance of therapists' sensitivity in conducting behavior therapy. Finally, Wolpe and Lazarus (1966) wrote that a close relationship between the therapist and the client was necessary but not sufficient for promoting positive therapeutic outcome, a position that has been reiterated many times (A. Beck, Freeman, & Associates, 1990; A. Beck, Rush, Shaw, & Emery, 1979; Persons & Burns, 1985; Sweet, 1984).

Why was the therapy relationship afforded so little importance early in the cognitive-behavioral tradition? Beyond the obvious answer that techniques were viewed as the central mechanisms of change, Wilson and Evans (1977) note that the concept of "relationship" is hard to define operationally and to measure. Given behaviorists' commitment to the scientific method, it makes sense that they focused their attention on observable therapist and client behaviors (i.e., techniques and clients' responses to those techniques). While observable behaviors surely constitute a part of the therapy relationship, one can study behaviors without generalizing to the concept of "therapeutic relationship." The early behavior therapists, by concentrating solely on observable behaviors, neglected other constituents of the therapy relationship—namely, clients' and therapists' feelings and attitudes. However, numerous changes in the field of behavior therapy, particularly its melding with cognitive approaches, have given rise to new perspectives on the nature and status of the therapy relationship.

The Current Scene

When the cognitive revolution occurred some quarter of a century ago, behavior theory began to embrace and incorporate principles related to nonobservable mental phenomena. Among the concepts that found their way into the developing cognitive-behavioral paradigm were several constructs from social psychology, such as expectancy, persuasion, and attraction (Safran & Segal, 1990). The influence of social psychology on cognitive-behavioral therapy has continued in that behavioral and cognitive therapists have demonstrated a growing recognition that behaviors are learned and cognitions develop in an interpersonal world. Moreover, cognitive-behavioral therapists are increasingly acknowledging that interpersonal factors play a role in the development and maintenance of many of the problems for which clients seek therapy (Mahoney, 1995). Thus, while human beings can be studied under isolated conditions, cognitive-behaviorists are recognizing that our thoughts and actions are perhaps best understood in the social context within which we live. This emerging view, quite naturally, has been accompanied by a realization that relationships, including the psychotherapy relationship, deserve and in fact require scientific attention and study (Borkovec & Newman, in press; Robins & Hayes, 1995). Consequently, it is no longer the case, if it ever was true, that cognitive-behavioral therapists are more interested in techniques than in the people with whom techniques are used. Furthermore, while behavioral and cognitive therapists have frequently debated the importance they attach to the therapy relationship, the literature is clear that the therapy relationship has always been important to the *clients* engaged in behavioral and cognitive therapy (Morris & Magrath, 1983; Persons & Burns, 1985). For example, Burns and Nolen-Hoeksma (1992) found that client ratings of empathy in cognitive-behavioral therapy predicted decreases in depression, even after technical factors, such as homework compliance, were controlled for. Furthermore, research has documented that the working alliance can be at least as strong in cognitive-behavioral therapy as in other approaches (Raue et al., 1993; Salvio et al., 1992).

TECHNICAL VERSUS RELATIONAL FACTORS IN THE THERAPY RELATIONSHIP

Given the recent changes in the cognitive-behavioral landscape, and particularly in regard to the somewhat elevated status of the therapy relationship, one may wonder about the importance of the relationship relative to techniques, which have typically held a prominent position in behavioral and cognitive theories. Despite the increased attention it has received relative to the past, the relationship is still widely considered to be secondary to techniques in promoting therapeutic outcome (Beck et al., 1990; Corey, 1996; Ellis, 1995). An analogy may help illuminate this point.

One of the authors recently had his house painted. His relationship with the painter, while cordial, was fairly unimportant in determining the appearance of the house when the painter was finished. The final product was largely a function of the painter's skill and effort. The same author also has been seeing a chiropractor for several weeks. Whereas the painter applied the tools of her trade to an inanimate object with which she had no relationship (at least as we would define it), the chiropractor has been executing his skills on a live human being who has not only lower back pain, but also a mix of apprehension, curiosity, and reserved optimism. Because the author (JAH) is the direct recipient of the chiropractor's interventions, his relationship with the chiropractor is of somewhat greater consequence than his relationship with the painter. After all, it requires considerable faith on a patient's part to allow another individual to manipulate one's body in such a way that fairly loud and peculiar noises emanate from one's vertebrae. Additionally, and more seriously, a patient's confidence in a chiropractor affects the patient's likelihood of returning for further treatment and adhering to the exercise regimen prescribed by the chiropractor. However, given that the chiropractor is directly treating the patient's back, not the patient's thoughts or desires or values or emotions, it seems reasonable to conclude that a successful outcome will largely be dictated by the efficacy of the chiropractor's techniques and not the quality of the patient-chiropractor relationship.

Cognitive-behavioral therapists generally would agree that the client-therapist relationship is of greater significance than the patient-chiropractor relationship, but not by much. Arnkoff (1983, p. 86) writes: "At least as important as the relationship as an end in itself . . . is the leverage the relationship provides the therapist to influence the client." Furthermore, Corey (1996) states that a strong therapy relationship is "viewed by cognitive therapists as being necessary, but not sufficient, to produce optimum therapeutic effect. Therapists must also have a cognitive conceptualization of cases, be creative and active, be able to engage clients through a process of Socratic questioning, and be knowledgeable and skilled in the use of cognitive and behavioral strategies" (p. 341). Because cognitive-behavioral therapists directly treat and affect clients' thoughts and behaviors, both of which are components of and influence the therapy relationship, the client-therapist relationship is relatively more important than the patient-chiropractor relationship. Nonetheless, cognitive-behavioral therapists contend that the relationship itself is not a central mechanism for change, and outcome is still largely dependent on techniques. Based on our review of the relevant literature, however, we propose that the relative importance of any therapist-client relationship in cognitive-behavioral work depends on a number of factors, four of which will be explored below.

To begin, the emphasis a therapist places on technical and relationship factors when working with a client will vary as a function of *time*, both within and across sessions (Arnkoff, 1983; Burns & Auerbach, 1996; Morris

& Magrath, 1983). For instance, Morris and Magrath suggest that the therapy relationship is especially important early in the work. In initial therapy sessions, establishing a strong working alliance creates a precondition for change that will more directly follow, later on, from the therapist's use of specific techniques. A client's faith in and adherence to these techniques are likely to be affected by the strength of this early working alliance. Safran and Segal (1990), warning against a static view of the therapeutic alliance, note that therapists must exercise care in attending to fluctuations in the alliance throughout the process of cognitive therapy.

A second factor that influences the relative importance of relational and technical factors in cognitive-behavioral therapy involves the *stability of the therapy relationship*. The more the client experiences difficulties within the therapy relationship, the more attention needs to be devoted to it rather than to techniques (Lazarus, 1989). For example, Burns and Auerbach (1996) state that relationship factors need attention when the client distrusts the therapist or expresses strong, and particularly hostile, emotions toward the therapist. Burns and Auerbach maintain that when instability arises in the relationship, it calls for a sensitive and empathic response on the part of the therapist. However, Burns's (1989) description of empathy seems to us to be more a manifestation of technique itself (e.g., reflection, paraphrasing, summarizing) than a genuine attempt on the therapist's behalf to deeply comprehend and convey an understanding of the client's subjective experience. When empathy is reduced to techniques, we would caution that therapists run the risk of being perceived by clients as formulaic and insincere.

A less technical and more comprehensive discussion of the role and nature of empathy in cognitive therapy is offered by Safran and Segal (1990). They note that empathy is critical to the process of cognitive therapy in that empathic relating involves the therapist's constant efforts to understand clients' phenomenological constructions of reality (i.e., clients' cognitions). Furthermore, empathy helps cognitive-behavioral therapists tailor their interventions to the needs of individual clients, taking into account the client's fears, skills, and self-efficacy. Safran and Segal compare the empathic resonance that can develop between therapist and client with a dance, describing the synergistic exchange that occurs and leaves the client feeling acknowledged, respected, and understood. Conversely, some cognitive-behavioral theorists argue that it is critical for therapists and clients alike to distinguish clients' *feeling* better from their actually *getting* better (Burns & Auerbach, 1996; Ellis & Dryden, 1997). Toward this end, Burns and Auerbach recommend that cognitive-behavioral therapists not preoccupy themselves with overt displays of empathy. Indeed, most cognitive-behaviorists would contend that empathy should be viewed as "a soothing background variable used to establish a relationship so that the client will comply with the therapist's treatment prescriptions" (Bohart & Greenberg, 1997, p. 4). However, Safran and Segal maintain that by empathizing with and accepting clients, cognitive-behavioral therapists can effectively challenge clients' dysfunctional schemas (e.g., "I need to be someone else or maintain a facade when I relate to others"). Thus, Safran and Segal conclude, "True empathy does more than provide the necessary precondition for effective cognitive intervention; in and of itself, it can be one of the most powerful means of challenging the patients' dysfunctional interpersonal schemas" (p. 189).

A third factor that affects the relative importance of the therapy relationship in cognitive-behavioral work is the *type of technique* to be implemented (Morris & Magrath, 1983). The quality of the therapy relationship acquires increased importance when the therapist hopes to employ techniques that require a high degree of trust and cooperation on the client's behalf. For example, the nature of the therapy relationship may be of relatively little consequence when a therapist asks a client to keep a daily record of behaviors such as watching television and doing homework. A task such as this involves a fairly low level of threat to most clients. On the other hand, the degree to which the client trusts and feels understood by the therapist may tremendously affect how likely the client is to participate in an intervention that demands greater vulnerability on the client's part, such as a shame-attacking exercise, or in some forms of in vivo desensitization. In either case, when a client is resistant to or does not comply with a particular technique, the stability of the therapy relationship is undermined and, as discussed previously, the relationship needs to be attended to (Rothstein & Robinson, 1991). For additional discussion of this topic, we encourage the reader to consult Beck et al. (1990, pp. 66–78), who offer excellent ideas for therapists to consider when clients are resistant to interventions (e.g., timing of intervention, client skill level, unclear relation between intervention and therapy goals, secondary gain from noncompliance).

The fourth and final factor that influences the relative importance of relational and technical factors in cognitive-behavioral therapy is the *complexity of the client problem* (Gelso & Carter, 1985; Padesky, 1996). Gelso and Carter note that simpler problems may be treated effectively by employing certain techniques (e.g., bibliotherapy) with relatively little consideration for relationship factors. Gelso and Carter do not imply that therapists can afford to be rude or altogether neglectful of relationship issues when treating relatively basic client problems, but rather that techniques themselves can be sufficient to produce change. However, when clients have problems with greater layers of complexity, therapists need to possess and demonstrate more overall clinical skill and sensitivity, including in the area of the therapeutic relationship. Along these lines, Beck et al. (1990) contend that clients with more chronic and complex issues need greater encouragement from the therapist to do homework assignments than clients with more acute and circumscribed problems. These latter clients are likely to benefit more rapidly from techniques and thus find them rewarding, whereas clients with more complicated and longstanding problems require reinforcement from within the therapy relationship itself to maintain their motivation to work on more entrenched issues.

Gelso and Carter (1985) discussed how the complexity of client problems typically has been restricted in research that examines the relative contributions of technical and relational factors in cognitive-behavioral therapy. In fact, Gelso and Carter asserted that research that has found technical factors to be more important to outcome than relational factors has tended to focus on:

> ... client problems that minimize the possible importance of relationship matters. For example, it seems safe to say that most desensitization studies employ marginally motivated and disturbed clients (such as college student volunteers) and attack relatively unimportant life problems—snake phobias, rat phobias, and the like. The latter might not be so troublesome if it represented what people sought help for in the real world of the clinic. But that is not the case. (1985, p. 228)

Although research conducted since Gelso and Carter's statement has increasingly focused on more complex, real-life problems, the relative contributions of technical and relational factors to outcome is still a matter of open debate.

Further addressing the manner in which problem complexity affects the relative importance of relational and technical factors, Padesky (1996) suggests that the therapy relationship is less consequential when therapists are working with clients who have anxiety and mood disorders than with clients who have personality disorders. Padesky argues that the dysfunctional schemas inherent in personality disorders tend to be revealed interpersonally, more so than is the case for clients with anxiety and mood disorders. As a result, Padesky contends that when treating a client with a personality disorder, the therapist needs to attend to relationship dynamics and address these dynamics skillfully.

We would agree with Padesky that clients who have personality disorders tend to manifest their dysfunctional cognitions interpersonally, but our own practice and supervision of therapy suggest that many clients with anxiety and mood disorders also possess problematic schemas of an interpersonal nature. Although we would submit that these schemas often are not revealed as strikingly as in the case of clients with personality disorders, we would not conclude that the therapy relationship is of less importance with anxious and mood-disordered clients. To the contrary, we would argue that the therapist needs to display a heightened sensitivity to the therapy relationship with anxious and mood-disordered clients, looking to detect the subtle ways in which problematic schemas might be manifested in the client-therapist relationship. We have found that the therapy relationship itself contains valuable information about anxious and depressed clients' schemas. For example, depressed clients frequently possess schemas related to a fear of rejection and isolation. When this cognitive schema is operative in depressed clients, it tends to be applied to the therapy relationship as well as to other relationships in the client's life. The therapist who is sensitive to detecting and exploring depressed clients' fears of being rejected by the therapist can help modify the problematic schema (Jacobson, 1989).

In discussing factors that influence the importance of relationship factors relative to technical factors, we have, for the sake of clarity, presented the two realms as dichotomous. This dichotomy between technical and relational factors is commonly found in the literature, where it sometimes takes the form of a debate between the efficacy of specific and nonspecific therapy factors (i.e., factors specific to a particular theoretical approach, such as systematic desensitization, versus nonspecific factors such as the therapy relationship). To the extent that we have presented technical and relational factors as orthogonal, we have oversimplified reality. S. Butler and Strupp (1986) argue persuasively that techniques are offered and have their effectiveness and meaning in the context of a client-therapist relationship. Furthermore, as we discussed in Chapter 6, the therapy relationship and the use of techniques have a reciprocal influence on one another. The type of relationship that a therapist hopes to establish with a client (e.g., provocative and experiential) will in large part dictate the techniques the therapist chooses (e.g., an empty chair dialogue). Alternatively, the use of particular techniques or interventions (e.g., advice giving) will influence the type of relationship that develops between the client and the therapist (e.g., authoritative). Even when techniques are to be practiced outside the therapist's office, as with homework assignments, they are still prescribed by a therapist within the context of a relationship to the client, they emanate from the existing relationship, and they in turn affect that relationship.

We would like to address one additional issue concerning the relative importance of technical and relational factors in cognitive-behavioral therapy. Behavioral and cognitive therapists tend to receive a fair amount of training on the use of particular technical interventions, but Safran and Segal (1990) raise an important question: Where and how do cognitive-behavioral therapists learn "nonspecific" therapy skills, such as forming and maintaining a strong therapy relationship? The training of cognitive-behavioral therapists on relational dimensions seems especially important, given the growing popularity of manualized approaches to treatment. From our perspective, manualized treatments run the risk of neglecting relationship factors in favor of a focus on well-defined and clearly operationalized techniques. Not only might some cognitive-behavioral therapists receive inadequate training in the area of the therapy relationship, but, according to Safran and Segal, none of the existing cognitive or behavioral theories satisfactorily addresses the integration of technical and relational factors. Safran and Segal attempt to redress the deficiencies they perceive both in training and in terms of the lack of integration of technical and relational factors in cognitive therapy.

THE THERAPY RELATIONSHIP AS A MEANS VERSUS AN END

As discussed in the previous chapter, the "means-end" conceptualization of the therapy relationship pertains to the extent to which the relationship is considered the primary mechanism for client change, as opposed to serving as a means of promoting the effectiveness of some method or technique that produces change. Currently, the most widely held position on the means-end continuum as it relates to the cognitive-behavioral therapy relationship is that establishing a strong and healthy relationship is a necessary, or at least useful, means for affecting client change (Beck et al., 1990; Lazarus, 1995; Meichenbaum, 1985; Morris & Magrath, 1983). As we noted earlier in this chapter, techniques are viewed as the primary change agents in cognitive-behavioral therapy, and the therapy relationship itself is not considered sufficient to affect change. Still, the "necessary but not sufficient" perspective raises the question: What is the relationship necessary for? Below, we explore three answers to this question.

THE RELATIONSHIP AS A MEANS OF ENHANCING
THE EFFICACY OF TECHNIQUES

A common perspective of the cognitive-behavioral therapy relationship holds that a positive relationship, marked by the client's and the therapist's shared commitment and respect, is likely to create or enhance client expectations that treatment, and the techniques on which treatment is based, will be effective (Arnkoff, 1983). For instance, Arnkoff described a case example of Aaron Beck's work with a female client who identified two factors that were pivotal to her recovery from depression: her trust in Beck and his confidence in her reasoning abilities. Arnkoff relates that the client "was responsive to cognitive therapy, was persuaded by its 'rationale and rituals,' only because she could trust and follow the therapist. . . . Her trust in Beck prompted her to listen to his appeal to her reason" (p. 86).

Beyond the importance of the relationship in fortifying client expectancy factors, Gelso and Carter (1985) note that, in learning theories, the relationship "gives the therapist a power base that facilitates appropriate persuasion, reinforcement, the use of techniques, and the client's revelation of the details of the problem so that techniques can be helpfully employed" (p. 225). Gelso and Carter's perspective on the cognitive-behavioral therapy relationship is consistent with social influence theory, which posits that a therapist's persuasive ability to affect change is a function of the degree to which the client perceives the therapist as expert, trustworthy, and attractive (Heppner & Claiborn, 1989; Strong, 1968). For example, therapists must work to help clients trust them, not because a trusting relationship is thought to be curative, but because the client's trust in the therapist will enable the therapist to more effectively employ the techniques that are viewed as curative (DeVoge & Beck, 1978; Rothstein & Robinson, 1991). In fact, research has found that clients' perceptions of therapists' expertness, trustworthiness, and attractiveness are related inversely to clients' likelihood of terminating therapy prematurely (McNeil, May, & Lee, 1987) and relate directly to clients' satisfaction with and gains from therapy (Chambers, 1986; Heppner & Heesacker, 1983; McNeil et al., 1987; Zamostny, Corrigan, & Eggert, 1981). Along similar lines, therapist warmth (a component of therapist attractiveness) has been found to enhance the effectiveness of systematic desensitization as well as the behavioral treatment of agoraphobia (Williams & Chambless, 1990; Wolowitz, 1975). More generally, Morris and Magrath (1983) reviewed several studies and concluded that therapist warmth positively influenced the outcome of behavior therapy.

Consistent with social influence theory, then, many cognitive-behavioral therapists view the establishment of a therapeutic relationship as a necessary precondition for subsequent client change. However, Safran and Segal (1990) offer a trenchant critique of the position that the psychotherapy relationship should be viewed as a precursor to change rather than an integral component of the change process itself. They argue that the prevailing cognitive-behavioral view of the relationship:

> . . . perpetuates a mechanistic approach to therapy that fails to recognize the fundamentally human nature of the therapeutic encounter and the change process. The assertion that psychotherapy is fundamentally a human encounter does not mean that there is no theory for therapists to learn and no skills for them to acquire. It does mean, however, that the relevant theory must clarify the process through which this human encounter brings about change, and that the relevant skills must include the ability to use one's own humanity as a therapeutic instrument. (p. 5)

THE RELATIONSHIP AS A MEANS OF OBTAINING A "BEHAVIOR SAMPLE"

In addition to the perspective that a strong therapy relationship facilitates the effectiveness of techniques, a second way in which the relationship is viewed as a "means" to some greater end is in terms of gathering useful data. Although cognitive-behavioral theorists generally would argue that using the therapy relationship to collect information is not a necessary means of conducting therapy, it is nonetheless a valuable option.

To begin with, Safran and Segal (1990, p. 86) note that "the quality of the therapeutic relationship always mediates the patient's ability to explore his or her own inner world." A caring, safe relationship promotes deeper exploration and more open sharing of information on the client's part, just as a poor therapy relationship can cause the client to limit inner exploration or withhold crucial data from the therapist (J. Beck, 1996). On the other hand, even when the relationship is less than ideal, critical information still can be culled from it. For instance, in the past two decades, cognitive theorists have increasingly advocated an approach to treatment in which evidence is sought within the therapy relationship itself about clients' core beliefs, automatic thoughts, cognitive schemas, and even clients' attachment patterns (Arnkoff, 1981; J. Beck, 1996; Jacobson, 1989; Liotti, 1991; Padesky, 1996; Robins & Hayes, 1995; Rothstein & Robinson, 1991; Safran & Segal, 1990). Drawing heavily from principles of interpersonal psychotherapy, these theorists contend that clients' here-and-now cognitions about the therapist and the therapy relationship can be explored to reveal the critical information needed to assess clients' more general problematic thinking. Gathering data on client cognitions about the therapy relationship itself affords the therapist the benefits of direct observation rather than having to rely on clients' self-reports of their extratherapy cognitions and behaviors. Furthermore, therapists can utilize their own reactions to a client to generate hypotheses about how significant others in the client's life may be affected by and react to the client. Aaron Beck refers to the therapist's personal reactions to a client as "experimental evidence" for how the client may affect others (e.g., Beck et al., 1990, p. 252), and encourages therapists to note their automatic thoughts, strong emotional responses, and client behaviors that elicit these reactions. Judith Beck (1996) advocated a similar type of interpersonal approach to the therapy relationship for cognitive-behavioral clinicians: "The therapeutic relationship poses . . . an opportunity for therapists to gain a 'window' into the patients' reactions to other people. And monitoring their own emotional responses to patients' behavior also provides therapists with a window into how others may in turn be reacting to the patient" (p. 176).

The degree to which one can accurately generalize from patterns within the therapy relationship to other relationships in the client's life is debatable. In fact, Bandura (1969) claimed that the therapist-client relationship is too artificial to be a suitable stimulus for strong, generalized responses outside the therapy relationship. Consequently, Bandura discouraged therapists from trying to use the therapy relationship itself as a vehicle for promoting client change. However, the growing popularity of interpersonal tenets within a cognitive-behavioral framework seems to suggest that Bandura's view is not currently prevalent. In addition, current research underscores the importance of addressing interpersonal factors in cognitive-behavioral therapy. In reviewing more than a dozen controlled therapy outcome studies involving clients with generalized anxiety disorder, Borkovec and Newman (in press) concluded that "interpersonal problems, if left unattended in therapy, may be especially associated with failure to maintain therapeutic gains obtained by intrapersonally oriented cognitive-behavioral therapy."

THE RELATIONSHIP AS A MEANS OF AFFECTING BEHAVIOR AND COGNITIONS

A third manner in which the cognitive-behavioral therapy relationship may be used as a means toward some other end is in terms of modifying the client's thoughts about and behaviors toward the therapist. It should be noted at the outset that, whereas affecting clients' thoughts and actions is generally considered the ultimate goal of cognitive-behavioral therapy, affecting clients' thoughts about and behaviors toward the therapist is viewed as only one possible, intermediate step; it is not the equivalent of successful outcome. In the long run, it matters little if the client thinks differently about and behaves differently toward the therapist. When clients seek therapy, and especially when they seek therapy because of problems with significant people in their lives, any changes demonstrated within the therapy relationship must generalize to these extratherapy relationships for outcome to be considered successful. Therefore, modifying clients' thoughts about and behaviors toward the therapist is simply one means toward achieving a larger end.

In what ways might the therapeutic relationship serve as a vehicle for changing a client's cognitions? The therapist can modify a client's automatic thoughts, irrational beliefs, and faulty cognitive schemas related to the therapist and the therapist's supposed attitudes and feelings toward the client (Arnkoff, 1983; J. Beck, 1996). For example, the therapist can directly challenge a client's assumption that the therapist will disapprove of the client if the client displays certain emotions. By exploring with the client the lack of evidence within the relationship for such a belief, the therapist can point out the irrational basis of the client's thinking. Furthermore, the therapist can help the client develop more realistic perceptions of and self-statements about the therapist and the client's relationship with the therapist. Again, the ultimate aim is to hypothesize about and change the extent to which the client applies similar dysfunctional schemas to other relationships in the client's life.

In addition to serving as a vehicle for modifying clients' cognitions, the therapy relationship can be used to influence clients' behaviors. DeVoge and Beck (1978) invoke Leary's (1957) interpersonal model in suggesting how therapists can best respond to and influence client behaviors. For instance, drawing from the principle that complementary responses are reinforcing, a therapist can reinforce a client's friendliness by responding in a friendly manner. Furthermore, a therapist can behave in a submissive fashion to reinforce a client's dominant behavior, or, if the goal is to help the client learn to be less dominant, the therapist can reinforce the client's submissiveness with dominant relating. Alternatively, therapists can use noncomplementary responses (e.g., responding to submissiveness with submissiveness or to hostility with friendliness) to help extinguish targeted client behaviors. Within this interpersonal context, the therapist can serve as a role model of healthy functioning by demonstrating flexible behavior, rational thinking, and positive interpersonal relating from which clients can learn vicariously (Arnkoff, 1983; Safran & Segal, 1990; Wilson & Evans, 1977).

REAL AND UNREAL COMPONENTS
OF THE RELATIONSHIP

Given that the therapy relationship may be used as a vehicle to foster change in cognitive-behavioral therapy, one may wonder about the relative emphasis on real and "unreal" components of the relationship in treatment. Suffice it to say at the outset that when the relationship is deemed significant in behavioral and cognitive approaches, it is the real and not the "unreal" constituents that are considered important. That is, the client's and therapist's genuine feelings toward and relatively undistorted perceptions of one another are considered more important than transferential aspects of the therapy relationship. In this section, we explore the nature of the real relationship in cognitive-behavioral therapy, as well as cognitive-behavioral views on the transference relationship in therapy.

QUALITIES OF THE REAL RELATIONSHIP IN
COGNITIVE-BEHAVIORAL THERAPY

As discussed in Chapter 5, the real relationship consists of clients' and therapists' reality-based perceptions of one another, as well as both participants' authentic expressions of thoughts and feelings. Deffenbacher (1985) noted that the real relationship is relevant to cognitive-behavioral therapy in that "at least moderate attention to real relationship parameters [is] important in dealing with complex client problems from a learning perspective" (p. 262). What is the nature of this real relationship that requires attention? Is the real relationship in cognitive-behavioral therapy essentially the same as in other approaches? Gelso and Carter (1985) argue that, compared to psychoanalytic and humanistic therapy relationships, the real relationship in cognitive and behavioral therapy tends to be less deep. For example, although both humanistic and cognitive theorists tend to give credence to the importance of a warm therapeutic relationship, for the cognitive therapist, the notion of warmth generally takes the form of establishing rapport with the client through displays of respect, concern, and commitment. By way of contrast, the concept of warmth in humanistic therapy typically extends beyond establishing rapport to the development of intimacy. Rollo May (1939/1989), for instance, describes the closeness that unfolds between a client and an existential therapist as so powerful as to be transformative *for the therapist.* Some existential therapists, furthermore, conceive of their work as a journey into the depths of a client's private hell (Assagioli, 1965). It would be unusual to find the therapy relationship described in as intense a fashion by cognitive-behavioral writers. Still, the fact that most cognitive-behavioral theorists would not describe the therapy relationship in such terms does not preclude cognitive-behavioral clinicians from actually establishing deep, intimate relationships with clients. Especially in the current era of eclecticism and theory integration, when few therapists adhere strictly to any one approach, many therapists who identify themselves as primarily cognitive-behavioral may, in practice, utilize cognitive-behavioral techniques while still developing powerfully intimate relationships with their clients. We would note, however, that the cognitive-behavioral literature, perhaps understandably, does not address ways in which clinicians may depart from their preferred theory when working with clients.

How do cognitive-behavioral writers describe the real relationship between client and therapist? Kelly (1955) referred to the client and therapist as "personal scientists" who work jointly to uncover and resolve clients' problems. This same ethos can be found in the writings of Beck, who depicts the real relationship as marked by a spirit of "collaborative empiricism" (Beck et al., 1990). The client and the therapist are "co-investigators" (Beck & Weishaar, 1995, p. 244) who together set goals, generate hypotheses, gather data, examine evidence, and derive conclusions. The therapist is less of an omniscient expert than a "guide" or "catalyst" for therapy. Consistent with this egalitarian view of the relationship, client feedback is sought about the process and progress of therapy. In addition, clients' apprehensions about the therapist are to be openly discussed, because trust is "one of the cardinal principles" of Beck's approach (Beck et al., 1990, p. 64). Furthermore, therapists are not discouraged from displaying warmth; such displays can challenge clients' beliefs that they are unlovable (Beck et al., 1979).

In contrast, Ellis's view of the therapy relationship is somewhat less collaborative or warm. Rational emotive therapy (RET) therapists are didactic, directive, and confrontational. Nonetheless, Ellis advocates a philosophy of complete acceptance of clients, who are not to be blamed for their inherent tendency toward irrational thought. Therapists' acceptance of clients, however, is not to be confused with overt expressions of warmth. Therapist warmth is considered by Ellis to be neither necessary nor sufficient for producing client change. In fact, Ellis believes that therapists' warmth can reinforce clients' problematic beliefs that they need to be loved by everyone with whom they have contact, and that they have little ability to tolerate frustration (Ellis & Dryden, 1997). Ellis claims that RET therapists often are perceived by clients as warm, largely because of their tolerant attitudes, but RET therapists are "much more interested in helping [clients] with their emotional problems than in relating to them personally" (Ellis, 1995, p. 190). Helping clients gain relief from the issues that bring them to therapy is more important to Ellis than establishing a personal relationship with clients.

Despite the differences between Beck's and Ellis's treatment of the therapy relationship, both seem to describe the therapy relationship in somewhat limited terms, as is true of most cognitive-behavioral writers. When the relationship is discussed at all in cognitive-behavioral theories, the discussion tends to be brief and focused more on therapists' behaviors than on therapists' or clients' feelings and attitudes. For example, Wilson's (1995) description of the therapy relationship occupies less than 1 of the 32 pages in his chapter on behavior therapy. In his brief synopsis of the behavior therapy relationship, Wilson calls a fair amount of attention to behavior therapists' activity levels (e.g., disclosure, directiveness), and he characterizes the typical behavior therapist as more "concerned" than the "neutral and detached" psychoanalytic therapist (p. 209). We would question Wilson's conception of the therapy relationship in psychoanalytic treatment; from our perspective, the psychoanalytic therapist's neutrality is not equivalent to, nor does it stem from, a lack of concern for the client. Although it is theoretically understandable that cognitive-behavioral writers concentrate more on techniques than on the therapy relationship, our impression is that most cognitive-behavioral therapists are cognizant of and sensitive to the importance that clients typically attach to the nature and quality of the client-therapist relationship.

COGNITIVE-BEHAVIORAL VIEWS OF TRANSFERENCE AND THE "UNREAL" RELATIONSHIP

To the extent that cognitive-behavioral therapists acknowledge that transference exists, it tends to be conceptualized as simply another "sample" of behavior and treated similarly to other client thoughts, feelings, and behaviors. For example, Deffenbacher (1985) writes that transference phenomena may be viewed as overgeneralized learning on the client's part that can be treated effectively via cognitive restructuring. Alternatively, transference may be conceptualized as an interpersonal skills deficit that can be remedied with skills training. According to Beck, cognitive-behavioral therapists should be alert for signs of transference but should not intentionally provoke it, as would a psychoanalytic therapist.

The cognitive-behavioral therapist, unlike the psychoanalytic clinician, is not interested in the historical origins of the client's distorted perceptions of the therapist (Arnkoff, 1983), except as they may be constituents of a relevant pattern of interpersonal reinforcement. Although cognitive-behavioral therapists may assess a client's reinforcement history, they tend not to concern themselves with intrapsychic, unconscious underpinnings of the client's transference. Consider the following statement from Ellis (1995, p. 190): "If a client tries to seduce a therapist, this is not usually explained in terms of 'transference' but in terms of (a) the dire needs for love, (b) normal attraction to a helpful person, and (c) the natural sex urges of two people who have intimate mental-emotional contact." Ellis does not find it necessary to spend time in therapy exploring the origins of the client's "dire needs for love," nor explaining why "normal attraction" and "natural urges" for a particular client manifest themselves in seductive behavior in a help-giving/receiving situation. In RET, when transference is recognized by the therapist, the therapist attacks the transference by quickly pointing out the client's irrational beliefs that are involved. In short, transference tends to be afforded no special status in cognitive-behavioral therapy, and it certainly is not viewed as an important mechanism of change. In fact, transference phenomena often represent a nuisance and a hindrance to the crux of cognitive-behavioral therapy (Gelso & Carter, 1985; Wilson & Evans, 1977).

Despite the obvious differences between psychoanalytic and cognitive-behavioral views of transference, Safran and Segal (1990) note that commonalities exist between the psychoanalyst's task of interpreting transference and the cognitive-behavioral therapist's role in helping clients distinguish between rational and irrational thinking. Safran and Segal remark that both types of therapists aim to help clients perceive their environments more realistically.

Beck et al. (1990) provide a notable exception to the typical conceptualization of transference in cognitive-behavioral therapy. Beck claims that transference reactions are likely to play an important role in cognitive-behavioral therapy with clients who have borderline personality disorder. Even though the cognitive-behavioral therapist is typically active and unambiguous, especially compared to psychoanalytic therapists, Beck contends that borderline clients' strong and rigid constructions of reality predispose them to overgeneralize their beliefs and expectancies regarding interpersonal interactions. Furthermore, clients with borderline personality disorder have a heightened tendency toward confirmation bias in that they are sensitive to information from therapists that might substantiate their convictions about people in general. When a borderline client distorts information about the therapist, Beck advocates that the therapist deal immediately and explicitly with the client's perceptions, as opposed to fostering the development of transference, a tactic that is in many ways similar to what psychoanalytic therapists would recommend with profoundly disturbed clients. If transference is not explored with clients, it will interfere with collaboration within the relationship. Beck also emphasizes the importance of therapists' maintaining an empathic sensitivity to clients who are experiencing transference reactions so as not to reject clients when confronting their transference thoughts and feelings.

Regarding the role of countertransference and its contributions to what we see as the transference configuration in therapy, cognitive-behavioral writers are noticeably silent on the topic. Rarely is countertransference addressed or even mentioned in the cognitive-behavioral literature, creating the impression that either countertransference is viewed as relatively unimportant, or it doesn't occur in cognitive-behavioral work. We would disagree with both positions. As discussed in Chapter 4, we consider countertransference to be present in and of potentially great significance to all approaches to therapy. We do not believe that therapists are less likely to have their unresolved issues provoked simply because they are practicing from one particular theoretical framework; nor do we believe that countertransference reactions will have no effect on one's work. However, we recognize that because cognitive-behavioral therapists typically do not use the therapy relationship as a direct mechanism of change, they may be less inclined to consider their countertransference reactions as valuable components of their work (see Proposition 4 in Chapter 4).

Consistent with the minimal attention paid to countertransference issues in cognitive-behavioral therapy, Burns and Auerbach (1996) downplay the importance of therapists' reactions to clients. Cognitive theory, Burns and Auerbach write, holds that an individual's perceptions dictate subsequent emotional reactions, and this holds true both for clients and therapists. Consequently, therapists' reactions are to be understood as reflecting more about the therapist and the therapist's perceptual set than about the client. Burns and Auerbach therefore hold that therapists' emotional reactions are of little utility because they cannot be trusted to correspond strongly to or reveal reliable information about the client's behavior. We recognize therapists' susceptibility to countertransference distortions, but we disagree with Burns and Auerbach's stance that therapists' perceptions are necessarily tainted to such a degree that they contain little valuable data about the client. Instead, we propose that therapists can work profitably to decipher the degree to which their reactions are personal manifestations of countertransference versus realistic reactions to the client's behavior.

POWER IN THE COGNITIVE-BEHAVIORAL THERAPY RELATIONSHIP

In his book *Persuasion and Healing,* Frank (1961) argues convincingly that therapists of all theoretical approaches exercise influence over their clients. The extent to which this influence is acknowledged and just how it is employed, however, varies among therapists of different schools. In a provocative discussion of this topic, Heller (1985) posits that psychoanalytic therapists neglect their power over clients, person-centered therapists deny their power, and behavior therapists intentionally use their power. Inherent throughout Heller's argument is the perspective that behavioral and cognitive therapists acknowledge more explicitly than do therapists of other orientations the authority and persuasive power that accompany the general role of therapist. Heller asserts that therapists' open acknowledgment and subsequent utilization of their power in the therapy relationship are for the best. When a power differential exists between two people but is neglected or denied by the person in power, the potential for exploitation increases. Because cognitive-behaviorists explicitly recognize and use the power differential between client and therapist, Heller maintains that power is less likely to be subtly abused by cognitive-behavioral therapists than by humanistic and psychodynamic therapists. If mistakes are made in cognitive-behavioral therapists' uses of power, they are likely to be more out in the open, and perhaps more easily identifiable and addressable, Heller asserts.

We agree with Heller's reasoning that the likelihood of exploitation increases when power imbalances are ignored, but we would also note that some cognitive-behavioral therapists seem both aware of their power and dangerously close to abusing it. For example, whereas Ellis states that one of the goals of RET is to "empower individuals" (1995, p. 165), Ellis also commonly advocates in his writing that RET therapists "attack," "annihilate," and "demolish" clients' irrational thinking. The forceful language that is scattered throughout Ellis's writing may translate into an aggressive approach to therapy that some clients (e.g., abuse survivors) could find objectionable. Further difficulties in the misuse of power in RET can be traced to Ellis's antagonistic views of clients' religious beliefs (Ellis,

1991, 1995, 1996). Not only does Ellis run the risk of appearing insensitive to religious clients' cultural values, but his stance also minimizes the fact that religion has been linked empirically to mental health. Not all RET therapists subscribe to Ellis's views on religion, or practice RET as Ellis does; nonetheless, we encourage clinicians who openly advocate the use of power-laden tactics in therapy to remain cognizant of their potential for harm.

Just as it would be unfair to lump all RET therapists with Ellis, it would be inaccurate to associate all cognitive-behavioral therapists with Ellis in terms of power dynamics in the therapy relationship. For example, Lazarus's (1989) espousal of "parity" in the therapy relationship and Beck's view of therapy as "collaborative empiricism" both seem to promote less overtly persuasive and forceful approaches than RET. To be specific, unlike Ellis, Beck does not believe that therapists should "attack" clients' thinking. Instead, Beck encourages the use of Socratic dialogue to more gently help clients arrive at logical conclusions to the questions posed by the therapist (Beck & Weishaar, 1995). Furthermore, Beck et al. (1990) explicitly acknowledge the power that *clients* have in therapy (e.g., to not comply with a homework assignment), and they discourage an authoritarian stance on the therapist's part when issues of control arise. Instead, Beck recommends that therapists disengage from the power struggle and collaboratively help clients weigh the benefits and drawbacks to choosing not to follow through with a recommended intervention.

From a more behavioral perspective, Kazdin (1980, p. 59) acknowledges: "Behavior modification is inherently controlling and by design attempts to influence behavior, although it does not necessarily rely on aversive means or act against an individual's volition." Kazdin notes that common misperceptions and fears of behavior therapists stem from concern about the application of behavior principles to society in general, as advocated by Skinner (1948, 1971) and made popular in books like *A Clockwork Orange* (Burgess, 1963). Implementing behavioral principles on a societal level raises legitimate ethical issues about restricting the autonomy of individuals who are not seeking help from someone with expertise in the use of behavioral techniques. Kazdin notes, however, that affecting change on other than an individual level is rarely the immediate concern of the behavioral therapist. As we discuss in Chapter 10, promoting societal change is much more the focus of feminist therapists than behavior therapists. Behavior therapy is no different from other approaches in that therapists use their knowledge and skill to help clients change their behaviors so that they can live more effectively. The difference between behavior therapy and other approaches stems from clients' perceived control over the change process. In behavior therapy, the use of externally applied techniques that are thought to produce change contrasts with the emphasis, in other approaches, of helping clients develop more internally regulated processes that lead to change (e.g., insight, self-acceptance). Behaviorists argue that the techniques they employ, rather than being controlling, actually free clients from conditions that inhibit clients' choices and behaviors (Kazdin, 1980). Consequently, behavior therapists would contend that their interventions ultimately impinge no more on clients' freedom than do empty chair techniques, minimal encouragers, or dream analysis. Although we agree with much of the behaviorists' perspective, we are left uneasy by the possible utilitarian rationale for using techniques that may be perceived by clients as controlling. We would echo, to behavioral as well as cognitive therapists, Maeder's (1989) general caution that a clinician "who wields power in the name of some perceived ultimate good is always potentially dangerous" (p. 44).

CONCLUSION

The client-therapist relationship in cognitive-behavioral approaches occupies a place of greater prominence than has been the case historically. Nevertheless, the relationship is seen as secondary to techniques in its ability to affect therapeutic change. Cognitive-behavioral theories tend to consider a strong therapy relationship to be a necessary precondition for change, in that a positive relationship minimizes clients' resistance and facilitates clients' cooperation and adherence to techniques. The therapy relationship may also be used to "gather data" about clients and to affect clients' therapy-specific cognitions and behaviors as a precursor to more generalized change. In general, cognitive-behavioral therapists advocate a client-therapist relationship characterized by mutual respect, acceptance, commitment, limited depth, and a varying degree of warmth. Transference phenomena are treated like other samples of client behavior and are not considered central to the change process. Finally, whereas many cognitive-behavioral therapists recognize and use therapeutically the power ascribed to them by clients, the intentional use of power in therapy carries with it the potential for exploitation, to which therapists must remain sensitive.

CHAPTER 9

The Humanistic and Existential Vision of the Therapeutic Relationship: The Real Relationship and More

T HIS CHAPTER addresses the nature of the psychotherapy relationship in the "Third Wave" of theories known collectively as the humanistic psychotherapies. Humanistic psychology in general, and the humanistic approaches to therapy in particular, grew out of dissatisfaction with the biological reductionism of psychoanalysis and behavioral psychology's rigid insistence on the objective study of observable phenomena. More specifically, humanistic psychologists refute the psychoanalytic notion that behavior is determined more by instinct than volition. In addition, humanists have taken issue with the prominence of the unconscious in psychoanalytic thought. On the other hand, behavioral psychology, and the learning theories more broadly, suffered historically from what humanistic psychologists might call "physics envy." That is, in attempting to emulate established sciences such as physics and chemistry, behaviorists adopted a philosophy and practice of research from disciplines whose objects of study are nonconscious. Humanistic psychologists maintain that the application of traditional scientific approaches to the study of human beings limits the potential understanding that can be gained from such undertakings. Furthermore, humanistic psychologists question the assumption underlying orthodox science that objective observation is even possible (G. Howard, 1986). As F. Perls (1947) pointed out, "Observations are dictated by specific interests, by preconceived ideas and by an . . . attitude which collects and selects facts accordingly. In other words: there is no such thing as objective science. . . . In psychology more than in any other science observer and observed facts are inseparable" (p. 14). Physicists themselves have come to recognize the inseparability of the observer and observed in discovering that one's approach to studying certain objects, such as subatomic particles, influences the very properties of that which is being investigated (Capra, 1991).

Humanistic psychology may be described in terms of its opposition to the tenets of psychoanalysis and behaviorism, but humanistic psychology is more usefully characterized in terms of what it stands for rather than what it is opposed to. Although a rich diversity of beliefs and practices typifies humanistic psychology, several common themes unite the field. Tageson (1982) identified seven philosophical components of humanistic psychology: (a) phenomenology, (b) self-determination, (c) holism (vs. reductionism), (d) humans' actualizing tendency, (e) the ideal of authenticity, (f) self-transcendence, and (g) person-centeredness. We refer the interested reader to Tageson's excellent text for greater detail on these distinguishing characteristics of humanistic psychology. Suffice it to say here that humanistic psychologists concern themselves with questions that, across time and across cultures, are of universal concern to human beings.

A multitude of approaches to psychotherapy trace their lineages back to humanistic psychology. They have in common, relative to other approaches to therapy, greater "attention to the client's (and therapist's) 'here-and-now' functioning, to the client's phenomenological-perceptual world, and to the client's inherent trustworthiness and capacity for actualization" (Gelso & Carter, 1985, p. 196). This chapter focuses primarily on the nature of the psychotherapy relationship within two approaches that we believe to be representative of the humanistic movement and to have greatly influenced its development and current practice: person-centered and gestalt psychotherapy. In addition, the therapy relationship will be examined briefly within a sampling of other humanistic approaches (existential and experiential) to provide a broader scope to the chapter. Each of the theories will be discussed in terms of how its central principles bear on the psychotherapy relationship. As in the previous two chapters, we also explore the therapy relationship within the humanistic theories along four dimensions: (a) the extent to which the relationship is considered to be central or peripheral, (b) whether the relationship is viewed as a means or an end, (c) the relative emphasis on real and "unreal" (i.e., transferential) components of the relationship, and (d) how power is conceptualized and used in the relationship. Recent research findings will be incorporated in relevant places throughout the chapter.

PERSON-CENTERED PSYCHOTHERAPY

Carl Rogers' theory of psychotherapy has evolved considerably since the 1942 publication of his revolutionary book *Counseling and Psychotherapy*. Each stage of development in Rogers' theory has been accompanied by a variation in the name of his theory. Initially, Rogers termed his approach "non-directive counseling" to emphasize his novel belief that clients should be responsible for directing the course of treatment. The counselor was to provide an atmosphere in which clients were free to express themselves, within clearly communicated limits, regarding time, aggression, and affection. "Limits are kept with a warm understanding of the client's need to break them," Rogers (1942, p. 89) wrote. Diagnosing, interpreting, and advising were strictly off-limits. The second phase of development in Rogers' theory was called "client-centered therapy," coinciding with the publication in 1951 of his book by the same name. In this stage of his theory, also sometimes referred to as "reflective psychotherapy" (Hart, 1970), Rogers stressed the importance of counselors' communicating their understanding of both the content and, more importantly, the underlying feelings related to clients' verbalizations. This "exclusive focus in therapy on the present phenomenal experience of the client is the meaning of the term 'client-centered'" (Rogers, 1951, p. 191). The third phase of Rogers' theory, known to some as "experiential psychotherapy" (Hart), prioritized therapist attitudes over specific techniques such as reflection. This emphasis on counselor attitudes can be traced to Rogers' classic 1957 paper in which he delineated his beliefs about the "necessary and sufficient conditions" for therapeutic change (to be discussed shortly). The fourth and most recent stage of his theory, marked by the 1980 publication of *A Way of Being*, has come to be known as the "person-centered approach." Rogers (1980) described the shift in both name and philosophy as follows: "The old concept of 'client-centered therapy' has been transformed into the 'person-centered approach.' In other words, I am no longer talking simply about psychotherapy, but about a point of view, a philosophy, an approach to life, a way of being, which fits any situation in which *growth*—of a person, a group, or a community—is part of the goal" (p. ix).

CHARACTERISTICS OF THE PERSON-CENTERED THERAPY RELATIONSHIP:
THE THERAPIST-OFFERED NECESSARY AND SUFFICIENT CONDITIONS

Since 1957, three concepts have embodied the person-centered perspective of the ideal therapy relationship: (a) therapists' empathy, (b) unconditional positive regard, and (c) congruence. Over the years, we have become so familiar with these constructs that, at times, the temptation exists to assume that little more needs to be said about them. Consider, however, what psychotherapy would be like if these three relationship ingredients were absent, or nearly so. Imagine, if you will, a therapist who was only slightly empathic, somewhat authentic, and had limited regard for a client. What would psychotherapy be like if some or all of these "nonfacilitative" qualities were present in the therapist? Rather than provide an answer to this question, we shall turn our attention to an exploration of how each of these three concepts influences and even defines the relationship in person-centered therapy. We shall present the three constructs separately, although it is useful to remember that, in practice, they work together, interacting to provide a climate that Rogers believed to be necessary and sufficient for therapeutic change. In fact, Rogers believed that the synthesis of the three facilitative conditions can create a state of being in the therapist in which healing is almost inevitable, as he expressed in the following passage: "I find that when I am closest to my inner, intuitive self, when I am somehow in touch with the unknown in me, when perhaps I am in a slightly altered state of consciousness in the relationship, then whatever I do seems to be full of healing. Then simply my *presence* is releasing and helpful" (Rogers, 1986, cited in Raskin & Rogers, 1995, p. 129).

The first of the three facilitative conditions to be discussed, empathy, results literally from the combination of a Greek prefix meaning "in" and the root word "pathos" which connotes an experience of deep feeling, often associated with suffering (May, 1939/1989). Thus, the word *empathy* itself connotes an entering into the feelings of another, with an associated willingness to experience fully and even suffer the other's emotions.

What type of a relationship is created when the therapist strives to be empathic? First, it might be said that such a relationship will be perceived by the client to be *special* rather than ordinary. Empathic understanding, according to Rogers (1961, p. 62), "is extremely rare. We neither receive it nor offer it with any great frequency. Instead we offer another type of understanding which is very different . . . an evaluative understanding from the outside." Shlien (1997) offers a different perspective. He contends that empathy itself is not rare, but wise and compassionate use of empathy is. Far too often, according to Shlien, empathy is not combined with sympathy and so is used for selfish purposes.

We agree with Shlien that empathy without sympathy or compassion has little therapeutic value, but we nonetheless favor Rogers' view that empathy itself is a scarce commodity in relationships. In fact, we would like to suggest three reasons that empathic understanding is rare. First, empathic relating is arduous work. To relate empathically is to swim against the natural and powerful currents of self-absorption. Empathic understanding, or cognitive empathy (Gladstein, 1983), requires a willingness to suspend one's own thoughts and opinions and interpretations to understand another. To relate with cognitive empathy is to persistently refine one's understanding of the other, to demonstrate a willingness to let one's present perceptions be inaccurate. Along these lines, Spence (1987) states: "Truly respectful listening requires a continual making and breaking of tentative assumptions and underlying metaphors in an effort to hear what the patient is 'really' saying" (p. 68). This type of relating, from our experience, is at once arduous and deeply rewarding. In addition to requiring effort, a second reason empathy is rare is that empathic relating on an emotional level, or affective empathy (Gladstein, 1983), involves pain—not continuously, but inevitably. To enter with affective empathy into the world of another is to experience the full range of human emotions. The willingness to share another person's suffering, when the human inclination is to escape pain, is indeed an uncommon quality. Finally, empathic relating is rare because it is perhaps more of an ideal than an actuality. It is never possible to fully understand another from his or her unique point of view or to completely feel another's exact feelings; it is only possible to strive for and approximate these conditions. In addition to the quality of being special, person-centered theorists maintain that empathic relationships can be characterized in terms of *freedom*. When the therapist is empathic, and the client perceives the therapist as such, the client "experiences a freedom to explore oneself at both conscious and unconscious levels, as rapidly as one can dare to embark on the dangerous quest. There is also a complete freedom from any type of moral or diagnostic evaluation, since all such evaluations are, I believe, always threatening" (C. Rogers, 1961, p. 34). According to person-centered theory, empathic relating creates in the client a sense of freedom from judgment precisely because empathy requires that the therapist adopt the client's internal frame of reference. In fact, Bozarth (1997) remarks that "empathic understanding is the unconditional acceptance of the individual's frame of reference" (p. 85). Judgment, to the contrary, involves the imposition of the therapist's external frame of reference on the client's experience. When a therapist suspends the human tendency to relate from without, rather than from within the client's world, the client is believed to experience an increased freedom to explore and express foreign aspects of the self.

In addition to being special and freeing, empathic relationships are likely to be perceived as *helpful*. The therapist's empathic relating is believed to be helpful, in part, because it provides a model for how clients might better relate to themselves, in terms of deepening both self-understanding and the experiencing of affect (Barrett-Lennard, 1997). Empathic relationships also are helpful in providing a sense of universality. If a client can be understood deeply and clearly by another human being, then there must be something about the client that is common to both client and therapist. In empathic relating, then, the client's feelings of being isolated or alienated can be dissipated by the experience of an empathic connection and resonance with the therapist. Rogers maintained that clients are apt to feel helped when they perceive a therapist to be empathic even to a small degree. "I am often impressed with the fact that even a minimal amount of empathic understanding—a bumbling and faulty attempt to catch the confused complexity of the client's meaning—is helpful" (Rogers, 1961, p. 53). Empathic relating is especially important in the therapy relationship because, according to Rogers, empathy is needed most when "the other person is hurting, confused, troubled, anxious, alienated, terrified, or when he or she is doubtful of self-worth, uncertain as to identity" (Rogers, 1980, p. 160), as many clients are.

In paying heed to the importance of these common client characteristics (hurting, confused, troubled, and so on), Rogers strayed from his usual emphasis on therapist characteristics as all-important determinants of the therapy relationship. It may be recalled that Rogers' (1957) original statement about the necessary and sufficient conditions included several stipulations about client characteristics: clients were to be anxious or vulnerable, in psychological contact with the therapist, and capable of recognizing and receiving the therapist-offered conditions. Over time, however, person-centered theory has moved away from consideration of client factors, almost neglecting the reciprocal influence that relationship participants have on one another. Raskin and Rogers (1995), for instance, wrote: "Certain attitudes in therapists constitute the necessary and sufficient conditions of therapeutic effectiveness" and, further downplaying the importance of client variables, stated: "The same principles of psychotherapy apply to all persons, whether they are categorized as psychotic, neurotic, or normal" (p. 131).

We agree with the person-centered perspective that empathy plays an immensely important, even curative, role in therapy. Nevertheless, we wonder whether the person-centered approach might benefit from returning to a consideration of the ways in which empathy is communicated effectively. For Rogers (1957), techniques were merely vehicles for conveying therapeutic attitudes and were of little to no importance otherwise. Rogers's position stemmed largely from his opposition to the common perception of empathy as equivalent to reflection. We would not advocate a return to the days of equating empathy with therapist reflection, but we nonetheless think it would be valuable for person-centered theorists to clearly articulate the myriad ways that deep, accurate empathy interacts with client factors and is communicated effectively to clients. L. Greenberg and Elliott's (1997) recent work represents an important step toward illuminating this issue. They note that empathy may be conveyed using a variety of therapist response modes, such as interpreting, evoking, reflecting, probing, and speculating. Greenberg and Elliott emphasize that the manner in which empathy is communicated depends largely on the therapist's intentions.

Despite the therapeutic value of empathy, we wonder about the merits of therapists' thoughtfully limiting their expression of empathy on occasion—a position not commonly endorsed by person-centered scholars. We would not encourage therapists to limit their empathic understanding per se, but we believe that there are times when it may be beneficial to withhold the *communication* of empathy. For example, if one adopts the position that clients can be "optimally frustrated" toward growth (F. Perls, 1969), withholding the overt communication of empathy may be helpful toward this end. What are the consequences of the "optimal provision" and "optimal withholding" of empathic expression in person-centered therapy? When are the critical moments in which therapists should consider refraining from displays of empathy? With what types of clients might suppression of empathic communication have adverse effects? Answers to these questions await theoretical and empirical advancements in the person-centered camp.

Closely related to the concept of empathy is that of unconditional positive regard, which refers to a valuing and respect for the client independent of the client's behaviors or feelings or attitudes. M. Kahn (1991) compares unconditional regard to the Greek term *agape*, a selfless, altruistic form of love. Unconditional regard also shares similarities with the philosophy of complete acceptance, characteristic of Hinduism and Mahayana Buddhism, and has some parallels with the Afrocentric principle of *umoja,* or unity (Phillips, 1990). Thus, the notion of unconditional regard seems to be a universal concept, with related concepts found on several continents. On a personal level, the notion of unconditional regard took on deeper meaning for one of the authors (JAH) hours after the birth of his first child. Sitting with his son in the hospital nursery, this author was filled with the conviction, as we suppose many parents are, that there is nothing his son could ever do that would cause his father not to love him. Whether this same attitude can or ought to be felt toward clients with equal purity and intensity is a matter of open debate.

Inherent in the Rogerian concept of unconditional regard is the distinction between behaviors and worth. Simply stated, certain behaviors are unacceptable in psychotherapy. However, it is probably not feasible to universally categorize unacceptable client behaviors; individual therapists must do this for themselves. When confronted by a client's unacceptable behavior, then, the person-centered therapist faces the delicate task of communicating to the client the unacceptability of the behavior without conveying to the client that *he* or *she* is unacceptable. Just as the person-centered therapist is to maintain and communicate an attitude of unconditional regard when the client behaves unacceptably, the therapist is not to convey greater valuing of the client when the client behaves in a manner approved of by the therapist. Damning and exalting both equate the client's behavior with his or her worth. When the person-centered therapist finds that she or he values the client more because the client expresses emotions freely or laughs at the therapist's jokes or seems to be improving, then it is a sign that the therapist's regard for the client is conditional.

We noted earlier the Rogerian perspective that it is difficult to be empathic if one's regard for another is conditional. That is, if the therapist is attempting to understand the client from an external frame of reference that involves judgment, empathic relating will be severely limited. Conversely, Bozarth (1997) maintains that empathy is the best way to exhibit unconditional positive regard; in fact, it might be said that with enough understanding inevitably comes compassion, or even that unconditional positive regard and empathy are ultimately one and the same. Thus, the person-centered perspective holds that when the therapist comprehends the client's experience sensitively and deeply, compassion is unavoidable. This perspective is consistent with the humanistic view of clients as inherently trustworthy, but it discounts the possibility that therapists might deeply understand and still genuinely dislike or even loathe clients (see Peck, 1983). Furthermore, whereas person-centered theory advocates unconditional positive regard for clients at all times, we wonder about the value of conditional positive regard. When might it be in the client's best interest for the therapist to "demand" the best from the client, expressing regard conditionally to reinforce the client's healthy behavior?

The last of Rogers's facilitative conditions, congruence, is considered by person-centered theorists to be the most important of the three. Rogers favored therapist authenticity over facades of warmth and caring. Speaking to the importance of therapist congruence, Rogers (1961, p. 33) remarked:

> I have found that the more that I can be genuine in the relationship, the more helpful it will be. This means that I need to be aware of my own feelings, in so far as possible, rather than presenting an outward facade of one attitude, while actually holding another attitude at a deeper or unconscious level. Being genuine also involves the willingness to be and to express, in my words and my behavior, the various feelings and attitudes which exist in me. It is only in this way that the relationship can have *reality,* and reality seems deeply important as a first condition. It is only by providing the genuine reality which is in me, that the other person can successfully seek for the reality in him. I have found this to be true even when the attitudes I feel are not attitudes with which I am pleased, or attitudes which seem conducive to a good relationship. It seems extremely important to be *real.*

What is the effect on the therapy relationship if the therapist is not congruent? First, person-centered theory holds that a lack of authenticity on the therapist's behalf provides unhealthy modeling to the client. Disingenuous relating communicates messages such as: "The way I am feeling right now is not OK"; "I need to behave as if I were someone other than who I am"; "I cannot let you know how I am feeling and who I am." Messages such as these, subtly transmitted to the client, run counter to the open and accepting environment the person-centered therapist aims to create. Second, if the therapist is inauthentic, the depth of the psychotherapy relationship is necessarily limited. Intimacy requires honesty, and incongruence, as a form of dishonesty, confines a relationship to superficiality. Finally, if a therapist is not congruent and the client senses it, the client is put in the difficult position of needing to choose which part of the therapist's presentation to respond to—the inauthentic behavior or the genuine feelings beneath the surface. Thus, the therapist's incongruence can be confusing for the client and can undermine the client's ability to trust his or her own judgment—and the therapist's as well.

One of the primary obstacles to congruence is that it necessitates self-acceptance on the part of the therapist. Trainees, and even some seasoned therapists, for instance, often experience a reluctance about being all of who they are with clients. It is as if these clinicians believe that they will be more effective with a client if they are only partially themselves, or if they are someone else altogether, and so they behave disingenuously. "Surely I don't have the resources within me to help this client. What would Carl Rogers do in this situation?" they occasionally say to themselves, looking outside themselves for direction in such moments. From a person-centered perspective, the process of looking outside oneself for guidance while conducting therapy takes a therapist's attention away from his or her inner feelings, thus increasing the chances that the therapist's behavior and feelings will be discrepant. Somewhat paradoxically, the greater fidelity therapists display to their own feelings, the more trust clients will show in them. Rogers wrote, "I have come to recognize that being trustworthy does not demand that I be rigidly consistent but that I be dependably real" (1961, p. 50).

We would argue that there are occasions in therapy when congruence is not called for, or, at least, when the therapist's transparency should be limited. For example, when therapists suspect that they are enmeshed in countertransference issues but cannot clearly discern or articulate their reactions as such, we would advocate quiet reserve on the part of the therapist until the countertransference has been understood. A limited amount of transparency also is called for, we believe, when working with clients whose fragility, whether temporary or characterological, interferes with their ability to benefit from interpersonal feedback. We would recommend that therapists be measured in how much they reveal of their reactions when working with such clients.

RECENT RESEARCH ON THE THERAPIST-OFFERED NECESSARY AND SUFFICIENT CONDITIONS

Are empathy, unconditional regard, and congruence necessary and sufficient for therapeutic change, as Rogers (1957) postulated? The empirical answer, after several decades of research, seems to be "No." That is, the therapist-offered facilitative conditions are neither necessary nor sufficient for positive outcome, although they are typically quite helpful (Gelso & Carter, 1985). For example, a recent review of more than 100 studies concluded that a slight majority of the studies supported the existence of a direct, moderate relationship between empathy and therapy outcome, especially when outcome is measured from the client's perspective (Orlinsky, Grawe, & Parks, 1994; see also Beutler, Machado, & Neufeldt, 1994, and Bohart & Greenberg, 1997, pp. 18–19). On the whole, however, evidence indicates that the therapist-offered facilitative conditions do not account for large gains in therapy outcome.

Several explanations exist as to why empathy, unconditional regard, and congruence seem to be neither necessary nor sufficient to bring about client change. First, a sole focus on conditions offered by the therapist minimizes the contributions of client variables (Rice, 1983). Not only are client variables important, but evidence exists to suggest that client characteristics account for more variance in outcome than do therapist characteristics (Orlinsky et al., 1994, p. 361). In addition, Rogers' hypotheses about the facilitative conditions diminish the importance of both the therapist techniques and the tasks in which clients in person-centered therapy are engaged (e.g., exploring and experiencing feelings, focusing on the present, and assuming responsibility for oneself; Rice, 1983). Furthermore, the possibility exists that Rogers' hypotheses have not enjoyed empirical support because they have yet to be adequately tested; measurement and methodological flaws plague existing research (Gelso & Carter, 1985). Perhaps, as the humanists have argued for years, we need to apply qualitative and other nontraditional research methodologies to the study of person-centered therapy to capture the subjective experience of clients and therapists before deciding about the validity of Rogers' hypotheses. Finally, maybe Rogers' hypotheses about the necessary and sufficient conditions are unrealistically bold. With growing evidence to suggest that a wide variety of pantheoretical factors promote outcome, it seems unreasonable to expect that any one, relatively small set of variables would account for more than a moderate amount of therapy outcome.

THE ROLE OF THE PERSON-CENTERED THERAPY RELATIONSHIP: CURATIVE AGENT

Whereas the *characteristics* of the person-centered therapy relationship are largely captured by Rogers' necessary and sufficient conditions, the *role* of the client-therapist relationship has only been hinted at so far. In short, the person-centered relationship is considered the central mechanism of therapeutic change. If the right conditions are offered by the therapist and received by the client, change is believed to occur inevitably, though perhaps not immediately. Because the relationship is regarded as healing in and of itself, techniques are eschewed, except as they contribute to the development and deepening of an authentic, accepting, empathic relationship. The role of the person-centered relationship in achieving positive therapeutic outcomes will be discussed more, toward the end of the chapter, when we consider "means-end" perspectives on the humanistic therapy relationship.

GESTALT PSYCHOTHERAPY

Gestalt psychotherapy, to many individuals, is synonymous with Fritz Perls. It seems important at the outset to both acknowledge and challenge this perception of gestalt therapy. Although no one would question the influence of Perls on the development of gestalt therapy, it would be unfair and inaccurate to associate the current practice of gestalt therapy strictly with "Perlsian" therapy. Recent advancements in the theory and practice of gestalt therapy have changed the landscape considerably. Therefore, in the pages that follow, we attempt to distinguish Perls's ideas about the therapy relationship from more contemporary thinking among gestalt theorists and practitioners.

In addition to the view that gestalt therapy is synonymous with Perls, another common perception of gestalt therapy is that it is technique-oriented, if not technique-driven. On the one hand, Perls denounced this point of view: "One of the objections I have against anyone calling himself a Gestalt Therapist is that he uses techniques. A technique is a gimmick. A gimmick should be used only in the extreme case" (F. Perls, 1969, p. 1). Perls preferred to think of gestalt therapy as one of the existential approaches to therapy, which are characterized by their explicit *lack* of techniques. On the other hand, even Laura Perls lamented that her husband became preoccupied with techniques late in his career. In a conversation with Friedman (1983, p. 89), Laura remarked, "What was very problematic in Fritz's approach was that he was not interested in the person as such but in what he could do with her." Laura Perls helped broaden the practice of gestalt therapy to emphasize the therapist's authentic relational style over the somewhat artificial use of techniques. She maintained: "A Gestalt therapist does not use techniques; he applies *himself in* and *to* a situation with whatever professional skill and life experience he has accumulated and integrated. There are as many styles as there are therapists and clients who discover themselves and each other and together invent their relationship" (L. Perls, 1976, cited in Hycner & Jacobs, 1995, p. xx). Current gestalt practitioners use techniques, or other interventions, as a natural extension of the type of relationship that has been established with a client (Hycner & Jacobs, 1995; Yontef, 1979). L. Greenberg (1983, p. 135) states that gestalt techniques "are always conducted in a relationship context in which the therapist suggests experiments designed from an appreciation of the client's readiness to experiment."

THE RELATIONSHIP IN GESTALT THERAPY: ROLES AND CHARACTERISTICS

There seems to be less agreement about the role of the relationship in gestalt therapy than about its characteristics (Hycner & Jacobs, 1995). First, we shall address controversy about the role of the gestalt therapy relationship; we will then discuss some of its common attributes.

Hycner and Jacobs (1995) contend that there are two primary viewpoints regarding the role of the relationship in gestalt therapy. The more traditional perspective favors using the relationship to foster client *awareness*; the more contemporary position views the relationship as an avenue for *contact*. To understand the notion of contact in gestalt therapy, a brief discussion of boundaries may be helpful. F. Perls (1969, p. 6) described relationship as "an everchanging boundary where two people meet. And when we meet there, then I change and you change, through the process of encountering each other." Whereas healthy boundaries allow for an authentic encounter between client and therapist, disturbances in the client's (and presumably the therapist's) boundaries can profoundly affect the therapy relationship. Boundary disturbances may take on several different forms. For example, when the client lacks clear boundaries, the condition of confluence exists; the client does not differentiate between self and therapist (F. Perls, Hefferline, & Goodman, 1951). At the other extreme, the condition of isolation occurs when the client's boundaries are too rigid, and the client experiences no contact with or connection to the therapist (Yontef & Simkin, 1989). A third condition, known as introjection, exists when "aspects of the environment are *identified* with, as if they were aspects of the self" (L. Greenberg, 1983, p. 130). When introjection occurs in the context of therapy, the therapist may be "swallowed whole" into the person of the client. Although this leads to the same end result as does confluence, the difference between the two conditions is that, in introjection, there is an initial recognition of the boundary between self and other. Finally, in retroflection, the self of the client is divided into subject and object and "impulses directed toward the environment become redirected toward the self as object" (L. Greenberg, 1983, p. 130). Retroflected anger, for instance, can take the form of "I'll show you, I'll hurt me," in which anger is directed back at the internalized object within the self instead of outward, leading to self-injurious behavior.

For gestalt therapists who view the therapy relationship primarily as a means of establishing contact with a client, the relationship is of central importance. However, the therapy relationship is considered secondary by those gestalt therapists who place a premium on client awareness. For these therapists, any technique or experiment that fosters awareness takes precedence over the nature of the therapy relationship. This stance follows from Perls's belief that "awareness per se—by and of itself—can be curative" (F. Perls, 1969, p. 16). Hycner and Jacobs (1995) offer a potential rapprochement between the two opposing camps in suggesting that *contact* is a necessary precondition for full *awareness.* "Therapy composed solely of awareness techniques, without the contactful engagement of the therapist/person with the patient/person, paradoxically limits the awareness possibilities for the patient and interrupts the becoming of both people" (Hycner & Jacobs, 1995, p. 84).

In addition to the role of the relationship in gestalt therapy, what are its distinguishing characteristics? Paramount among the defining features of gestalt relating is an I-Thou attitude on the part of the therapist. I-Thou relating includes elements of empathic inclusion, noncoercive respect, affirmation, genuine caring, and a willingness to be fully present in the moment. I-Thou relating, then, shares strong similarities with Rogers' facilitative conditions of empathy, congruence, and positive regard. In gestalt theory, I-Thou relating is contrasted with I-It relating, which makes authentic encounter impossible because it reduces the client to an object. Buber (1958) believed that I-Thou relating was necessary for healing: "The regeneration of an atrophied personal center . . . can only be attained in the person-to-person attitude of a partner, not by the consideration and examination of an object" (cited in Friedman, 1983, p. 132). L. Greenberg (1983) maintains that when gestalt therapists emphasize technique over relationship, they engage in I-It relating, functioning as teachers of the gestalt method. Once a client has demonstrated an understanding of basic gestalt principles, such as awareness and responsibility, some technique-oriented therapists make the shift to enter into I-Thou relating, having "prepared" the client for such a relationship. Other gestalt therapists adopt an I-Thou orientation toward their clients from the outset, regardless of whether the client is able to engage in an I-Thou relationship. The underlying belief is that an I-Thou relationship is:

     . . . necessary both to affirm the client's experience and to provide a context in which any disturbances of free-flowing, authentic contact can become phenomena of interest for therapeutic exploration. If the client experiences herself or himself authentically, an I-Thou encounter with the therapist will ensue. If, however, the therapist notices a contact boundary disturbance, such as a projection or retroflection . . . then the next therapeutic step is to have the client pay attention to the boundary disturbance. The I-Thou relationship, in providing a context for the organism to become aware of its emerging needs, express them, and move on, thereby becomes an important vehicle for identifying disturbances in this process of contacting. (L. Greenberg, 1983, p. 142)

Consistent with the notion of an I-Thou relationship, gestalt therapists place a premium on authenticity in relating to clients. For Perls, therapist authenticity is needed to combat clients' game playing. "Anybody who goes to a therapist has something up his sleeve," F. Perls (1969, p. 75) wrote. "I would say 90% don't go to a therapist to be cured, but to get more adequate in their neurosis." When gestalt therapists are genuine, they both refuse to engage in clients' games and discourage clients from playing games. Authenticity on the therapists' behalf also serves a modeling function for clients, many of whom play roles rather than living genuinely. A final point: therapist authenticity is considered more important than an empathic understanding of the client. Although the same is true of person-centered therapy, as discussed earlier, empathy is far less important than genuineness in gestalt therapy (Gelso & Carter, 1985). F. Perls (1973) makes clear that if a therapist is too empathic, the therapist may lose himself or herself in overidentifying with the client, making true contact impossible.

We would like to raise one additional issue about characteristics of the gestalt therapy relationship. For F. Perls (1973), the therapy relationship could be described as ideally oscillating between a source of support and of frustration for the client; Perls occasionally referred to the therapeutic encounter as a "safe emergency." The gestalt therapist's supportive stance fosters a climate of safety, even as attempts to frustrate the client are aimed at creating "emergencies" that provoke discovery. Frustrating clients toward discovery can take the form of confronting clients, intentionally confusing clients, and refusing to answer clients' questions. F. Perls (1969) maintained: "Every time you refuse to answer a question, you help the other person to develop his own resources" (p. 27). However, when clients are being frustrated rather than supported by the therapist, and when clients are not supporting themselves (i.e., they are facing an impasse), the therapist must be prepared for clients to try to elicit from the therapist what clients are not mobilizing in themselves. In essence, the client will project disowned parts of the self onto the therapist in an attempt to manipulate the therapist to meet the client's needs. The gestalt therapist's task is to recognize the pulls that she or he is experiencing from the client, and use them as cues for what the client needs to provide to himself or herself. F. Perls (1969, p. 37) referred to this task as "skillful frustration" in the service of helping clients to mature.

RECENT RESEARCH ON GESTALT PSYCHOTHERAPY

As has been the case historically, virtually no studies have been published on gestalt psychotherapy since Gelso and Carter (1985) reviewed research on the psychotherapy relationship (for exceptions, see Beutler et al., 1991, and Clarke & Greenberg, 1986). Consequently, current understanding of the gestalt therapy relationship remains minimally informed by empirical data. Why has there been such scientific neglect of the relationship in gestalt therapy? Gelso and Fretz (1992, p. 288) note: "Few outcome studies have been conducted to support its effectiveness, partly because of the indifference among gestaltists to scientific study. Perhaps the deemphasis of intellect in gestalt therapy was inappropriately applied to research. If we should 'lose our minds and come to our senses,' perhaps scientific study is unnecessary." However, we see no sound reason why fruitful research could not be conducted on the relationship in gestalt therapy, and we hope that future research endeavors foster an empirical understanding of gestalt relationship factors.

OTHER HUMANISTIC APPROACHES: EXISTENTIAL AND EXPERIENTIAL THERAPIES

In this section, we review the psychotherapy relationship in two additional humanistic theories: existential and experiential psychotherapy. Our coverage of these two theories, though brief, is intended to broaden the scope of the chapter, providing further evidence of the diversity of ways in which the therapy relationship is viewed within humanistic approaches. We will begin with the more established of the two theories, existential psychotherapy, and then address the experiential psychotherapy relationship.

EXISTENTIAL PSYCHOTHERAPY

Existential psychotherapy is rooted in the existential philosophy of individuals such as Heidegger, Tillich, Sartre, Buber, Kierkegaard, Dostoyevski, and Nietzsche (Corey, 1996). These philosophers were concerned about issues basic to human existence: freedom, responsibility, anxiety, death, identity, and relatedness. Existential therapists listen for these themes and address them in their work with clients, seeking to promote clients' awareness and responsibility. Because some of these themes also are the focus of person-centered and gestalt therapists, an inclusive use of the term *existential therapy* might encompass several humanistic theories. However, we will restrict our focus to existential theorists and therapists who would not readily be classified in any other humanistic camp.

The therapy relationship within existential psychotherapy has been likened to that between a traveler and a fellow companion or guide (Bugental, 1987). Assagioli (1965) used the journeying metaphor from Dante's *Inferno* to describe his approach to existential psychotherapy. According to Assagioli, therapists must be willing to descend with clients into their private hells before clients can ascend toward personal liberation and spiritual growth. Furthermore, the depth of the therapy is largely determined by how far the therapist is willing to descend. When clients begin their "descent," exploring painful and neglected aspects of themselves, existential therapists do not remain on the surface, bidding clients well on their journeys. Instead, the therapists must be willing to journey with the clients, facing both the clients' pain and the therapists' own demons that may be encountered along the way. Thus, existential therapists need to accept the possibility of being transformed by the therapy process. "In effective therapy a change occurs in *both* the therapist and the patient; unless the therapist is open to change the patient will not be either" (May, 1983, p. 22).

To extend the journey metaphor, the role of empathy is critical to the relationship between the travelers. May (1939/1989) described empathy as:

> ... learning to relax, mentally and spiritually as well as physically, learning to let one's self go into the other person with a willingness to be changed in the process. It is a dying to one's self in order to live with others. It is the great giving up of one's self, losing one's own personality temporarily and then finding it a hundredfold richer in the other person. (p. 79)

Empathy allows the therapist to remain connected to the client as the client explores the depths of his or her existence. Like climbers descending or ascending in tandem, client and therapist ideally work together as a single unit. May (1939/1989) wrote: "The counselor works basically through the process of empathy. Both the counselor and the counselee are taken out of themselves and become merged in a common psychic entity" (p. 67). The interconnectedness of client and therapist in existential therapy has been further expressed by Yalom (1989, p. 14): "We psychotherapists cannot cluck with sympathy and exhort patients to struggle resolutely with their problems. We cannot say to them *you* and *your* problems. Instead we must speak of *us* and *our* problems, because our life, our existence, will always be riveted to death, love to loss, freedom to fear, and growth to separation. We are, all of us, in this together."

Existential therapy, as mentioned earlier in the chapter, is marked by an explicit lack of techniques. In fact, Rollo May believed that techniques often are invented by therapists to offset a boredom that arises from therapists' and clients' failure to deal with issues at the core of human existence. To be clear, existential therapists do use techniques, but existential therapy is not characterized by particular techniques. A wide variety of techniques may be used by the existential therapist, but techniques are seen as less critical to outcome than the therapy relationship. As in the person-centered perspective, the therapy relationship itself is considered curative (Yalom, 1980). Even though the psychotherapy relationship is necessarily temporary, Yalom believes that clients change permanently by learning to relate deeply to the therapist. Furthermore, the therapy relationship provides an opportunity for clients to learn about other significant relationships in their lives, and it provides them with a healing source of intimacy. We agree that the therapy relationship can be restorative in all of these—and other—ways, though we consider the existentialists, like person-centered therapists, to excessively minimize the value of technical factors. Techniques can be used both to enhance the relationship and to facilitate change directly.

EXPERIENTIAL PSYCHOTHERAPY

The term *experiential psychotherapy* has been used to refer collectively to theories that place a premium on affective and sensate experiencing, including, for example, gestalt and person-centered therapy. We wish to make clear, therefore, that we are limiting our use of the term to a specific and relatively new brand of therapy, sometimes referred to as "process-experiential therapy," whose primary proponents are Mahrer (1983, 1986, 1989, 1996) and Greenberg (L. Greenberg & Elliott, 1997; L. Greenberg & Goldman, 1988; L. Greenberg, Rice, & Elliott, 1993). Experiential therapy, even in the narrow manner in which we are using the term, is difficult to characterize. For example, Bohart and Greenberg

(1997) describe Mahrer's theory as having existential roots but containing psychodynamic and behavioral influences. Greenberg's approach, on the other hand, contains a mix of person-centered and gestalt qualities (L. Greenberg et al., 1993). Nonetheless, Mahrer's and Greenberg's experiential approaches possess some common features. "Experiential therapies differ from their predecessors in (a) their more explicit emphasis on working at the experiential and emotional level and (b) their more specific emphasis on how particular therapist operations can facilitate specific client processes at specific times" (Bohart & Greenberg, 1997, p. 8). Furthermore, both Mahrer's and Greenberg's approaches are phenomenological and present-focused, and they share these characteristics with all other humanistic theories.

Empathy plays a central role in experiential therapy. For Mahrer (1986), empathy takes the form of a complete, rather than partial, identification with the client. With eyes closed and bodies prone, facing in the same direction, the therapist and client fix their attention "out there" on some meaningful experience of the client's. When the therapist becomes properly aligned with the client and succeeds in entering fully into the client's immediate world, the therapist's boundaries dissipate:

> There is little if any of the two of you attending mainly to each other. The vaunted therapist-patient "relationship" is all but washed away. You have stepped away from helping alliances, transferences, and relationships in which each party is attending mainly to the other. Even when you address the patient, it is generally with most of your attention out there, on something other than mainly that person. When you are aligned, the two of you have departed from the mutual attending to and relating to each other. (Mahrer, 1997, p. 195)

The merger between therapist and client, which is to last throughout the session rather than occurring periodically, is so complete that the therapist loses a sense of identity separate from the client. In addition to this loss of self:

> [T]he aligned therapist loses the whole array of therapist roles and personal experiencings that may be a major feature in most face-to-face therapies. The aligned therapist generally loses the opportunity of being the patient's best friend, someone the patient looks up to, someone who provides valuable insights and understandings, a trusted confidante, someone with wisdom about life, an exemplar of mental health, a solid rock of reality, someone who values and treasures the patient's preciousness, the rescuer from catastrophic psychopathology, the expert in behavior change. (Mahrer, 1997, p. 202)

In Greenberg's approach, empathic attunement is paramount, in terms of both establishing contact with the client and communicating accurate understanding (L. Greenberg & Elliott, 1997; L. Greenberg et al., 1993). "Empathic attunement to affect is one of the core ways of being therapeutic because empathic attunement and its communication are key aids in the construction of self experience. They help the client to symbolize inchoate emotional meaning, and this aids affect regulation and strengthening of the self as well as exploration and discovery" (L. Greenberg & Elliott, 1997, p. 185). Empathic responses can target affect or cognition and can vary in form from empathic understanding to empathic exploration to empathic interpretation, based on the therapist's intent.

Although empathy is critical in both experiential approaches, the psychotherapy relationship itself is not a central component of Mahrer's theory. Mahrer believes that preset ideas about roles within the therapy relationship (e.g., being a blank screen) unduly influence clients' decisions about which material to bring forth, and interfere with the client's full experiencing and processing of emotions. Furthermore, Mahrer believes that focusing on and using the therapy relationship in one's work is of little value. "The therapist-patient relationship opens only a minuscule of early deeper material related to the relationship itself, and thereby misses virtually the whole universe of experientially meaningful early life events" (Mahrer, 1986, p. 49). Experiencing is all-important in Mahrer's approach, and Mahrer advocates that clients actually *relive* early life events rather than *relate* them as a client talking to a therapist. "The current therapist-patient relationship is incredibly less useful than the actual earlier situational context. Carrying forward the experiencing of having surgery at age two years or of a near-drowning at four years is much more effectively negotiated when the patient is being a two-year-old or four-year-old child, actually existing and fully being in those feeling-filled situations, rather than being a patient relating to a . . . psychotherapist" (Mahrer, 1986, p. 49).

In Mahrer's approach, techniques for deepening client experiencing are emphasized over the therapy relationship. In this way, Mahrer's theory is similar to the strain of gestalt therapy that emphasizes awareness (versus contact). Even some of the techniques in Mahrer's approach resemble those found in gestalt work (e.g., focusing attention, affective expression). However, more than is true of gestalt therapists, Mahrer advocates therapists' using self-disclosure, following the client's lead, and focusing on discrete behavior change.

Mahrer downplays the role of the therapy relationship but he does not disregard it altogether. He writes that the relationship between experiential therapist and client is ideally marked by a "genuine, full, heartfelt liking of the patient" akin to a "wonderful friendship between two best friends who have known each other a long time and who unabashedly like one another" (Mahrer, 1986, p. 126). In addition, the therapy relationship is one to which the therapist is committed fully, without conditions, come what may in terms of hardships, surprises, and disappointments. We agree with Mahrer's emphasis on commitment within the therapy relationship, but his comparison between the therapy relationship and a longtime friendship is difficult for us to integrate with our own experience. It is not clear how the therapist is to have genuine feelings of affection for a client, akin to "best friends," if the therapist has only recently met the client or if the client manipulates or continually rages against the therapist. Furthermore, Mahrer's likening the therapy relationship to being best friends contradicts his earlier statement that the aligned therapist loses the opportunity to be the client's best friend.

The therapy relationship within Greenberg's experiential therapy reflects both person-centered and gestalt influences. Therapist empathy, congruence, and warmth are emphasized and seen as curative, and an I-Thou attitude on the part of the therapist is espoused. Greenberg's approach also includes gestaltlike techniques involving an empty chair, although nongestalt techniques also may be employed (Greenberg et al., 1993). On a different note, Greenberg underscores the importance of collaboration between therapist and client in ways that are similar to Beck's notion of "collaborative empiricism" (described in Chapter 8).

Because experiential therapy is a relatively new approach to therapy, research to date has been limited. The few studies that have been published hold promise for the efficacy of experiential therapy, but none sheds direct light on the nature or role of the therapy relationship (see Greenberg et al., 1993). We see this area as fertile ground for future psychotherapy research.

COMPARING THE PSYCHOTHERAPY RELATIONSHIP ACROSS THE HUMANISTIC THEORIES

To conclude the chapter, we shall compare the various humanistic theories on four dimensions: (a) the centrality of the psychotherapy relationship, (b) the extent to which it is a means or an end, (c) whether real or "unreal" components of the relationship are emphasized, and (d) the conceptualization and use of power in the relationship. We begin with the centrality of the psychotherapy relationship.

The psychotherapy relationship generally holds a place of prominence in the humanistic theories, with some notable departures. From the outset of his work, Rogers considered the relationship itself to be a powerful source of healing. In *Counseling and Psychotherapy,* Rogers (1942) wrote:

> This approach lays stress upon the therapeutic relationship itself as a growth experience. . . . Here the individual learns to understand himself, to make significant independent choices, to relate himself successfully to another person in a more adult fashion. In some respects this may be the most important aspect of the approach we shall describe. (p. 30)

Rogers' position on the fundamental importance of the relationship has been maintained, if not strengthened, in the years since publication of this statement (e.g., Rogers, 1980). Although emphasized less than in Rogers' theory, the relationship is still a central component of existential therapy and Greenberg's approach to experiential therapy. The therapy relationship is of varying importance to gestalt therapists, depending on whether they emphasize contact (the therapy relationship is then the primary avenue for establishing connection with the client) or awareness (techniques or experiments are prioritized). Similarly, Mahrer's experiential therapy, with its almost exclusive focus on awareness and experiencing, places the therapy relationship in a tangential role. For Mahrer, the therapy relationship is, at best, of limited therapeutic value and, at worst, constricting and interfering.

Just as they consider the therapy relationship to be central, most humanistic writers tend to view the relationship as an end unto itself, as opposed to a means to achieving some other end. The relationship in humanistic therapy is itself curative; it is not considered a means for the therapist to do something else that is healing (e.g., use certain techniques). Gelso and Carter (1985, p. 217) note that, in person-centered therapy, for example, "the relationship per se is viewed as the *sine qua non* of constructive personality and behavior change." Indeed, Rogers (1951, p. 172) wrote: "The process of therapy is seen as being synonymous with the experiential relationship between client and therapist." The gestalt camp, once again, is divided on the means-end issue. The relationship may be considered an end in itself—a way to establish contact—or a means for enhancing clients' awareness and teaching them gestalt principles (e.g., assuming responsibility, focusing attention). The view of the gestalt relationship as an end in itself is captured in the following passage: "What unites us as humans is not necessarily the visible and the tangible, but rather the invisible intangible dimension 'between us.' It is the human spirit that permeates our every interaction. . . . *It is the source of healing"* (Hycner & Jacobs, 1995, p. 3). The alternative perspective, in which the relationship does not directly lead to change, is expressed by L. Greenberg (1983, p. 146): "Even though the I-Thou relationship in some form or another is regarded as essential to therapy, a good relationship is not seen as sufficient for therapeutic change. In both the written and the oral Gestalt therapy tradition, there is a greater emphasis on the role of awareness and technical considerations than on the significance of the therapeutic relationship to change." For the existentialists, such as May (1983), the relationship is "our most useful medium of understanding the patient as well as our most efficacious instrument for helping him open himself to the possibility of change" (p. 22). Expressing his opposition to reliance on techniques, May (1983, p. 162) warns that "The *technical* view of the other person is perhaps the therapist's most handy anxiety-reducing device. This has its legitimate place. The therapist is presumably an expert. But technique must not be used as a way of blocking presence." Finally, in the experiential approaches, Greenberg's theory seems to view the establishment of an empathic relationship as curative in and of itself, whereas Mahrer, to the extent that he considers the relationship of any value whatsoever, clearly would see it as a means to get the client to participate in and make use of his experiential therapy, and not curative in and of itself.

Perhaps the one dimension on which all of the humanistic theories are united involves the primacy of the real relationship. As Gelso and Carter (1985) stated, authentic relating "is the hallmark of all of the humanistic approaches to therapy. That is, healing occurs through experiencing an intensely human interaction within the context of an emotionally 'real' relationship" (p. 213). Regarding authenticity, Rogers, for example, underscored the need for therapist congruence, the gestalt therapists highlight the value of a genuine I-Thou encounter, and May (1983) acknowledged that "in the therapeutic hour a total relationship is going on between two people which includes a number of different levels. One level is that of real persons" (p. 21). From the experiential perspective, Greenberg emphasizes the therapist's authentic empathic relating, and Mahrer, while minimizing the role of the therapy relationship, real or otherwise, at least concedes that the therapist should like the client.

The humanistic theorists are similarly like-minded in their oppositional stance toward transference. Rogers recognized that transference relationships may occur in person-centered therapy, but the therapist does not encourage their development. Rogers believed that:

[T]ransference relationships develop in an evaluative atmosphere in which the client feels the therapist knows more about the client than the client knows about him- or herself, and therefore the client becomes dependent. Person-centered therapists tend to avoid evaluation. . . . Person-centered therapists have not found the transference relationship, central to psychoanalysis, a necessary part of a client's growth or change. (Meador & Rogers, 1984, p. 159)

With regard to transference, gestalt therapists maintain that it is not necessary to interpret the client's current feelings toward the therapist, including transference, in the context of the client's distant history. In gestalt therapy, it is enough to recognize in the moment how the client projects parts of the self onto the therapist. "The therapeutic meaning of [transference] is not that it is the same old story, but precisely that it is now differently worked through as a present adventure: the analyst is not the same kind of parent" (F. Perls, 1958, p. 234). Furthermore, gestalt therapists do not get into the "why" of transference interpretation, nor are they interested in "explaining away the powerful force of present action and feeling, substituting once-upon-a-time for right now" (Polster & Polster, 1973, p. 7).

From an existential perspective, May (1983) refers to transference as "one of Freud's great contributions" that has "vast implications for therapy" (p. 18). May also agrees with Freud that a client's personal past is influential in that "one's ancestors, like Hamlet's father, are always coming on to the edge of the stage with various ghostly challenges and imprecations" (p. 18). However, May notes that the concept of transference can be used as a defense by the therapist, to hide "from the anxiety of direct encounter" (p. 19), a belief expressed by Yalom (1980) as well. Along these same lines, existential scholars emphasize that a therapist's preoccupation with transference can undermine vitally necessary attention to the real relationship. Yalom contends, "Viewing the therapist-patient relationship primarily in terms of transference negates the truly human, and truly mutative, nature of the relationship" (p. 404). Similarly, May considers the real relationship to be figure, and transference to be ground: "Transference is to be understood as the distortion of encounter. . . . How is it possible that one being relates to another? What is the nature of human beings that two persons can communicate, can grasp each other as beings, have genuine concern with the welfare and fulfillment of the other, and experience some genuine trust? The answer to these questions will tell us of what transference is a distortion" (pp. 19–20). Attention to the real and unreal components of the relationship in existential therapy is thus a matter of degree, not mutual exclusion, from May's perspective. Yalom, however, seems to have difficulty accepting that transference and the real relationship can coexist without one negating the other. From our vantage point, both can and always do exist simultaneously in therapy relationships. We think that May offers existential therapists a useful position on transference: "The emphasis on the reality of presence does not obviate the exceedingly significant truths in Freud's concept of transference. . . . But in existential therapy 'transference' gets placed in the new context of *an event occurring in a real relationship between two people*" (May, 1983, p. 160). Thus, even when transference is recognized to occur, it is viewed within the larger framework of the real relationship.

In experiential therapy, transference phenomena are not considered grist for the therapeutic mill. Greenberg recommends the empathic understanding of transference phenomena so that transference dissipates, and Mahrer (1986) takes an almost hostile stance toward transference: "Transference phenomena are largely a function of the psychoanalytic therapist in mutual co-construction with the patient. In terms of illuminating that which is experientially earlier and deeper in the patient, such material is far from either significant or useful" (p. 48).

The last dimension on which we compare the humanistic theories concerns the power dynamics in the therapy relationship. We begin with a postulate: the extent to which the therapist aims to influence or control a client is inversely related to how fundamentally trustworthy the therapist considers the client to be. Because the humanistic theories tend to view clients as inherently trustworthy, these theories also downplay the role of power in psychotherapy. For example, in formulating his nondirective approach to counseling, Rogers sought to reverse what he perceived to be the prevalent practice by which therapists assumed responsibility for directing the focus of treatment. Rogers believed that the type of directive therapy in which he was trained and to which he objected was "built largely on the persuasive powers of the counselor" (1942, p. 118). Furthermore, Rogers sought to eradicate the power imbalance between therapist and client, positing that "therapy and authority cannot be coexistent in the same relationship. . . . There cannot be an atmosphere of complete permissiveness when the relationship is authoritative" (p. 109).

However, the point could be made that the Rogerian approach to therapy imbues the therapist with a subtle, almost deceptive power. By contending that the client should lead the session (even when the client may not wish to), focus on the present, express his or her feelings, and be genuine, the person-centered therapist exerts considerable influence over both the therapy process and the client. Furthermore, whereas clients are expected to reveal themselves, the therapist remains largely hidden (M. Kahn, 1991), contributing to the power imbalance in the relationship. Rogers maintained that the conditions of person-centered therapy are "in no way manipulative or controlling in the relationship" (Rogers, 1977, p. 11). However, in a famous debate, theologian Martin Buber disagreed with Rogers about power dynamics in the therapy relationship. Buber maintained that the inherent lack of mutuality in the therapy relationship precluded true I-Thou relating, though Rogers (1957, 1980) professed that I-Thou relating is an achievable ideal. The client, Buber (1966) stated, "comes for help to you. You don't come for help to him. And not only this, but you are *able,* more or less, to help him. He can do different things to you, but not help you. . . . He is not interested in you" (p. 171). Thus, whereas person-centered therapy is egalitarian in theory, the actual practice of person-centered therapy may be discrepant from ideology in terms of the power that the therapist possesses and frequently exercises (Heller, 1985).

The same critique may be made of gestalt therapy. On one side of the coin, Yontef and Simkin (1989, p. 327) claim that, in gestalt therapy, "the power and responsibility for the present are in the hands of the patient." While theoretically the client may be responsible for what transpires in the present, on the other side of the coin, in practice—especially in the technique-oriented, awareness-focused type of gestalt therapy—the therapist wields a tremendous amount of power. L. Greenberg (1983, p. 144) notes: "A number of people both orally and in the literature criticize Gestalt techniques as manipulative and controlling." In defense of gestalt therapy, however, Greenberg goes on to say: "Gestalt techniques can be used coercively, but their true use as experiments suggests a different form of relationship characterized by partnership rather than force" (1983, p. 144). Ideally, according to Greenberg, the gestalt experiment results in a synergistic dance between therapist and client, in which the partners take turns leading. However, from our vantage point, it is almost always the therapist who suggests the experiments and thus initially leads the dance.

In existential therapy, power is ideally shared between therapist and client, as between fellow travelers. However, the lack of explicit attention to techniques and the resulting wide variety of interventions employed by existential therapists make generalizations about the actual practice of existential therapy difficult, including any conclusions about power dynamics. The role of power in existential therapy could profitably be explored in the future by existential writers. Finally, in the experiential approaches, Mahrer and Greenberg differ slightly in their treatment of power. Greenberg et al. (1993) thoughtfully describe the delicate balance that therapists must demonstrate in occasionally being directive without being authoritative. The therapist is recognized as the expert on therapy process, but the client is regarded as the expert on his or her experience, which is the "ultimate reference point" in experiential therapy (Greenberg et al., 1993, p. 22). The client's experience also serves as the focal point in Mahrer's approach, although it seems to us that the therapist must exert at least some power to persuade uninformed clients to focus on their experience in the ways that Mahrer perceives as beneficial (e.g., meeting for one to four hours in a reclined position with eyes closed).

CONCLUSION

The therapy relationship within the humanistic approaches is generally viewed as central and curative. The real relationship is given precedence over transference components of the relationship, which are worked with in the "here and now" or not at all. In theory, power is shared in the humanistic relationship. In practice, however, the therapist often exerts considerable influence over the client, with varying degrees of subtlety across theories. Research has supported the curative effects of therapist empathy, congruence, and regard, although not to the extent hypothesized by Rogers. Research is greatly needed on the relationship within gestalt, existential, and experiential therapies.

CHAPTER 10

Feminist Therapy:
Beyond the Third Force

A CHAPTER on the client-therapist relationship in feminist therapy might well begin with the question of whether feminist therapy represents a unique theoretical approach to clinical work. On the one hand, feminist therapy may be considered a singular approach that constitutes a fourth major theory cluster, following psychoanalytic, cognitive-behavioral, and humanistic systems. Like these other theories, feminist therapy theory possesses a set of guiding philosophical principles, both about human development and about psychotherapy. In addition, as is true for psychoanalytic, cognitive-behavioral, and humanistic approaches, feminist therapy emerged out of dissatisfaction with existing theories, was influenced by historical events that tilled the soil for its evolution, and was pioneered by a relatively small number of clearly identifiable individuals. Laura Brown, prominent feminist scholar and spokesperson, has defined feminist therapy as:

> ... the practice of therapy informed by feminist political philosophy and analysis, grounded in multicultural feminist scholarship on the psychology of women and gender, which leads both therapist and client toward strategies and solutions advancing feminist resistance, transformation, and social change in daily personal life, and in relationships with the social, emotional, and political environment. (Brown, 1994b, pp. 21–22)

In short, there is ample support for the position that "feminist therapy is a free-standing, established therapy" (Cammaert & Larsen, 1988, p. 14).

On the other hand, feminist therapy may be considered a system that possesses tenets of its own but also shares attributes with other approaches and can be combined with them. From this perspective, feminist therapy is characterized more by the clinician's critical feminist analysis and understanding of psychotherapy, in whatever form it is practiced, than by the clinician's adherence to a particular doctrine or circumscribed set of techniques. Thus, the distinguishing feature of this broader interpretation of feminist therapy is the utilization of feminist theory and scholarship to challenge traditional conceptualizations of mental health and psychotherapy.

Depending on one's perspective, then, feminist therapy may be construed as a pure form of therapy or an approach that informs and may be combined thoughtfully with other systems of therapy. In fact, the major theory clusters covered in the previous three chapters (psychoanalytic, cognitive-behavioral, and humanistic) could be viewed as existing on a vertical axis, with feminist and other culturally informed approaches existing on a horizontal axis. The theories on either axis could be studied and employed separately, as is often the case, or they could be carefully integrated. For example, numerous authors have offered models for a feminist-psychoanalytic approach to therapy (Benjamin, 1984; Chodorow, 1989; Daugherty & Lees, 1988; Eichenbaum & Orbach 1983, 1984; Prozan, 1993). Worrell and Remer (1992) and Fodor (1988) have suggested ways in which feminist and cognitive-behavioral theories can be combined. Finally, concerning the compatibility of feminist and humanistic approaches, Enns (1987) has offered guidelines for the integration of feminist and gestalt therapies, and Waterhouse (1993) raises points to consider in synthesizing feminist and person-centered approaches. Even when feminist therapy is viewed as an independent theoretical system, it would be a mistake to presume that only one form of feminist therapy exists (Dutton-Douglas & Walker, 1988). Enns and Hackett (1993) note that there is no "monolithic" version of feminist therapy. The term *feminist therapy* subsumes radical, liberal, socialist, conservative, lesbian separatist, and cultural feminist approaches, each with varying emphases on individual and societal change (Cammaert & Larsen, 1988; Enns, 1997). Given that multiple forms of feminist therapy exist, it may be helpful to consider briefly what the various feminist approaches have in common.

To begin with, feminist approaches to therapy possess a common history. Feminist therapy arose out of discontent with prevailing theories of personality, mental health, and psychotherapy that were considered androcentric and misogynistic. Furthermore, feminist therapy was fueled by the climate of social unrest and change in the United States in the late 1960s and early 1970s. During this time, grassroots community efforts were undertaken to establish agencies designed to meet the needs of women (e.g., rape crisis centers, shelters for battered women, abortion referral services). These agencies were marked by a collective rather than a hierarchical power structure, and they were intended to be accessible to all women, not just to women who were economically privileged (Enns, 1993). At approximately the same time, an emerging body of literature appeared on the particular mental health needs of women and effective forms of psychotherapy for women. Much of this writing, which was influential to the development of feminist therapy, was published in relatively new and specialized journals such as *Psychology of Women Quarterly, Women and Therapy,* and *Feminism and Psychology* (Cammaert & Larsen, 1988; Enns, 1993; Russell, 1984).

In addition to a common history, the various forms of feminist therapy share a set of underlying assumptions. One of these beliefs is that the relationship between feminist therapist and client should be egalitarian (Gilbert, 1980; Mowbray, 1995), or, as some feminist writers prefer, "equalitarian" (M. Butler, 1985; Douglas, 1985). An egalitarian (or equalitarian) relationship implies that the therapist and client have equal worth and dignity, though not equal power (more on this later in the chapter). Furthermore, egalitarianism dictates that therapists make clear to prospective clients their approach to therapy, fees, guiding philosophies, and associated techniques so that clients can be maximally informed consumers of therapy (Enns & Hackett, 1990; Laidlaw & Malmo, 1990). An additional component of egalitarianism is that the client, not the therapist, is considered the expert on the client's history, needs, and goals (Enns, 1997; Laidlaw & Malmo, 1990).

A final assumption of feminist therapy is that external attributions for the client's problems are considered potentially valid. A therapist cannot focus solely on intrapsychic factors in accurately determining full responsibility for the client's problems. As Brown (1994b) has stated succinctly, "The nature of the problem must not be assumed to lie solely or even primarily within the client" (p. 49). Feminist therapists contend that it is important to account for the interaction between a client's cultural characteristics and relevant societal forces when therapists attempt to understand, assess, and effectively intervene with clients. For example, while they tend to focus on gender and the effects of sexism on the client, feminist therapists also recognize how a client's race, sexual orientation, social class, religion, and age predict the degree to which the client's mental health is affected by racism, heterosexism, classism, religious prejudices, and ageism (Brown, 1994b; Gannon, 1982). Such factors may or may not be directly responsible for a client's presenting problem, but these various forms of oppression, bias, and discrimination clearly have a negative impact on the societally marginalized client's mental health. Thus, whereas clients may blame themselves fully for their problems, the feminist therapist seeks to discern when clients are attributing to themselves too much responsibility for their problems. By doing so, feminist therapists attempt to alleviate clients' inappropriate self-blame by pointing to the role that external factors play in causing, sustaining, and exacerbating problems. Eichenbaum and Orbach (1983) provide an example of how reattributing a client's problems to external sources may be helpful in working with a woman who is trying to come to terms with her lesbian identity:

THERAPIST: Can you say what is the hardest thing for you to accept—the thing that stands in the way of your embracing your gay identity?

CLIENT: That I have failed . . . that I can't seem to get on with men. . . . Perhaps I don't try properly.

THERAPIST: Has it ever occurred to you that perhaps it is the men who have disappointed you . . . that you are not at fault per se? (p. 132)

We find that determining the validity of clients' attributions, especially external ones, is tricky business. We recognize that external forces, including oppression and discrimination, certainly impinge on clients' well-being, but it is no easy matter for therapists to accurately assess the relative contributions of external and internal factors to clients' problems. Therapists need, but often lack, authentic data that would verify the accuracy of clients' external attributions. Consider the example in which a therapist is working with a client who complains of relationship difficulties with his or her partner. The client's version of reality is such that the client's partner is largely to blame for problems in their relationship. Now imagine that the client's partner is invited to join the client for couples therapy. As often happens, when the therapist observes firsthand the manner in which both clients contribute to difficulties in the relationship, the purely external attributions made originally by the client lose validity. The therapist recognizes that the client both is affected by and contributes to a problematic system—in this case, the couple's relationship.

Therapists are generally in a difficult position because all of the information about the cause of a client's problem, and sometimes even the crucial information, is not readily available to the therapist. To avoid playing the role of detective, therapists must decide on the basis of limited information the extent to which the client's external and internal attributions are valid. Therapists must also decide when it is in clients' best interests to challenge them to assume more (or, sometimes, less) responsibility for the causes of their problems. When clients blame themselves too much, or externalize blame too much, these attributions themselves are problematic. Along these lines, we find it useful to distinguish between clients' responsibility for causing their problems and clients' responsibility for solving their problems, as Brickman et al. (1982) suggested. Therapists often lack sufficient data to effectively challenge clients' beliefs about the causes of their problems, but therapists can effectively help clients assume appropriate levels of responsibility for generating and implementing solutions to their problems, which may be far more critical to determining outcome than attributions about causality.

Returning to the assumptions that unite different forms of feminist therapy, these various suppositions are captured in the popular feminist expression, "The personal is political." One implication of this phrase is that individuals' problems are due, at least in part, to political and societal factors, such as oppression, economic injustice, discrimination, and prejudice. The aim is to "deprivatize and politicize" clients' experiences in helping them understand how "personal experience is the lived version of political reality" (Brown, 1994b, p. 50). The role of feminist therapy, then, is twofold. First, feminist therapists realize that effecting change within the individual has a transformative effect however slight, on society (Enns, 1993). Brown, a leading spokesperson for feminist therapy, expressed feminist therapy's benefit to society in concise fashion: "People empowered to value themselves will find it difficult to participate in the oppression of others" (p. 103). J. Miller (1976) expressed a similar ideal of feminist therapy: "The greater the development of each individual, the more able, more effective, and less needy of limiting or restricting others she or he will be" (p. 116). However, it is equally true, and at least as important from a feminist perspective, that affecting change within society may enhance the well-being of its members. That is, feminist therapists seek to promote the mental health of individuals, especially those who do not enjoy power or privileged status in society, by challenging oppressive norms, institutions, philosophies, and roles. The work of feminist therapists takes place, then, both within and outside the clinician's office. Within the office, "therapists need to reconstruct the meaning of psychotherapy so that it looks beyond the individual, beyond the family, to a society where privilege is based on gender, race, and class" (Mirkin, 1994, p. 1). Outside the office, feminist therapists appreciate the importance of working to modify systems that have a negative impact on clients' mental health. Dutton-Douglas and Walker (1988) express this sentiment eloquently:

> Feminist therapy is less interested in the psychotherapy client's conformity to the mainstream than in helping to identify and overcome rampant oppressive social pressures for both women and men. Thus the ultimate goal of the feminist psychotherapist is primarily the elimination of the patriarchal power structure so as to facilitate both women's and men's personal growth. (p. 4)

In addition to the ultimate goal of eliminating oppressive patriarchal systems rather than adjusting to them, the goals of feminist therapy include more personal ways of empowering clients. These "subgoals" do not distinguish feminist therapy from other approaches as much as the overarching goal of eradicating oppression does. Nonetheless, feminist therapists aim to empower clients directly by working toward various ends. For example, feminist therapists seek to help clients reduce symptomatology, raise their awareness, improve interpersonal relationships (Cammaert & Larsen, 1988), increase self-esteem, redefine themselves according to terms that clients choose, and develop a more flexible repertoire of behaviors, including communication skills, vocational choices, and emotional expressiveness (Collier, 1982).

Whereas the preceding paragraphs have described the foundations of feminist therapy, the remainder of the chapter will be devoted to exploring the therapist-client relationship in feminist therapy along the four dimensions examined in the previous three chapters: (a) the centrality of the therapy relationship, (b) the degree to which it is a means versus an end, (c) real and "unreal" components of the relationship, and (d) how power is conceptualized and used within the relationship. Before turning our attention to these four dimensions, however, a word is in order about research on the feminist therapy relationship. To the best of our knowledge, no research has been conducted that examines the relationship in feminist therapy. Some published studies have examined other aspects of feminist therapy (e.g., the effects of identifying a therapist's approach as feminist or making a feminist therapist's values explicit; see Enns & Hackett, 1990, 1993), but research on the feminist therapy relationship itself appears to be lacking. It may be that many feminist therapists and scholars devalue empirical research in favor of alternative ways of knowing (see for example, Belenky, Clinchy, Goldberger, & Tarule, 1986). Whatever the reason, we view the shortage of research on the feminist therapy relationship as both a detriment to the current state of knowledge in this area and a rich opportunity for critical future research.

CENTRALITY OF THE FEMINIST THERAPY RELATIONSHIP

Relationships in general, and the therapy relationship in particular, are viewed by feminist therapists as potential sources of strength, support, and competence. In fact, relationships are considered to play a critical role in healthy psychological development and functioning for both men and women (McLeod, 1994; Stiver, 1994). More specifically, women's self-esteem is often a function of their ability to empathize, nurture, and attend to the needs of others (Stiver, 1994). Furthermore, women's self-identity may be shaped in large part by their relationships with others. J. B. Miller (1976), for example, has written: "Women's sense of self becomes very much organized around being able to make and maintain affiliation in relationships" (p. 83). Gilligan (1982) and Josselson (1987) have challenged the validity, for women, of Erikson's developmental theory by positing that, for many women, self-definition does not necessarily precede the capacity for intimate relationships. Rather than following a linear movement from Stage 5 (identity vs. confusion) to Stage 6 (intimacy vs. isolation), women's development may involve an interplay between defining the self and cultivating the capacity for intimate relating. That is, many women develop self-identities through their intimate relations with others, and the emerging and deepening sense of self fosters the capacity for intimate relating.

Given the importance of relationships in the lives of most women, it is perhaps not surprising that the client-therapist relationship is deemed highly significant in feminist therapy. In fact, Brown (1994b) actually equates feminist therapy with the therapy relationship itself. In the introduction to her comprehensive and insightful chapter on the feminist therapy relationship, Brown writes: "Therapy is a relationship ..." (p. 92). While Brown goes on to describe features of the therapy relationship, it is important to note here that the therapy relationship is itself defined as the very essence of therapy. Brown does not say, "Therapy involves a relationship" or "Therapy includes a relationship," but rather: "Therapy is a relationship." Feminist therapy is viewed as a relational enterprise, and the client-therapist relationship is considered central to this endeavor.

Consistent with this perspective, feminist therapists attach deep meaning to the therapy relationship. Not only is the therapy relationship accorded value as a vehicle for therapeutic change, as discussed in the next section of the chapter, but feminist therapists also acknowledge the importance of their relationships with clients on a personal, private level. Brown (1994b) writes that feminist therapists strive to:

> . . . honor the reality of the psychotherapy relationship as an entity in their own lives. . . . In practice, it means being honest about the transformative effect of the work in their lives, the ways in which they are moved to rage, pain, excitement, joy by the people they work with, the manner in which their own wounds are mirrored or reopened, the dreams they dream of their clients' traumas, the exasperation and fatigue they may feel when it seems as if they are struggling against the oppressors internalized within this other person. . . . (p. 120)

Because of the general importance that women attach to relationships, when feminist therapy is practiced with female clients, the therapy relationship is likely to be viewed as significant by the client. However, when feminist therapy is conducted with a male client, as we believe it fruitfully can be, the therapy relationship may be more important to the therapist than to the client. The socialization of men tends to emphasize separation and independence more than affiliation and interdependence. Traditional male socialization has certain virtues (e.g., assertiveness, self-reliance, logical thinking; see Whitley, 1985), but one of its costs is the devaluing of intimate forms of relating, which are generally deemed to be feminine (Cournoyer & Mahalik, 1995). Feminist scholars contend that one of the consequences of the devaluation of intimate relationships by men in a patriarchal society is a sense of alienation among individuals (Brown, 1994b). The pervasive sense of alienation contributes to many of the problems for which men and women seek therapy, and it heightens the need for a relational therapy in which clients feel connected to their therapists (Brown, 1994b). A male client may at some level sense this need for greater connection to others, including his therapist, but he may not be able to articulate this need and may even deny it. Furthermore, a traditionally socialized male client may resist the development of an intimate therapy relationship (e.g., by becoming aloof, or sexualizing the intimacy) because of the threat it represents to his masculinity. Consequently, the feminist therapist may need to work harder with male clients than with female clients in overcoming the clients' resistance and forming a close therapy relationship.

We would note, however, that because wide variation exists in the socialization of men—and, of course, in men's individual characteristics— we caution against any overgeneralizing about male clients. In fact, by remaining cognizant of the variability in men's socialization and ascertaining the degree to which men's attitudes are traditionally masculine, therapists can derive information that may be helpful to their treatment decisions (Wisch, Mahalik, Hayes, & Nutt, 1995). Finally, although men's gender role attitudes can be assessed informally by therapists, useful and psychometrically sound instruments exist that can assist a therapist in this process (see Eisler & Skidmore, 1987; O'Neil, Helms, Gable, David, & Wrightsman, 1986).

THE FEMINIST THERAPY RELATIONSHIP: MEANS OR END?

Feminist therapy is characterized more by its commitment to feminist theory and principles than by adherence to any particular set of techniques. As with most other approaches, feminist therapy techniques are viewed as natural extensions of underlying theory. One of the primary tenets of the theory underlying feminist therapy is that egalitarianism and shared power represent ideals in virtually all relationships, including the therapy relationship. With egalitarianism as a focal point, the bulk of existing writings on the feminist therapy relationship has been devoted to two objectives: (a) understanding how sociopolitical factors affect the client-therapist relationship, and (b) critiquing existing models of the therapy relationship. As a result of concentrating on these two aims, and because of the relative youth of the feminist therapy literature, feminist scholars have yet to commit their full attention to a discussion of the relative contributions of the therapy relationship and techniques to outcome. Nonetheless, it is possible to infer from various writings how the feminist therapy relationship proportionally affects outcome, and, consequently, how the relationship may be conceptualized on a "means- end" continuum.

Before discussing the "means-end" dimension of the feminist therapy relationship, it might be instructive to briefly examine some of the techniques that feminist therapists commonly employ. In particular, we shall address teaching, advocacy, self-disclosure, and metacommunication. Each of these techniques ultimately is geared toward empowering clients.

Teaching, for example, may involve the transmission from therapist to client of factual information that raises clients' awareness, challenges their stereotypes, or reframes beliefs about themselves. Teaching may also take the form of helping clients develop the skills of critical social analysis so that clients might better understand the ways in which, historically and currently, societal forces affect their mental health (Russell, 1984). Alternatively, feminist therapists may teach clients about the process of therapy so as to enable current and potential clients to make informed choices about the services they receive.

In addition to teaching, feminist therapists may employ advocacy as a technique to empower their clients. By expanding traditional therapist roles to include that of advocate, feminist therapists demonstrate their willingness to help clients overcome the institutional or societal obstacles they may face. Advocating for a client, for instance, may entail writing a letter of support on a client's behalf, or accompanying a client to court to obtain a restraining order against an abusive partner.

A third feminist therapy technique, self-disclosure, when used judiciously, can serve to effectively demystify the therapy process, convey one's feelings about or reactions to a client, allow therapists to admit when they have made a therapeutic mistake, and provide a sense of universality to clients (Enns, 1997; Russell, 1984). Feminist therapists, like many others, warn against the potential misuses of self-disclosure, particularly in terms of indulging therapists' needs at the expense of the client.

A final feminist therapy technique, metacommunication—or communicating about the communication process—may be used by feminist therapists to help clients and therapists get unstuck when they have hit an impasse, or to assist clients in making continual choices about the direction and duration of therapy.

As mentioned earlier in the chapter, these and other feminist therapy techniques are utilized in a manner that is consistent with feminist theory and dictated by the welfare of the client. The techniques also are recognized to be employed within, affected by, and influential on the client-therapist relationship. That is, the techniques used by a feminist therapist are always employed within the context of a relationship with a client and will shape that relationship. As discussed in Chapters 6 and 8, the reverse is also true: the nature of the therapy relationship will determine, in part, the appropriateness and effectiveness of various techniques. For instance, the therapist who tries to raise a client's consciousness by teaching the client in the first session may find the client resistant to the therapist's efforts. Until the client is convinced, or willing to simply trust, that the therapist has the client's best interests in mind, the client may be reluctant to follow the therapist's techniques.

Beyond the use of specific techniques, the feminist therapy relationship itself is viewed as an avenue for empowering the client. Brown (1994b), for instance, states that heightened client awareness is "construed as a good outcome *of the therapeutic relationship*" in feminist therapy (p. 30, italics added). How does the feminist therapy relationship promote or otherwise affect outcome? The feminist therapist provides a healing, healthy presence to clients in myriad responses that demonstrate: reverence for a fellow human being's worth and dignity; appreciation for that person's cultural characteristics; knowledge of and confidence in the client's capabilities; interest in the client's history; and respect for the client's capacity to choose. Any one of the aforementioned features of the feminist therapy relationship is believed to be a potential source of empowerment, but when received as a whole by clients, these combined relationship qualities are considered, at a minimum, to be supportive, and, at a maximum, to have the potential to reduce clients' suffering and free up their inner competencies. Furthermore, by working toward, though never actually achieving, an egalitarian therapy relationship, feminist therapists help clients cultivate constructive relationships in other realms of their lives (Enns, 1997). Thus, "egalitarian relationships are important as both an outcome of therapy and as a condition of the psychotherapy relationship" (Enns, 1997, p. 15).

In summary, it may be said that the feminist therapy relationship is both a means and an end, though more of the latter than the former. Feminist therapists employ a variety of techniques to empower clients, although the effectiveness of these techniques is dependent, to some extent, on the quality and nature of the therapy relationship. Furthermore, the therapy relationship itself is viewed as a therapeutic change agent in directly providing to clients the empowering experience of being respected, supported, and valued. The feminist therapy relationship, then, appears to be situated between the psychoanalytic and humanistic therapy relationships on the "means-end" continuum. The cognitive-behavioral relationship clearly is the most "means" oriented of the four approaches, and, as discussed in Chapter 7, we view the psychoanalytic relationship as being more of a "means" than an end in itself, though less so than is true of cognitive-behavioral theories. Moving along the continuum, we would classify the feminist therapy relationship as falling on the "end" portion. However, because of the potentially healing and empowering role afforded to techniques in feminist therapy, we envision the feminist relationship as occupying a more moderate position on the "end" dimension than the humanistic theories, and especially person-centered therapy, where techniques are almost ignored and the relationship is believed to be virtually the sole change agent. In feminist therapy, the relationship is considered a primary, but not the only, source of therapeutic change.

THE REAL AND "UNREAL" RELATIONSHIP IN FEMINIST THERAPY

HISTORICAL CONSIDERATIONS

Because most feminist therapists are initially educated, trained, and supervised by nonfeminist therapists in traditional modes of therapy, when feminist therapists "emerge," they often lack a clearly delineated framework for what the "real" feminist therapy relationship is or ought to be (Brown, 1994b). This was especially true for early feminist therapists. In rebelling against patriarchal models of the therapy relationship, feminist therapy pioneers rejected the notion that a power differential between client and therapist was inevitable. Thus, one early conceptualization of the relationship between feminist therapist and client was that of a "consciousness raising group of two" (Brown, 1994b, p. 95). Feminist therapist and client were considered co-equals, each with her own contributions to make to the welfare of the other. In an attempt to avoid the power imbalance between therapist and client that feminists perceived to be both inherent in predominant approaches and inimical to clients' well-being, innovators of feminist therapy attempted to create a relationship between therapist and client that was egalitarian in every regard. These early formulations of the feminist therapy relationship helped enlighten the field about numerous unnecessary and problematic asymmetries involving power in the client-therapist relationship, but, according to Brown, these novel feminist therapy relationships tended not to work because they ignored the intrinsic power imbalance between therapist and client. Given that clients typically seek out and pay therapists, and given that the reverse is not true, an unavoidable power differential exists between the two parties. As this realization spread among feminist therapists, attempts were undertaken to rename therapy "consultation" or "facilitation" in an effort to circumvent the perceived difficulties associated with the power differential between "therapists" and "clients." However, these ventures amounted to little more than semantic changes. The disparity in power inherent in the roles of help-giver and help-seeker remained, requiring feminist writers and clinicians to continue to address and refine the nature of the relationship in feminist therapy (Brown, 1994b; Enns, 1997).

Feminist therapy practitioners and writers now recognize that a power imbalance between therapists and clients exists in both traditional and feminist versions of the therapy relationship. We address issues of power in more depth in the next section of the chapter; for now, we turn our attention, as feminist scholars and therapists are increasingly doing, to examining other aspects of the feminist therapy relationship. More specifically, we shall explore feminist therapists' conceptualizations and treatment of the real relationship and the transference configuration in feminist therapy.

Feminist therapists acknowledge that the therapy relationship contains both real elements and components that are less grounded in the immediate reality of the client and therapist (Berman, 1985; Brown, 1984, 1994b; Eichenbaum & Orbach, 1984). Brown (1994b) refers to the less reality-based aspects of the feminist therapy relationship as the "symbolic relationship." She writes that feminist therapists "have identified the importance of attending both to the symbolic relationship—that which is usually referred to in the psychotherapy literature as transference and countertransference—and to the real, in-the-world-now encounter" (p. 94).

Of the many different influences on the therapy relationship, feminist writers pay particular attention to the client's and therapist's cultures. A therapist's cultural characteristics may be obvious to the client, or they may be conveyed more subtly—for example, through the therapist's language, clothing, observance of holidays, and office decor. The real relationship in feminist therapy also is recognized to be potentially affected by extratherapy events, especially those with cultural overtones (e.g., the O. J. Simpson trials' effect on the therapy relationship between Black and White members of a therapy dyad). Brown, a lesbian feminist therapist, described the strain on the real relationship in her work with a Christian fundamentalist client when an anti-gay-rights bill was being considered in a neighboring state and was receiving considerable public attention. The cultural contrast between Brown and her client was cast into the spotlight in a way that compelled them to openly discuss their differences, acknowledge their similarities, and draw closer as a result.

Below, we examine in greater detail feminist scholars' notions about both the real relationship and the transference relationship in feminist theory. Because Brown's writing contains what we perceive to be the most thorough treatment of the relationship in feminist therapy, and because

Brown is recognized as a leading scholar on feminist therapy, we draw heavily from her thinking in our formulations that follow.

CHARACTERISTICS OF THE REAL RELATIONSHIP IN FEMINIST THERAPY

As we have defined it throughout the book, the real relationship consists of two dimensions: (a) the client's and therapist's *genuine* attitudes and feelings toward one another, and (b) each participant's *realistic* perceptions of and reactions to the other. Consistent with our definition, Eichenbaum and Orbach (1984) offer a helpful description and illumination of the real relationship in feminist therapy:

> We stress that this relationship is a real one and that the most meaningful moments in therapy take place when that realness is acknowledged and felt between client and therapist. By real relationship we mean that there are genuine feelings between the two people engaged in the process of therapy. . . . There are feelings of concern, love, and empathy that build over the time together, and to call it merely a professional relationship gives it overtones of clinical sterility which misrepresent the human exchange of feelings and care in the room. (p. 52)

In addition to the "feelings of concern, love, and empathy," other therapist emotions that often characterize real relationships with a positive valence in feminist therapy include respect, caring, compassion, nurturance, and reverence (Brown, 1984; Eichenbaum & Orbach, 1983). From virtually any theoretical vantage point, these traditionally maternal qualities are considered crucial to the role of the therapist. Nonetheless, except in some psychoanalytic circles, the view of therapist as mother typically has been denigrated and discouraged (Layton, 1994). Layton claims that much of the reason for therapists' being dissuaded from conceiving of themselves as mothers (or, more broadly, as parents) arises out of concern for maintaining healthy boundaries with clients. However, Layton contends that therapists' preoccupation with maintaining appropriate clinical boundaries has resulted in professional neglect of therapists' potential to heal via nurturing. Layton does not argue that therapists should act primarily like parents; rather, she asserts that the therapy relationship can be informed and enhanced by the therapist's thoughtful consideration of the life-sustaining and nurturing characteristics of a mother. "It behooves us to question and compare what we know about caretaking: caretaking as a skill, as a philosophy, as a kind of thinking and behavior shaped by the demands of caring for growing people" (Layton, 1994, p. 486).

Layton's position is only one of many regarding the role of boundaries in the feminist therapy relationship. Because healthy boundaries are part and parcel of an ideal real relationship in feminist therapy, and because feminist scholars have generated provocative insights regarding therapeutic boundaries, we shall pursue this topic in greater detail.

THE ROLE OF BOUNDARIES

Across a wide range of theoretical orientations, the establishment and maintenance of appropriate boundaries in the therapy relationship are considered important. Healthy boundaries provide clients with a therapy experience that is predictable and consistent enough to be beneficial. Furthermore, boundaries minimize the likelihood of role confusion for both therapy participants, decrease the probability of therapist burnout, and lower the chances that the client will be exploited. Boundaries are especially important for women clients, many of whom seek therapy because their boundaries have been violated previously in the form of rape, sexual harassment, and other forms of abuse (Margolies, 1990). For these clients, in particular, therapists' maintenance of consistent boundaries may instill clients' trust and provide positive modeling.

The importance of consistent boundaries was brought to life for one of the authors (JAH) when working with a female client who had been sexually abused as a child. The client was informed that when she was in crisis, she could call the author's emergency voice-mail service, which would then immediately page the author. The author explained that, as a matter of course, he did not make his home phone number (which was unlisted) directly available to any of his clients. Despite being aware of this fact, the client asked the therapist for his home phone number at least monthly during the two years in which he worked with her. The author dealt with each request by uniformly reminding the client that he was available to her in times of crisis, but as a matter of policy, he did not give his home phone number to any of his clients. The client often responded to the author's patient but unwavering stance with frustration and increasingly desperate pleas for an exception to his established practice regarding his phone number. The author, in turn, attempted to empathize with the client's frustration and encouraged her not to view his policy personally—that is, as a reflection of her importance to him. During one of the final therapy sessions, as termination was approaching, the therapist asked this woman what stood out for her as a significant contributor to the progress that she had made. Without hesitating, the client replied, "The fact that you never gave me your home phone number." Somewhat perplexed, the therapist asked, "Then why did you continually ask for it?" The client responded, "I needed to know that you were predictable." Upon reflection, it became clear that the times at which the client would ask for the therapist's phone number preceded periods of increased vulnerability on the client's behalf. The therapist's consistency in maintaining boundaries facilitated the client's deepening of trust in the therapist.

Given that, on the one hand, Layton (1994) and other feminists have questioned the rigidity of traditional conceptions of therapeutic boundaries, and, on the other hand, feminist therapists are particularly sensitive to the exploitation of clients, one might wonder what feminist therapists consider to be "appropriate" boundaries. Consistent with the feminist view that multiple perspectives of reality are valid, feminist writers do not advocate one exclusive set of therapy boundaries (Berman, 1985; Brown, 1994a). Feminist writers maintain that therapists must decide for themselves what constitutes acceptable and healthy boundaries, taking into consideration the client's presenting concern, personality, and history, and the interaction of the client's and therapist's cultural characteristics. Feminist therapists tend not to adopt so conservative a stance with regard to possible boundary violations that therapists are likely to be perceived by clients as cold and aloof (Brown, 1994a; A. Rogers, 1991). In fact, therapists cannot avoid any and all behaviors that may be construed by clients as potential boundary violations. Because therapists cannot *not* act in a way that clients might perceive as violating, and, at the same time, because a practical set of universal rules about boundaries is not possible, therapists must resort to following certain guidelines in determining for each client the behaviors that comprise appropriate boundaries. Brown (1994a) frames these guidelines in the form of three overarching questions regarding therapist behavior that is likely to contribute to unhealthy boundaries:

1. Does the therapist's behavior objectify the client by meeting the therapist's needs (e.g., for power, for intimacy)?
2. Even if the therapist does not objectify the client, does the therapist's behavior meet the therapist's needs at the expense of the client's needs?
3. Is the behavior impulsive?

Brown believes: "Impulsivity on the part of the therapist ignores the relational and interpersonal as well as symbolic components of our behavior" (p. 35).

Although we would not encourage therapists to act impulsively, we do believe that therapist *spontaneity* can be a valuable clinical asset. Differentiating between impulsive and spontaneous therapist behavior, however, is no easy task, whether one is reflecting on one's own actions or those of a supervisee or colleague. Our tentatively offered distinction between therapist impulsivity and spontaneity concerns the degree of thoughtfulness involved. Spontaneous behavior may not be premeditated, but it is preceded by at least some thoughtful consideration of the needs of the client and the intended and likely consequences of the behavior. Impulsive behavior, in contrast, is carried out with little or no regard for the client's needs or the probable effects of the behavior. In either case, but especially when a therapist feels the urge to act impulsively, feminist therapists caution therapists to remain mindful that therapy, at all times, is an interpersonal endeavor with significant repercussions for clients. Toward this end, Brown (1994a) writes: "Boundary violations . . . often occur when the *relational* nature of therapy is forgotten" (p. 37).

THE TRANSFERENCE CONFIGURATION IN FEMINIST THERAPY

Although most feminist therapy writers acknowledge that transference exists, some are hesitant to use the term. Brown (1984), for example, believes that feminist therapists should be cautious about using psychoanalytic terminology because, in her view, doing so promotes Freud's misogynist theory. Brown (1984, p. 76) has written: "If we use such terminology to describe the process of feminist therapy, we do violence to the term feminist." In particular, the terms *transference* and *countertransference* are viewed by Brown as dangerous in that they "carry the risk of transforming the therapist's perceptions to concepts less firmly rooted in feminism" (Brown, 1994b, p. 98).

We would agree with Brown that elements of Freud's theory are sexist and potentially offensive to women, but Brown seems to disregard her own advice not to "throw the psychodynamic baby out with its patriarchal bathwater" (Brown, 1984, p. 78). In fact, some of the bases for Brown's renunciation of psychoanalytic theory—and thus, psychoanalytic terminology—seem to stem from oversimplifications and misinterpretations of Freud's writing, as well as a lack of familiarity with contemporary psychoanalytic thinking. For example, Brown objects to the power imbalance that is typically present between a psychoanalytic therapist and a client. She claims that for the "entirely self-disclosing client" to successfully work through transference, the therapist must be "entirely unknown and mysterious" (Brown, 1984, p. 76). Whereas psychoanalytic therapists may attempt to remain neutral and ambiguous, to facilitate the development of transference, we—and many current psychoanalytic writers—would argue that therapists never can be, nor should they ever be, "entirely unknown," and that they need not be nearly so for clients to resolve transference successfully (see Chapters 3 and 7). Brown also objects to the emphasis that psychoanalytic systems place on transference and countertransference. By accenting the roles of transference and countertransference in therapy, Brown contends that psychoanalytic therapists create an environment in which clients cannot trust what they perceive to be authentic. "What is there in therapy is not 'really' there. . . . Any feelings that the client may have about the therapist are not genuine feelings. . . . And what the therapist says and does is equally not real; it only has meaning as meaning is projected onto it by the client. . . . There is no genuine, human-to-human response of therapist to client" (Brown, 1984, p. 76). As we discussed in Chapters 3 and 7, however, Freud and other psychoanalysts acknowledge that the therapy relationship contains not only transference components but elements of the real relationship as well, and the real relationship is of increasing significance in contemporary psychoanalytic thought. Not only is everything not transference, but, contrary to Brown's assertion, transference relations may be tremendously genuine, even though they are not reality-based. That is, although a client's perceptions of a therapist may be distorted by transference, the client's feelings, attitudes, and behaviors based on those perceptions may be quite authentic and sincere. Brown herself has stated: "The magic-feeling connections that occur in feminist therapy are as real as the concrete ones" (Brown, 1984, pp. 78–79). Finally, it is not true, as Brown claims, that psychoanalytic therapists do not distinguish between the client's reality-based and transferential feelings toward the therapist, nor is it true that analytic therapists themselves do not possess and occasionally express genuine feelings for their clients (e.g., Eichenbaum & Orbach, 1983, pp. 122–123). In psychoanalytic therapy, as in feminist therapy, "[not] all passionate responses of therapist to client and client to therapist [are] defined as necessarily derived from disrupted or disturbed elements in each person's past" (Brown, 1994b, p. 98). Thus, Brown's basis for rejecting psychoanalytic terminology on the grounds that it promotes Freudian theory seems misguided to the extent that her criticism of psychoanalytic theory is ill-founded and not consistent with contemporary psychoanalytic perspectives.

On the basis of Brown's hesitancy to combine feminist and psychoanalytic concepts, she prefers the phrase "symbolic relationship" over "transference relationship." Not only does Brown replace the words *transference* and *countertransference* with new terminology, she also adds to traditional notions of these constructs by describing an extra dimension of the distorted client-therapist relationship. For Brown (1994b), the symbolic relationship between client and therapist not only includes distortions based on one's intrapsychic conflict and personal history, but also encompasses elements of what the other represents in terms of that person's sociocultural group memberships. That is, the therapist does not merely symbolize a significant figure from the client's past but, consciously or unconsciously, the client may also transfer onto the therapist feelings that the client has for most or all members of a cultural group to which the client perceives the therapist to belong. Brown (1994b) states the issue in the following way:

> The vision of the symbolic relationship in therapy moves beyond that of transference and countertransference by placing the relationship in a broader sociopolitical context. The client's response to the therapist is not only about how the therapist symbolizes a parent or other caregiver; it is also about the various social meanings developed by this client regarding the therapist's actual or assumed group memberships. Feminist therapy theory argues that to strip the symbolic relationship of these sociocultural factors is to decontextualize this non-conscious component of psychotherapy in a manner that denies its relevance to the events of the world outside the therapy office. (p. 103)

An example of the symbolic therapy relationship from our own clinical experience may help illuminate Brown's point. Years ago, one of the authors cofacilitated a therapy group for women survivors of sexual abuse. As a male, the therapist was the recipient of a fair amount of symbolic reactions from the group members, owing both to feelings they had toward their male perpetrators in particular and to men more generally. These symbolic reactions were often hostile, sometimes intensely so. The author understood these reactions to be extensions of the women's history of abuse by men rather than targeted attacks on him personally. This perspective was underscored by the fact that the symbolic reactions occurred from the outset of therapy. Furthermore, the cofacilitator of the group (a woman) shared the author's interpretation of the group members' reactions to him. It might be noted that the author's intentionally gentle and nondefensive responses to the group members challenged their symbolic relationships with the author in a way that enhanced the development of real relationships and ultimately proved helpful to a number of women in the group.

Unlike Brown, many other feminist scholars (e.g., Berman, 1985; Prozan, 1993) use the terms *transference* and *countertransference*, retaining their analytic definitions but approaching the treatment of these constructs from a feminist perspective. Schlachet (1984) and Prozan, for example, argue that an understanding of transference dynamics in the therapist-client relationship needs to include an analysis of both the gender and the sex role socialization of the members of the dyad. The nature of the transference is likely to differ for the four possible combinations of therapist and client gender. For instance, when working with a woman who has been traditionally socialized, a male therapist who has been socialized to aspire toward dominance may, knowingly or otherwise, foster dependent transference dynamics. Alternatively, when a female therapist works with a male client who is oriented toward a traditionally masculine sex role, the client may be prone to sexualize intimacy in the relationship and develop an eroticized transference toward the therapist (Schlachet, 1984). When female therapists work with clients who are women, Eichenbaum and Orbach (1983) contend that "the most critical relationship that is going to come up in the transference is that between mother and daughter. . . . This will not always be the first thing that is talked about in therapy or that is immediately obvious in the transference relationship, but sooner or later it will be addressed at great length during the course of therapy" (p. 72). Often, a female client will develop a yearning to nurture and attend to the needs of her female therapist, a transference dynamic born out of an experience familiar to many women of needing to take care of their mothers, even from an early age (Eichenbaum & Orbach, 1983).

As is true of the real relationship and the transference configuration in feminist therapy, gender dynamics contribute significantly to feminist conceptualizations of the role of power in the therapy relationship. In the final section of the chapter, we examine issues pertaining to power in the feminist therapy relationship.

POWER IN THE FEMINIST THERAPY RELATIONSHIP

Feminist authors remark that many women are apprehensive about power and uneasy about being associated with positions of power (Enns, 1997;

J. B. Miller, 1976). Historically, numerous familiar images of powerful women—witch, sorceress, seductress, Eve—carry connotations of evil (Collier, 1982; J. B. Miller, 1976). Even feminist therapists themselves frequently seem uncomfortable with power. "Few feminist therapists seem willing to be caught in the act of being powerful. It seems as if our encounters with power in its official guises have been so damaging to us, or to those people and cultures important to us, that we shrink from any association with it" (Brown, 1994b, p. 106). The word *power,* as the preceding quote implies, often conveys something negative, such as dominance, violence, and tyranny, all of which involve power over others (Collier, 1982; J. B. Miller, 1976). Feminists describe and espouse a different type of power, one that is concerned less with power over others and more with power for oneself (Collier, 1982; J. B. Miller, 1976). J. B. Miller (1976, p. 116), for example, has defined power as "the capacity to implement" (e.g., to implement one's abilities) and as "the capacity to produce a change" (J. B. Miller, 1992, p. 198). Feminist scholars reject conventional notions of therapist authority as stemming from "powers to diagnose, define, and determine the reality of the client" (Brown, 1994b, p. 110). Instead, feminists give heed to the rarely considered power inherent in therapists' attending, nurturing, listening, witnessing, and perceiving that which is hidden in clients (Brown, 1994b).

As discussed previously, feminist therapists have come to recognize that power differences between client and therapist exist and are inevitable, due to the intrinsic vulnerability in the client's help-seeking role. However, feminist writers call attention to various other potential origins of power imbalance in the therapy relationship. Douglas (1985), for example, describes myriad types of power that therapists possess and that therapists may use for good or ill. "Reward power" stems from the therapist's capacity to validate, support, and encourage the client. "Coercive power" results from the therapist's potential to persuade the client by expressing disapproval, anger, or impatience regarding the client's behaviors or attitudes. "Informational power" is a function of the therapist's knowledge base; "expert power" derives from the therapist's proficiency in conducting therapy; and "legitimate power" emanates from the authority granted to therapists by society (e.g., to hospitalize a client involuntarily). Therapists' power may also be a function of the power associated with their various cultural characteristics. Disparities between therapists' and clients' power in the therapy relationship may be magnified when the therapist is male, White, wealthy, and/or heterosexual, and the client is a woman, non-White, poor, and/or gay, lesbian, or bisexual.

Any of the various sources of therapist power may be used to enhance or undermine a client's sense of personal power. Feminist therapists strive to be aware of these diverse forms of power and to use them to empower rather than disempower clients. In doing so, feminist writers caution that therapists must be sensitive to the possible effect of the therapist-client power differential on female clients. Because of the way many women are socialized to show deference to authority figures, the power imbalance in the therapy relationship may cause some women to defer too readily to the therapist. Alternatively, women who have been abused by people in positions of authority may be wary of what could be "done to them" in therapy (Eichenbaum & Orbach, 1983).

In addition to acknowledging the power that therapists possess, feminist therapists recognize the power of the clients. Clients are understood to have the power to select and reject their therapists, set treatment goals, shape the course of therapy, and decide when to terminate therapy (Brown, 1994b). A client's choice is thus considered central to her or his power. Along these lines, Collier (1982) has written:

> *Reacting* to change leaves a woman powerless; *choosing* breeds in her a feeling of power. . . . Choosing and acting always means development of a sense of power. . . . Negotiation, bargaining, and compromising give a level of control and power over the outcome that is essential to the development of self. When we act instead of reacting, when we choose instead of responding, we become an important ingredient in every event of our lives. The person who feels powerless in the face of change has to find points where she or he has the power to choose. (p. 113)

Further illuminating the importance of therapists' appreciating clients' power in feminist therapy, Brown (1994b) writes:

> Acknowledging the client's power lies at the heart of the egalitarian relationship in feminist therapy. Such relationships happen when the therapist knows and embraces the reality of her own power and uses it responsibly, as an agent for justice and change, and when, simultaneously, the power of the client is made manifest and strengthened. (p. 121)

As the above excerpt suggests, although feminist therapists recognize that a power imbalance between clients and therapists is unavoidable, feminist therapists nevertheless espouse an egalitarian therapy relationship as the ideal. From a feminist perspective, an egalitarian therapy relationship implies that therapist and client have equal worth and dignity but not equal power. In addition, the client is recognized to be the expert on her or his life and capable of self-determination while still being affected by societal oppression (Enns, 1997). Furthermore, egalitarianism requires of feminist therapists an explicit understanding of the power differential that does exist with clients. To ignore the power that therapists have relative to clients is to increase the likelihood of client exploitation. Brown (1994b) notes that the most grievous abuses of power committed by feminist therapists often occur when the therapist denies having power or authority. Brown believes that "it is essential that feminist therapists, in understanding the nature of the relationship in therapy, acknowledge and own the extraordinary degree of power that they do possess *in the context of that particular relationship.* . . . Denial of this power can be dangerous, both to the theoretical construct of egalitarianism and to the welfare of their clients and themselves" (Brown, 1994a, p. 108).

Because the overarching goal of feminist therapy is client empowerment, feminist therapists seek to use the power differential in the therapy relationship toward this end. That is, feminist therapists generally adopt a bilateral rather than unilateral power strategy, exerting control over the client only when absolutely necessary (e.g., when the client's physical welfare is endangered; Douglas, 1985). Consistent with the notion of a bilateral power strategy, feminist therapists seek to continually "give away" their power to clients. A power imbalance between a client and a therapist lasts throughout the duration of therapy, but feminist therapists aim to gradually decrease this inequity. Feminist therapists give away their power continually until clients no longer need to be empowered by the therapist. At this point, therapy is terminated and a greater mutuality exists between two human beings who are no longer restricted to the roles of client and therapist (Douglas, 1985; J. B. Miller, 1976).

How do feminist therapists give away their power? The feminist therapy literature is replete with examples. For starters, a feminist therapist may actively disclaim the role of being the expert about the client (M. Butler, 1985). Feminist therapists may have proficiency in the practice of therapy, but this expertise does not extend to the realm of determining what is true or right or best for clients. "Feminist therapy theory defines clients as the experts about the meaning of their lives and their pain" (Brown, 1994b, p. 115). A second way in which feminist therapists give away their power is by openly discussing with clients the power differential in the therapy relationship (Eichenbaum & Orbach, 1983). This type of discussion can help demystify the therapy process and clarify for clients their rights, responsibilities, and privileges in the therapy relationship. Third, feminist therapists are open to sharing their theoretical orientations and values with both current and potential clients (M. But-ler, 1985). Feminist therapists should be able and willing to articulate how their "political view of the world shapes a psychological view of women and how this in turn provides a particular viewpoint" (Eichen-baum & Orbach, 1983, p. 130). Another way in which feminist therapists share their power with clients is through self-disclosure. When used judi-ciously, therapist self-disclosure can promote "a sense of communality of experience" (M. Butler, 1985, p. 36) and dispel the myth that, unlike the client, the therapist has no problems (Gannon, 1982). By admitting their own issues to clients, feminist therapists heighten the likelihood that clients will identify with them and will see them as role models who have successfully worked through personal problems. Another manner in which feminist therapists can give away their power is through a willing-ness to be addressed by clients on a first-name basis (Burtle, 1985). Clients may not exercise this option, but knowing that it is available to them can be empowering in and of itself. Along similar lines, feminist therapists avoid using jargon and diagnostic labels with clients (Enns, 1997; Fitzgerald & Nutt, 1986; Gannon, 1982). (We would note that, from our perspective, good therapists of all persuasions avoid using jargon and labels with clients. A friend of one of the authors, for example, is a well-known psychoanalyst who was in analysis with an even more famous an-alyst for nine years. In all the time they worked together, the client never once heard his analyst utter the word *transference*.) In all of these ways, then, "the client is explicitly, carefully, and persistently given back the power to define self, and the meaning of self, in the manner most attuned to the person's present identity and cultural context and heritage" (Brown, 1994b, p. 115). Collier (1982) adopts a slightly different view-point. She believes that therapists "do not give women power or even teach it to them; they help them to uncover it within themselves" (p. 261) by allowing clients to freely express emotions, make choices, and receive the therapist's affirmation and validation. Smith and Siegel (1985) echo Collier's point, suggesting that feminist therapists can promote healing by reminding clients that they possess power of which they may be cur-rently unaware.

Although feminist therapists can give away their power in many ways, the differences between therapists' and clients' cultural characteristics contribute to a power imbalance in the relationship that can be difficult to overcome. To minimize the culturally based power differential be-tween clients and therapists, Douglas (1985) suggests that therapists consider restricting the practice of feminist therapy to clients of the same sex. Although we recognize that women clients are likely to experience less of a power imbalance with female therapists than with male therapists, we are inclined to believe that limiting the practice of feminist therapy to same-sex dyads is neither practical nor even in some clients' best interests. Given that one of the primary goals of feminist therapy is the empowerment of clients, and given that feminist therapists accomplish this goal in part by "giving away" their power to clients, it would follow logically that male therapists, who are accorded a fair amount of power in society, would be in an advantageous position to empower female clients. We have found from our own clinical and supervisory work that when a male therapist provides what proves to be an atypical relationship for a female client—one in which he respects and affirms both her independence and her possible need for interdependence, and conveys in a validating rather than a patronizing fashion his belief in her capabilities—the relationship can be extremely therapeutic for the client. Along similar lines, Enns (1997) notes that "feminists who espouse a liberal feminist position are likely to believe that men who have examined their own gender behavior, have developed sensitivity to and awareness of gender role issues, and endorse egalitarian roles can work effectively as feminist or gender-aware therapists" (p. 159). Believing that men can effectively practice feminist therapy does not negate the unique and empowering position that female therapists have in serving as role models for women clients.

CONCLUSION

Feminist therapy constitutes a singular approach to therapy that nonetheless may be integrated with other distinct theoretical systems. Because of the importance of relationships to women generally, the therapy relationship occupies a place of prominence in the theory and practice of feminist therapy. However, no research has been published to date on the feminist therapy relationship. The client-therapist relationship is viewed as a source of empowerment for clients, and, because empowerment is one of the primary goals of feminist therapy, the relationship may be viewed as directly promoting outcome more than as an indirect means to this end. However, client empowerment also may be facilitated through the use of certain therapist techniques, such as teaching, advocacy, self-disclosure, and metacommunication. Within the feminist therapy relationship, both the real relationship and the transference configuration are deemed important. The role of boundaries is central to feminist conceptualizations of the real relationship, and feminist writers contend that transference and countertransference dynamics are influenced not only by the client's and therapist's personal pasts but also by present sociopolitical factors. For this and other reasons, Brown (1994b) has argued for replacing the terms *transference* and *countertransference* with the phrase *symbolic relationship*. Finally, feminist scholars have devoted tremendous attention to analyzing the power imbalance between therapists and clients. Egalitarian relationships are considered the ideal in feminist therapy, where therapists and clients are recognized to possess equal dignity and worth though they are unequal in power. Feminist therapists look for ways to give away their power to clients to reduce unnecessary power differentials and to enhance positive outcomes. The feminist therapy relationship, then, is a complex, evolving phenomenon that challenges the assumptions and ground rules regarding the relationship in more established theories. It requires ingenuity and flexibility in its practice, needs pioneering efforts to be undertaken by researchers, and demands continued theoretical development by feminist scholars.

References

Adelstein, D. M., Gelso, C. J., Haws, J. R., Reed, K. G., & Spiegel, S. B. (1983). The change process following time-limited therapy. In C. J. Gelso & D. H. Johnson (Eds.), *Explorations in time-limited counseling and psychotherapy.* (pp. 63–81). New York: Teachers College Press.

Ainsworth, M. D. S., Blehar, M. C., Waters, E., & Wall, S. (1978). *Patterns of attachment: A psychological study of strange situation.* Hillsdale, NJ: Erlbaum.

Al-Darmaki, F., & Kivlighan, D. M. (1993). Congruence in client-counselor expectations for relationship and the working alliance. *Journal of Counseling Psychology, 40,* 379–384.

Andersen, S. M., & Berk, M. S. (1998). Transference in everyday experience: Implications of experimental research for relevant clinical phenomena. *Review of General Psychology, 2,* 81–120.

Arnkoff, D. B. (1981). Flexibility in practicing cognitive therapy. In G. Emery, S. Hollon, & R. Bedrosian (Eds.), *New directions in cognitive therapy* (pp. 203–223). New York: Guilford Press.

Arnkoff, D. B. (1983). Common and specific factors in cognitive therapy. In M. J. Lambert (Ed.), *Psychotherapy and patient relationships* (pp. 85–125). Homewood, IL: Dow Jones-Irwin.

Aron, L. (1996). *A meeting of minds and mutuality in psychoanalysis.* New York: Analytic Press.

Assagioli, R. (1965). *Psychosynthesis.* New York: Penguin Books.

Ayllon, T., & Michael, J. (1959). The psychiatric nurse as a behavioral engineer. *Journal of the Experimental Analysis of Behavior, 2,* 323–334.

Bacal, H. A., & Newman, K. M. (1990). *Theories of object relations: Bridges to self psychology.* New York: Columbia University Press.

Bachelor, A. (1995). Client's perceptions of the therapeutic alliance: A qualitative analysis. *Journal of Counseling Psychology, 42,* 323–337.

Bandura, A. (1969). *Principles of behavior modification.* New York: Holt, Rinehart and Winston.

Bandura, A., Lipsher, D. H., & Miller, P. E. (1960). Psychotherapists' approach-avoidance reactions to patients' expressions of hostility. *Journal of Consulting Psychology, 24,* 1–8.

Barrett-Lennard, G. T. (1985). The helping relationship: Crisis and advance in theory and research. *The Counseling Psychologist, 13,* 279–294.

Barrett-Lennard, G. T. (1997). The recovery of empathy toward others and self. In A. C. Bohart & L. S. Greenberg (Eds.), *Empathy reconsidered: New directions in psychotherapy* (pp. 103–121). Washington, DC: American Psychological Association.

Bartholomew, K., & Horowitz, L. M. (1991). Attachment styles among young adults: A test of a four-category model. *Journal of Personality and Social Psychology, 61,* 226–244.

Bartlett, F. C. (1932). *Remembering: A study in experimental and social psychology.* London: Cambridge University Press.

Beck, A. T. (1967). *Depression: Causes and treatment.* Philadelphia: University of Pennsylvania.

Beck, A. T. (1991). Cognitive therapy as *the* integrative therapy. *Journal of Psychotherapy Integration, 1,* 191–198.

Beck, A. T., Freeman, A. F., & Associates. (1990). *Cognitive therapy of personality disorders.* New York: Guilford Press.

Beck, A. T., Rush, A. J., Shaw, B. F., & Emery, G. (1979). *Cognitive therapy of depression.* New York: Guilford Press.

Beck, A. T., & Weishaar, M. E. (1995). Cognitive therapy. In R. J. Corsini & D. Wedding (Eds.), *Current psychotherapies* (5th ed., pp. 229–261). Itasca, IL: Peacock.

Beck, J. S. (1996). Cognitive therapy of personality disorders. In P. M. Salkovskis (Ed.), *Frontiers of cognitive therapy* (pp. 165–181). New York: Guilford Press.

Belenky, M. F., Clinchy, B. M., Goldberger, N. R., & Tarule, J. M. (1986). *Women's ways of knowing.* New York: Basic Books.

Benjamin, J. (1984). The convergence of psychoanalysis and feminism: Gender identity and autonomy. In C. M. Brody (Ed.), *Women therapists working with women* (pp. 37–45). New York: Springer.

Beres, D., & Arlow, J. A. (1974). Fantasy and identification in empathy. *Psychiatric Quarterly, 43,* 26–50.

Berman, J. R. S. (1985). Ethical feminist perspectives on dual relationships with clients. In L. B. Rosewater & L. E. A. Walker (Eds.), *Handbook of feminist therapy* (pp. 287–296). New York: Springer.

Beutler, L. E., Crago, M., & Arizmendi, T. G. (1986). Research on therapist variables in psychotherapy. In S. Garfield & A. Bergin (Eds.), *Handbook of psychotherapy and behavior change* (3rd ed., pp. 257–310). New York: Wiley.

Beutler, L. E., Engle, D., Mohr, D., Daldrup, R. J., Bergan, J., Meredith, K., & Merry, W. (1991). Predictors of differential response to cognitive, experiential, and self-directed psychotherapeutic procedures. *Journal of Consulting and Clinical Psychology, 59,* 333–340.

Beutler, L. E., Machado, P. P. P., & Neufeldt, S. A. (1994). Therapist variables. In A. E. Bergin & S. L. Garfield (Eds.), *Handbook of psychotherapy and behavior change* (4th ed., pp. 229–269). New York: Wiley.

Beutler, L. E., & Sandowicz, M. (1994). The counseling relationship: What is it? *The Counseling Psychologist, 22,* 98–103.

Blanck, G., & Blanck, R. (1979). *Ego psychology: II. Psychoanalytic developmental psychology.* New York: Columbia University Press.

Bohart, A. C., & Greenberg, L. S. (1997). Empathy and psychotherapy: An introductory overview. In A. C. Bohart & L. S. Greenberg (Eds.), *Empathy reconsidered:*

New directions in psychotherapy (pp. 3–31). Washington, DC: American Psychological Association.

Bordin, E. S. (1975). *The working alliance and bases for a general theory of psychotherapy.* Paper presented at the annual meeting of American Psychological Association, Washington DC.

Bordin, E. S. (1979). The generalizability of the psychoanalytic concept of the working alliance. *Psychotherapy: Theory, Research, and Practice, 16,* 252–260.

Bordin, E. S. (1989, June). *Building therapeutic alliances: The base for integration.* Paper presented at the annual meeting of the Society for Psychotherapy Research, Berkeley, CA.

Bordin, E. S. (1994). Theory and research on the therapeutic working alliance: New directions. In A. Horvath & L. Greenberg (Eds.), *The working alliance: Theory, research, and practice* (pp. 13–37). New York: Wiley.

Borkovec, T. D., & Newman, M. G. (in press). Worry and generalized anxiety disorder. In P. Salkovskis (Ed.), *Comprehensive clinical psychology.* Oxford, England: Elsevier Science.

Bouchard, M. A., Normandin, L., & Seguin, M. H. (1995). Countertransference as instrument and obstacle: A comprehensive and descriptive framework. *Psychoanalytic Quarterly, 64,* 717–745.

Bowlby, J. (1969). *Attachment and loss: Vol. 1: Attachment.* New York: Basic Books.

Bowlby, J. (1973). *Attachment and loss: Vol. 2. Separation—Anxiety and anger.* New York: Basic Books.

Bowlby, J. (1979). *The making and breaking of affectional bonds.* New York: Routledge & Kegan Paul.

Bowlby, J. (1980). *Attachment and loss: Vol. 3. Loss, sadness, and depression.* New York: Basic Books.

Bowlby, J. (Ed.). (1988a). *A secure base: Parent-child attachments and healthy human development.* New York: Basic Books.

Bowlby, J. (1988b). Attachment, communication, and the therapeutic process. In J. Bowlby (Ed.), *A secure base: Parent-child attachment and healthy human development* (pp. 137–157). New York: Basic Books.

Boyer, S. P., & Hoffman, M. A. (1993). Therapists' affective reactions to termination: Impact of therapist loss history and client sensitivity to loss. *Journal of Counseling Psychology, 40,* 271–277.

Bozarth, J. D. (1984). Beyond reflection: Emergent modes of empathy. In R. Levant & J. Shlien (Eds.), *Client-centered therapy and the person-centered approach.* New York: Praeger.

Bozarth, J. D. (1997). Empathy from the framework of client-centered theory and the Rogerian hypotheses. In A. C. Bohart & L. S. Greenberg (Eds.), *Empathy reconsidered: New directions in psychotherapy* (pp. 81–102). Washington, DC: American Psychological Association.

Brammer, L., & Shostrom, E. (1968). *Therapeutic psychology* (2nd ed.). Englewood Cliffs, NJ: Prentice-Hall.

Brickman, P., Rabinowitz, V. C., Karuza, J., Coates, D., Cohn, E., & Kidder, L. (1982). Models of helping and coping. *American Psychologist, 37,* 368–384.

Brown, L. S. (1984). Finding new language: Getting beyond analytic verbal shorthand in feminist therapy. *Women and Therapy, 3,* 73–80.

Brown, L. S. (1994a). Boundaries in feminist therapy: A conceptual formulation. *Women and Therapy, 15,* 29–38.

Brown, L. S. (1994b). *Subversive dialogues.* New York: Basic Books.

Buber, M. (1958). *I and thou*. New York: Scribners.

Buber, M. (1966). *The knowledge of man: A philosophy of the interhuman*. New York: Harper & Row.

Bugental, J. F. T. (1987). *The art of the psychotherapist*. New York: Norton.

Burgess, A. (1963). *A clockwork orange*. New York: Norton.

Burlingame, G. M., & Fuhriman, A. (1987). Conceptualizing short-term treatment: A comparative approach. *The Counseling Psychologist, 15*, 557–595.

Burns, D. D. (1989). *The feeling good handbook*. New York: Morrow.

Burns, D. D., & Auerbach, A. (1996). Therapeutic empathy in cognitive-behavioral therapy: Does it really make a difference? In P. M. Salkovskis (Ed.), *Frontiers of cognitive therapy* (pp. 135–164). New York: Guilford Press.

Burns, D. D., & Nolen-Hoeksma, S. (1992). Therapeutic empathy and recovery from depression in cognitive-behavioral therapy: A structural equation model. *Journal of Consulting and Clinical Psychology, 59*, 305–311.

Burtle, V. (1985). Therapeutic anger in women. In L. B. Rosewater & L. E. A. Walker (Eds.), *Handbook of feminist therapy* (pp. 71–79). New York: Springer.

Butler, M. (1985). Guidelines for feminist therapy. In L. B. Rosewater & L. E. A. Walker (Eds.), *Handbook of feminist therapy* (pp. 32–38). New York: Springer.

Butler, S. F., & Strupp, H. H. (1986). Specific and nonspecific factors in psychotherapy: A problematic paradigm for psychotherapy research. *Psychotherapy, 23*, 30–40.

Cammaert, L. P., & Larsen, C. C. (1988). Feminist frameworks of psychotherapy. In M. A. Dutton-Douglas & L. E. A. Walker (Eds.), *Feminist psychotherapies* (pp. 12–36). Norwood, NJ: ABLEX.

Capra, F. (1991). *Tao of physics*. New York: Sham.

Chambers, A. A. (1986). *Client judgements of therapist characteristics: A factor in the treatment of anxiety*. Unpublished doctoral dissertation, Pennsylvania State University, University Park.

Chesler, P. (1972). *Women and madness*. San Diego: Harcourt Brace Jovanovich.

Chodorow, N. J. (1989). *Feminism and psychoanalytic theory*. New Haven, CT: Yale University Press.

Clarke, K. M., & Greenberg, L. S. (1986). Differential effects of the Gestalt two-chair intervention and problem solving in resolving decisional conflict. *Journal of Counseling Psychology, 33*, 11–15.

Cohen, M. B. (1952). Countertransference and anxiety. *Psychiatry, 15*, 231–243.

Collier, H. V. (1982). *Counseling women*. New York: Free Press.

Collins, N. L., & Read, S. J. (1990). Adult attachment, working models, and relationship quality in dating couples. *Journal of Personality and Social Psychology, 58*, 644–663.

Corey, G. (1996). *Theory and practice of counseling and psychotherapy* (5th ed.). Pacific Grove, CA: Brooks/Cole.

Cournoyer, R. J., & Mahalik, J. R. (1995). Cross-sectional study of gender role conflict examining college-aged and middle-aged men. *Journal of Counseling Psychology, 42*, 11–19.

Cutler, R. L. (1958). Countertransference effects in psychotherapy. *Journal of Consulting Psychology, 22*, 349–356.

Daugherty, C., & Lees, M. (1988). Feminist psychodynamic therapies. In M. A. Dutton-Douglas & L. E. A. Walker (Eds.), *Feminist psychotherapies* (pp. 68–90). Norwood, NJ: ABLEX.

Deffenbacher, J. L. (1985). A cognitive-behavioral response and a modest proposal. *The Counseling Psychologist, 13*, 261–269.

DeVoge, J. T., & Beck, S. (1978). The therapist-client relationship in behavior therapy. In M. Hersen, R. M. Eisler, & P. M. Miller (Eds.), *Progress in behavior modification* (Vol. 6, pp. 203–248). New York: Academic Press.

Dolan, R. T., Arnkoff, D. B., & Glass, C. R. (1993). Client attachment style and the psychotherapeutic interpersonal stance. *Psychotherapy, 30,* 408–412.

Dollard, J., & Miller, N. E. (1950). *Personality and psychotherapy.* New York: McGraw-Hill.

Douglas, M. A. (1985). The role of power in feminist therapy: A reformulation. In L. B. Rosewater & L. E. A. Walker (Eds.), *Handbook of feminist therapy* (pp. 2241–249). New York: Springer.

Dutton-Douglas, M. A., & Walker, L. E. A. (1988). Introduction to feminist therapies. In M. A. Dutton-Douglas & L. E. A. Walker (Eds.), *Feminist psychotherapies* (pp. 3–11). Norwood, NJ: ABLEX.

Eagle, M. N. (1984). *Recent developments in psychoanalysis.* New York: McGraw-Hill.

Eagle, M. N., & Wolitzky, D. L. (1997). Empathy: A psychoanalytic perspective. In A. C. Bohart & L. S. Greenberg (Eds.), *Empathy reconsidered: New directions in psychotherapy* (pp. 217–244). Washington, DC: American Psychological Association.

Eichenbaum, L., & Orbach, S. (1983). *Understanding women: A feminist psychoanalytic approach.* New York: Basic Books.

Eichenbaum, L., & Orbach, S. (1984). Feminist psychoanalysis: Theory and practice. In C. M. Brody (Ed.), *Women therapists working with women* (pp. 46–55). New York: Springer.

Eisler, R. M., & Skidmore, J. R. (1987). MGRS: Scale development and component factors in the appraisal of stressful situations. *Behavior Modification, 11,* 123–136.

Elicker, J., Englund, M., & Stroufe, L. A. (1992). Predicting peer competence and peer relationships in childhood from early parent-child relationships. In R. Parke & G. Ladd (Eds.), *Handbook of social support and the family.* New York: Plenum Press.

Elliott, R., Hill, C. E., Stiles, W. B., Friedlander, M. L., Mahrer, A. R., & Margison, F. R. (1987). Primary response modes: A comparison of six rating systems. *Journal of Consulting and Clinical Psychology, 55,* 218–223.

Ellis, A. (1991). *The case against religiosity.* New York: Institute for Rational-Emotive Therapy.

Ellis, A. (1995). Rational-emotive therapy. In R. J. Corsini & D. Wedding (Eds.), *Current psychotherapies* (5th ed., pp. 162–196). Itasca, IL: Peacock.

Ellis, A. (1996). *Better, deeper, and more enduring brief therapy.* New York: Brunner/Mazel.

Ellis, A., & Dryden, W. (1997). *The practice of rational emotive behavior therapy.* New York: Springer.

Enns, C. Z. (1987). Gestalt therapy and feminist therapy: A proposed integration. *Journal of Counseling and Development, 66,* 93–95.

Enns, C. Z. (1993). Twenty years of feminist counseling and therapy. *The Counseling Psychologist, 21,* 3–87.

Enns, C. Z. (1997). *Feminist theories and feminist psychotherapies.* Binghamton, NY: Harrington Park.

Enns, C. Z., & Hackett, G. (1990). Comparison of feminist and nonfeminist women's reactions to variants of nonsexist and feminist counseling. *Journal of Counseling Psychology, 37,* 33–40.

Enns, C. Z., & Hackett, G. (1993). A comparison of feminist and nonfeminist women's and men's reactions to nonsexist and feminist counseling: A replication and extension. *Journal of Counseling and Development, 71,* 499–509.

Eugster, S. L., & Wampold, B. E. (1996). Systematic effects of participant role on evaluation of the psychotherapy session. *Journal of Consulting and Clinical Psychology, 64,* 1020–1028.

Eysenck, H. J. (1960). *Behavior therapy and the neuroses.* Oxford, England: Pergamon Press.

Eysenck, H. J. (1975). Some comments on the relation between A-B status of behavior therapists and success of treatment. *Journal of Consulting and Clinical Psychology, 43,* 86–87.

Farber, B. A., Lippert, R. A., & Nevas, D. B. (1995). The therapist as an attachment figure. *Psychotherapy, 32,* 204–212.

Fenichel, O. (1941). *The psychoanalytic theory of the neurosis.* New York: Norton.

Fenichel, O. (1945). *The psychoanalytic theory of the neurosis.* New York: Norton.

Fiedler, F. E. (1951). On different types of countertransference. *Journal of Clinical Psychology, 7,* 101–107.

Fine, R. (1990). *The history of psychoanalysis.* New York: Continuum.

Fitzgerald, L. F., & Nutt, R. (1986). The Division 17 principles concerning the counseling/psychotherapy of women. *The Counseling Psychologist, 14,* 180–216.

Flannery, J. (1995). Boredom in the therapist: Countertransference issues. *British Journal of Psychotherapy, 11,* 536–544.

Fodor, I. G. (1988). Cognitive behavior therapy: Evaluation of theory and practice for addressing women's issues. In M. A. Dutton-Douglas & L. E. A. Walker (Eds.), *Feminist psychotherapies* (pp. 91–117). Norwood, NJ: ABLEX.

Fonaghy, P., Leigh, T., Steele, M., Steele, H., Kennedy, R., Mattoon, G., Target, M., & Gerber, A. (1996). The relation of attachment status, psychiatric classification, and response to psychotherapy. *Journal of Consulting and Clinical Psychology, 64,* 22–31.

Frank, J. (1961). *Persuasion and healing.* Baltimore: Johns Hopkins University Press.

Freud, A. (1936). The ego and the mechanisms of defense. In *The writings of Anna Freud* (Vol. 2). New York: International Universities Press.

Freud, A. (1954). The widening scope of indications for psychoanalysis: Discussion. *Journal of the American Psychoanalytic Association, 2,* 607–620.

Freud, S. (1912). Recommendations for physicians on the psycho-analytic method of treatment. In J. Riviere (Trans. & Ed.), *Collected papers* (Vol. 2, pp. 323–333). New York: Basic Books.

Freud, S. (1913). On the beginning of treatment: Further recommendations on the technique of psychoanalysis. In J. Strachey (Ed.), *Standard edition of the complete psychological works of Sigmund Freud* (pp. 122–144). London: Hogarth Press.

Freud, S. (1915). Further recommendations in the technique of psycho-analysis: Observations on transference love. In J. Riviere (Trans. & Ed.), *Collected papers* (Vol. 2, pp. 377–390). New York: Basic Books.

Freud, S. (1919). Lines of advance in psychoanalytic therapy. In J. Strachey (Ed.). *Standard edition of the complete psychological works of Sigmund Freud* (Vol. 17, pp. 157–168). London: Hogarth Press.

Freud, S. (1923). The ego and the id. In J. Strachey (Ed.), *Standard edition of the complete psychological works of Sigmund Freud* (Vol. 19, pp. 3–66). London: Hogarth Press.

Freud, S. (1937). Analysis terminable and interminable. In J. Strachey (Ed.), *Standard edition of the complete psychological works of Sigmund Freud* (Vol. 23, pp. 209–253). London: Hogarth Press.

Freud, S. (1953). Fragment of an analysis of a case of hysteria. In J. Strachey (Ed.), *Standard edition of the complete psychological works of Sigmund Freud* (Vol. 7, pp. 15–122). London: Hogarth Press. (Original work published in 1905).

Freud, S. (1958). Remembering, repeating, and working through. In J. Strachey (Ed.), *Standard edition of the complete psychological works of Sigmund Freud* (Vol. 12, pp. 147–156). London: Hogarth Press. (Original work published in 1914).

Freud, S. (1959a). Fragment of an analysis of a case of hysteria. In E. Jones (Ed.) & J. Riviere (Trans.), *Collected papers* (Vol. 2, pp. 13–146). New York: Basic Books. (Original work published 1905)

Freud, S. (1959b). Future prospects of psychoanalytic psychotherapy. In J. Strachey (Ed.), *Standard edition of the complete psychological works of Sigmund Freud* (Vol. 20, pp. 87–172). London: Hogarth Press. (Original work published 1910)

Freud, S. (1959c). The dynamics of transference. In E. Jones (Ed.) & J. Riviere (Trans.), *Collected papers* (Vol. 2, pp. 312–322). New York: Basic Books. (Original work published in 1912)

Friedman, M. (1983). *The healing dialogue in psychotherapy.* New York: Jason Aronson.

Friedman, S., & Gelso, C. J. (1997, August). Development of the inventory of countertransference behavior. In J. A. Hayes (Chair.), *Exploring the therapist's inner world: Current research on countertransference.* Symposium conducted at the annual convention of the American Psychological Association, Chicago.

Fromm-Reichman, F. (1950). *Principles of intensive psychotherapy.* Chicago: University of Chicago Press.

Gabbard, G. O. (1995). Countertransference: The emerging common ground. *International Journal of Psychoanalysis, 76,* 475–485.

Gannon, L. (1982). The role of power in psychotherapy. *Women and Therapy, 1,* 3–11.

Gaston, L. (1990). The concept of the alliance and its role in psychotherapy: Theoretical and empirical considerations. *Psychotherapy, 27,* 143–153.

Gaston, L., & Marmar, C. R. (1994). The California Psychotherapy Alliance Scales. In A. O. Horvath & L. Greenberg (Eds.), *The working alliance: Theory, research, and practice* (pp. 85–108). New York: Wiley.

Gelso, C. J. (1992). Realities and emerging myths about brief therapy. *The Counseling Psychologist, 20,* 464–471.

Gelso, C. J. (1995). Theories, theoretical orientation, and theoretical dimensions: Comment on Poznanski & McLennan (1995). *Journal of Counseling Psychology, 42,* 426–427.

Gelso, C. J., & Carter, J. A. (1985). The relationship in counseling and psychotherapy: Components, consequences, and theoretical antecedents. *The Counseling Psychologist, 13,* 155–243.

Gelso, C. J., & Carter, J. A. (1994a). Components of the psychotherapy relationship: Their interaction and unfolding during treatment. *Journal of Counseling Psychology, 41,* 296–306.

Gelso, C. J., & Carter, J. A. (1994b). Level of generality and clear thinking in theory construction and theory evaluation: A reply to Greenberg (1994) and Patton (1994). *Journal of Counseling Psychology, 41,* 313–314.

Gelso, C. J., Fassinger, R. E., Gomez, M. J., & Latts, M. G. (1995). Countertransference reactions to lesbian clients: The role of homophobia, counselor gender, and countertransference management. *Journal of Counseling Psychology, 42,* 356–364.

Gelso, C. J., & Fretz, B. R. (1992). *Counseling psychology.* Fort Worth: Harcourt Brace Jovanovich.

Gelso, C. J., Hill, C. E., & Kivlighan, D. M. (1991). Transference, insight, and the counselor's intentions during a counseling hour. *Journal of Counseling and Development, 69,* 428–433.

Gelso, C. J., Hill, C. E., Mohr, J., Rochlen, A., & Zack, J. (1998). *The face of transference in long-term psychotherapy: A qualitative study.* Manuscript submitted for review.

Gelso, C. J., & Johnson, D. H. (1983). *Explorations in time-limited counseling and psychotherapy.* New York: Columbia University, Teachers College Press.

Gelso, C. J., Kivlighan, D. M., Wine, B., Jones, A., & Friedman, S. C. (1997). Transference, insight, and the course of time-limited therapy. *Journal of Counseling Psychology, 44,* 209–217.

Gelso, C. J., Mills, D. H., & Spiegel, S. B. (1983). Client and therapist factors influencing the outcome of time-limited counseling one and 18 months after treatment. In C. J. Gelso & D. H. Johnson (Eds.), *Explorations in time-limited counseling and psychotherapy.* New York: Columbia University, Teachers College Press.

George, C., Kaplan, N., & Main, M. (1996). *Adult attachment interview.* Unpublished protocol, Department of Psychology, University of California, Berkeley.

Gilbert, L. A. (1980). Feminist therapy. In A. Brodsky & R. T. Hare-Mustin (Eds.), *Women and psychotherapy* (pp. 245–265). New York: Guilford Press.

Gill, M. M. (1954). Psychoanalysis and exploratory psychotherapy. *Journal of the American Psychoanalytic Association, 2,* 771–797.

Gill, M. M. (1982). *Analysis of transference* (Vol. 1). New York: International Universities Press.

Gill, M. M. (1984). Psychoanalysis and psychotherapy: A revision. *International Review of Psychoanalysis, 11,* 161–179.

Gill, M. M. (1985). The interactional aspect of transference: Range of application. In E. A. Schwaber (Ed.), *The transference in psychotherapy: Clinical management* (pp. 87–102). New York: International Universities Press.

Gilligan, C. (1982). *In a different voice.* Cambridge, MA: Harvard University Press.

Gladstein, G. A. (1983). Understanding empathy: Integrating counseling, developmental, and social psychology perspectives. *Journal of Counseling Psychology, 30,* 467–482.

Glover, E. (1955). *The technique of psychoanalysis.* New York: International Universities Press.

Goldberg, A. (1988). *A fresh look at psychoanalysis: The view from self psychology.* Hillsdale, NJ: Analytic Press.

Golden, B. R., & Robbins, S. B. (1990). The working alliance within time-limited therapy: A case analysis. *Professional Psychology Research and Practice, 21,* 476–481.

Gorkin, M. (1987). *The uses of countertranference.* Northvale, NJ: Jason Aronson.

Graff, H., & Luborsky, L. L. (1977). Long-term trends in transference and resistance: A report on a quantitative-analytic method applied to four psychoanalyses. *Journal of the American Psychoanalytic Association, 25,* 471–490.

Greenberg, J., & Mitchell, S. A. (1983). *Object relations in psychoanalytic theory.* Cambridge, MA: Harvard University Press.

Greenberg, L. (1985). An integrative approach to the relationship in counseling and psychotherapy. *The Counseling Psychologist, 13,* 251–259.

Greenberg, L. S. (1983). The relationship in Gestalt therapy. In M. J. Lambert (Ed.), *Psychotherapy and patient relationships* (pp. 126–153). Homewood, IL: Dow Jones-Irwin.

Greenberg, L. S. (1994). What is "real" in the relationship? Comment of Gelso & Carter (1994). *Journal of Counseling Psychology, 41,* 307–309.

Greenberg, L. S., & Elliott, R. (1997). Varieties of empathic responding. In A. C. Bohart & L. S. Greenberg (Eds.), *Empathy reconsidered: New directions in psychotherapy* (pp. 167–186). Washington, DC: American Psychological Association.

Greenberg, L. S., & Goldman, R. (1988). Training in experiential psychotherapy. *Journal of Consulting and Clinical Psychology, 56,* 696–702.

Greenberg, L. S., Rice, L. N., & Elliott, R. (1993). *Process-experiential therapy: Facilitating emotional change.* New York: Guilford Press.

Greenson, R. R. (1965). The working alliance and the transference neurosis. *Psychoanalysis Quarterly, 34,* 155–181.

Greenson, R. R. (1967). *The technique and practice of psychoanalysis* (Vol. 1). New York: International Universities Press.

Greenson, R. R. (1978). *Explorations in psychoanalysis.* New York: International Universities Press.

Harper, F. D., & Bruce-Sanford, G. C. (1989). *Counseling techniques: An outline and overview.* Alexandria, VA: Douglass.

Harper, R. A. (1959). *Psychoanalysis and psychotherapy: 36 systems.* Englewood Cliffs, NJ: Prentice-Hall.

Hart, J. T. (1970). The development of client-centered therapy. In J. T. Hart & T. M. Tomlinson (Eds.), *New directions in client-centered therapy.* Boston: Houghton Mifflin.

Hartmann, H. (1964). Psychoanalysis and the concept of health. In H. Hartmann (Ed.), *Essays on ego psychology* (pp. 1–18). New York: International Universities Press. (Original work published 1939)

Hayes, J. A. (1992, August). *The current status of theoretical and empirical literature on countertransference.* Paper presented at the annual convention of the American Psychological Association, Washington, DC.

Hayes, J. A. (1995). Countertransference in group psychotherapy: Waking a sleeping dog. *International Journal of Group Psychotherapy, 45,* 521–535.

Hayes, J. A., & Gelso, C. J. (1991). Effects of therapist-trainees' anxiety and empathy on countertransference behavior. *Journal of Clinical Psychology, 47,* 284–290.

Hayes, J. A., & Gelso, C. J. (1993). Counselors' discomfort with gay and HIV-infected clients. *Journal of Counseling Psychology, 40,* 86–93.

Hayes, J. A., Gelso, C. J., Van Wagoner, S. L., & Diemer, R. A. (1991). Managing countertransference: What the experts think. *Psychological Reports, 69,* 139–148.

Hayes, J. A., McCracken, J. E., McClanahan, M. K., Hill, C. E., Harp, J. S., & Carozzoni, P. (1998). *Therapist perspectives on countertransference: Qualitative data in search of a theory.* Manuscript in preparation.

Hayes, J. A., Riker, J. R., & Ingram, K. M. (1997). Countertransference behavior and management in brief counseling: A field study. *Psychotherapy Research, 7,* 145–153.

Heimann, P. (1950). On countertranference. *International Journal of Psychoanalysis, 31,* 81–84.

Heimann, P. (1960). Countertransference. *British Journal of Medical Psychology, 33,* 9–15.

Heller, D. (1985). *Power in psychotherapeutic practice.* New York: Human Sciences.

Henry, W. P., & Strupp, H. H. (1994). The therapeutic alliance as interpersonal process. In A. O. Horvath & L. Greenberg (Eds.), *The working alliance: Theory, research, and practice* (pp. 51–84). New York: Wiley.

Heppner, P. P., & Claiborn, C. D. (1989). Social influence research in counseling: A review and critique. *Journal of Counseling Psychology, 36,* 365–387.

Heppner, P. P., & Heesacker, M. (1983). Perceived counselor characteristics, client expectations, and client satisfaction with counseling. *Journal of Counseling Psychology, 30,* 31–39.

Hill, C. E. (1990). Review of exploratory in-session process research. *Journal of Consulting and Clinical Psychology, 58,* 288–294.

Hill, C. E. (1994). What is the therapeutic relationship? A reaction to Sexton and Whiston. *The Counseling Psychologist, 22,* 90–97.

Hill, C. E., Nutt-Williams, E., Heaton, K. J., Thompson, B. J., & Rhodes, R. H. (1996). Therapist retrospective recall of impasses in long-term psychotherapy: A qualitative analysis. *Journal of Counseling Psychology, 43,* 207–217.

Hill, C. E., Thompson, B. J., & Williams, E. N. (1997). A guide to conducting consensual qualitative research. *The Counseling Psychologist, 25,* 517–572.

Holmes, J. (1993). *John Bowlby and the attachment theory.* London: Routledge & Kegan Paul.

Horvath, A. O. (1982). *Users' manual of the Working Alliance Inventory.* Unpublished manuscript No. 82:2, Simon Fraser University, Canada.

Horvath, A. O. (1991, June). *What do we know about the alliance and what do we still have to find out?* Paper presented at the annual meeting of the Society for Psychotherapy Research, Lyon, France.

Horvath, A. O., Gaston, L., & Luborsky, L. (1993). The therapeutic alliance and its measures. In N. E. Miller, L. Luborsky, J. P. Barber, & J. P. Docherty (Eds.), *Psychoanalytic treatment research: A handbook for clinical practice* (pp. 247–273). New York: Basic Books.

Horvath, A. O., & Greenberg, L. (1989). Development and validation of the Working Alliance Inventory. *Journal of Counseling Psychology, 36,* 223–232.

Horvath, A. O., & Greenberg, L. (1994). *The working alliance: Theory, research, and practice.* New York: Wiley.

Horvath A. O., & Marx, R. W. (1990). The development and decay of the working alliance during time-limited counselling. *Canadian Journal of Counselling, 24,* 240–260.

Horvath, A. O., & Symonds, B. D. (1991). Relation between working alliance and outcome in psychotherapy: A meta-analysis. *Journal of Counseling Psychology, 38,* 133–149.

Horwitz, L. (1974). *Clinical prediction in psychotherapy.* New York: Jason Aronson.

Hoshmand, L. T., & Martin, J. (1994). Naturalizing the epistemology of psychological research. *Journal of Theoretical and Philosophical Psychology, 14,* 171–189.

Howard, D. V. (1983). *Cognitive psychology.* New York: Macmillan.

Howard, G. S. (1986). *Dare we develop a human science?* Notre Dame, IN: Academic Press.

Hycner, R., & Jacobs, L. (1995). *The healing relationship in Gestalt therapy.* Highland, NY: Gestalt Journal Press.

Jacobson, N. (1989). The therapist-client relationship in cognitive behavior therapy: Implications for treating depression. *Journal of Cognitive Psychotherapy, 3,* 85–96.

Josselson, S. (1987). *Finding herself: Pathways to identity development in women.* San Francisco: Jossey-Bass.

Kahn, E. (1989). Carl Rogers and Heins Kohut: Toward a constructive collaboration. *Psychotherapy, 26,* 555–563.

Kahn, E. (1996). The intersubjective perspective and the client-centered approach: Are they one at the core. *Psychotherapy, 33,* 30–42.

Kahn, M. (1991). *Between therapist and client.* New York: Freeman.

Kanfer, F., & Phillips, J. (1966). Behavior therapy. *Archives of General Psychiatry, 15,* 114–128.

Kazdin, A. (1980). *Behavior modification in applied settings.* Homewood, IL: Dorsey Press.

Kelly, G. A. (1955). *The psychology of personal constructs.* New York: Norton.

Kernberg, O. (1965). Notes on countertransference. *Journal of the American Psychoanalytic Association, 13,* 38–56.

Kernberg, O. (1975). *Borderline conditions and pathological narcissism.* New York: Jason Aronson.

Kiesler, D. J. (1982). Interpersonal theory for personality and psychotherapy. In J. C. Anchin & D. J. Kiesler (Eds.), *Handbook of interpersonal psychotherapy* (pp. 3–24). New York: Pergamon Press.

Kiesler, D. J. (1996). *Contemporary interpersonal theory and research.* New York: Wiley.

Kivlighan, D. M., Gelso, C. J., Wine, B., & Jones-Cady, A. (1987, August). *The development of working alliance, transference, and countertransference in time-limited psychotherapy.* Paper presented at the annual meeting of the American Psychological Association, New York.

Kivlighan, D. M., & Shaugnessy, P. (1995). *Temporal dimensions of working alliance: A cluster analytic typology of client working alliance ratings.* Paper presented at the annual convention of American Psychological Association, New York.

Knox, S., Hess, S. A., Petersen, D. A., & Hill, C. E. (1997). A qualitative analysis of client perceptions of the effects of helpful therapist self-disclosure in long-term therapy. *Journal of Counseling Psychology, 44,* 274–283.

Kohut, H. (1959). Introspection, empathy, and psychoanalysis: An examination of the relationship between mode of observation and theory. In P. H. Ornstein (Ed.), *The search for the self* (Vol. 1, pp. 205–232). New York: International Universities Press.

Kohut, H. (1971). *The analysis of the self* (The Psychoanalytic Study of the Child, Monograph No. 4). New York: International Universities Press.

Kohut, H. (1977). *The restoration of the self.* New York: International Universities Press.

Kohut, H. (1984). *How does analysis cure?* Chicago: University of Chicago Press.

Kokotovic, A. M., & Tracey, T. J. (1990). Working alliance in the early phase of counseling. *Journal of Counseling Psychology, 37,* 16–21.

Krupnick, J., Stotsky, S., Simmens, S., & Moyer, J. (1992, June). *The role of therapeutic alliance in psychotherapy and pharmacology outcome: Findings in the NIMH treatment of depression collaborative research program.* Paper presented at the annual meeting of the Society for Psychotherapy Research, Berkeley, CA.

Lachmann, F. M., & Beebe, B. (1992). Reformulations of early development and transference: Implications for psychic structure formation. In J. W. Barron, M. N. Eagle, & D. L. Wolitzky (Eds.), *Interface of psychoanalysis and psychology* (pp. 133–153). Washington, DC: American Psychological Association.

Laidlaw, T. A., & Malmo, C. (1990). Introduction: Feminist therapy and psychological healing. In T. A. Laidlaw & C. Malmo (Eds.), *Healing voices: Feminist approaches to therapy with women* (pp. 1–11). San Francisco: Jossey-Bass.

Lambert, M. J. (Ed.). (1983). *A guide to psychotherapy and patient relationships.* Homewood, IL: Dow Jones-Irwin.

Lambert, M. J., & Bergin, A. E. (1994). The effectiveness of psychotherapy. In A. E. Bergin & S. L. Garfield (Eds.) *Handbook of psychotherapy and behavior change* (4th ed., pp. 143–189). New York: Wiley.

Lang, P. (1969). The mechanics of desensitization and the laboratory study of human fear. In C. Franks (Ed.), *Behavior therapy: Appraisal and status.* New York: McGraw-Hill.

Langs, R. J. (1974). *The technique of psychoanalytic psychotherapy* (Vol. 2). New York: Jason Aronson.

Latts, M. G., & Gelso, C. J. (1995). Countertransference behavior and management with survivors of sexual assault. *Psychotherapy, 32,* 405–415.

Latts, M. G., Gelso, C. J., Gomez, M. J., & Fassinger, R. E. (1997). *The management of countertransference as related to therapy outcome.* Manuscript in preparation.

Layton, M. (1994). Epilogue: The maternal presence in psychotherapy. In M. P. Mirkin (Ed.), *Women in context* (pp. 482–491). New York: Guilford Press.

Lazarus, A. A. (1989). *The practice of multimodal therapy.* New York: McGraw-Hill.

Lazarus, A. A. (1995). Multimodal therapy. In R. J. Corsini & D. Wedding (Eds.), *Current psychotherapies* (5th ed., pp. 322–355). Itasca, IL: Peacock.

Lazarus, A. A., & Abramowitz, A. (1962). The use of emotive imagery in the treatment of a children's phobia. *Journal of Mental Science, 108,* 191–195.

Leary, T. (1957). *Interpersonal diagnosis of personality.* New York: Ronald Press.

Lecours, S., Bouchard, M., & Normandin, L. (1995). Countertransference as the therapist's mental activity: Experience and gender differences among psychoanalytically oriented psychologists. *Psychoanalytic Psychology, 12,* 259–280.

Linden, J. A. (1994). Gratification and provision in psychoanalysis: Should we get rid of the "rule of abstinence"? *Psychoanalytic Dialogues, 4,* 549–582.

Liotti, G. (1991). Patterns of attachment and the assessment of interpersonal schemata: Understanding and changing difficult patient-therapist relationships in cognitive psychotherapy. *Journal of Cognitive Psychotherapy, 5,* 105–114.

Little, M. (1951). Countertransference and the patient's response to it. *International Journal of Psychoanalysis, 32,* 32–40.

Little, M. (1960). Countertransference. *British Journal of Medical Psychology, 33,* 29–31.

London, P. (1972). The end of ideology in behavior modification. *American Psychologist, 27,* 913–920.

Lopez, F. G. (1995). Contemporary attachment theory: An introduction with implications for counseling psychology. *The Counseling Psychologist, 23,* 395–415.

Luborsky, L. (1976). Helping alliances in psychotherapy. In J. L. Cleghorn (Ed.), *Successful psychotherapy* (pp. 92–116). New York: Brunner/Mazel.

Luborsky, L. (1977). Measuring a pervasive psychic structure in psychotherapy: The core conflictual relationship theme. In L. Freedman & S. Grand (Eds.), *Communicative structures and psychic structures* (pp. 367–395). New York: Plenum Press.

Luborsky, L. (1993). Documenting symptom formation during psychotherapy. In N. E. Miller, L. Luborsky, J. P. Barber, & J. Doherty (Eds.), *Psychodynamic treatment research* (pp. 3–13). New York: Basic Books.

Luborsky, L., & Barber, J. P. (1994). Perspectives on seven transference-related measures applied to the interview with Ms. Smithfield. *Psychotherapy Research, 3/4,* 172–183.

Luborsky, L., Barber, J. P., Binder, J., Curtis, J., Dahl, H., Horowitz, L. M., Horowitz, M., Perry, J. C., Schacht, T., Silberschatz, G., & Teller, V. (1993). Transference-related measures: A new class based on psychotherapy sessions. In N. E. Miller, L. Luborsky, J. P. Barber, & J. P. Docherty (Eds.), *Psychodynamic treatment research: A handbook for clinical practice* (pp. 326–341). New York: Basic Books.

Luborsky, L., Crits-Christoph, P. (1990). *Understanding transferences.* New York, Basic Books.

Luborsky, L., Popp, C., Luborsky, E., & Mark, D. (1994). The core conflictual relationship theme. *Psychotherapy Research, 4,* 172–183.

Maeder, T. (1989, January). Wounded healers. *Atlantic Monthly,* 37–47.

Mahoney, M. J. (1995). Theoretical developments in the cognitive and constructive psychotherapies. In M. J. Mahoney (Ed.), *Cognitive and constructive psychotherapies* (pp. 3–19). New York: Springer.

Mahrer, A. R. (1983). *Experiential psychotherapy: Basic practices.* New York: Brunner/Mazel.

Mahrer, A. R. (1986). *Therapeutic experiencing.* New York: Norton.

Mahrer, A. R. (1989). *How to do experiential psychotherapy: A manual for practitioners.* Ottawa, Canada: University of Ottawa Press.

Mahrer, A. R. (1996). *The complete guide to experiential psychotherapy.* New York: Wiley.

Mahrer, A. R. (1997). Empathy as therapist-client alignment. In A. C. Bohart & L. S. Greenberg (Eds.), *Empathy reconsidered: New directions in psychotherapy* (pp. 187–213). Washington, DC: American Psychological Association.

Main, M. (1996). Introduction to the special section on attachment and psychopathology: 2. Overview of the field of attachment. *Journal of Consulting and Clinical Psychology, 64,* 237–243.

Main, M., Kaplan, N., & Cassidy J. (1985). Security in infancy, childhood, and adulthood: A move to the level of representation. In I. Bretherton & E. Waters (Eds.), Growing points of attachment theory and research. *Monographs of the Society for Research in Child Development, 50*(1/2, Serial No. 209), 66–104.

Mallinckrodt, B., Coble, H. M., & Gantt, D. L. (1995a). Toward differentiating client attachment from working alliance and transference: A reply to Robbins. *Journal of Counseling Psychology, 42,* 320–322.

Mallinckrodt, B., Coble, H. M., & Gantt, D. G. (1995b). Working alliance, attachment memories, and social competencies of women in brief therapy. *Journal of Counseling Psychology, 42,* 79–84.

Mallinckrodt, B., Gantt, D. L., & Coble, H. M. (1995). Attachment patterns in the psychotherapy relationship: Development of the Client Attachment to Therapist Scale. *Journal of Counseling Psychology, 42,* 307–317.

Mann, J. (1973). *Time-limited psychotherapy.* Cambridge, MA: Harvard University Press.

Margolies, L. (1990). Cracks in the frame: Feminism and the boundaries of therapy. *Women and Therapy, 9,* 19–35.

Marmar, C. R., Horowitz, M. J., Weiss, D. S., & Marziali, E. (1986). The development of the therapeutic alliance rating system. In L. S. Greenberg & W. M. Pinsof (Eds.), *The psychotherapeutic process: A research handbook* (pp. 367–390). New York: Guilford Press.

May, R. (1983). *The discovery of being.* New York: Norton.

May, R. (1989). *The art of counseling* (Rev. ed.). New York: Gardner Press. (Original work published 1939)

McClure, B. A., & Hodge, R. W. (1987). Measuring countertransference and attitude in therapeutic relationships. *Psychotherapy, 24,* 325–335.

McLeod, E. (1994). *Women's experience of feminist therapy and counselling.* Buckingham, England: Open University.

McNeil, B. W., May, R. J., & Lee, V. E. (1987). Perceptions of counselor source characteristics by premature and successful terminators. *Journal of Counseling Psychology, 34,* 86–89.

Meador, B. D., & Rogers, C. R. (1984). Person-centered therapy. In R. J. Corsini (Ed.), *Current psychotherapies* (3rd ed., pp. 142–195). Itasca, IL: Peacock.

Meichenbaum, D. (1985). *Stress inoculation training.* New York: Pergamon Press.

Meissner, W. W. (1991). A decade of psychoanalytic praxis. *Psychoanalytic Inquiry, 11,* 30–64.

Menaker, E. (1942). The masochistic factor in the psychoanalytic situation. *Psychoanalytic Quarterly, 11,* 171–186.

Miller, J. B. (1976). *Toward a new psychology of women.* Boston: Beacon Press.

Miller, J. B. (1992). Women and power. In J. V. Jordan, A. G. Kaplan, J. B. Miller, I. P. Stiver, & J. L. Surrey (Eds.), *Women's growth in connection: Writings from the Stone Center* (pp. 197–205). New York: Guilford Press.

Miller, J. M., Courtois, C. A., Pelham, J. P., Riddle, P. E., Spiegel, S. B., Gelso, C. J., & Johnson, D. H. (1983). The process of time-limited therapy. In C. J. Gelso & D. H. Johnson (Eds.), *Explorations in time-limited counseling and psychotherapy* (pp. 175–184). New York: Teachers College Press.

Miller, N. E., Luborsky, L., Barber, J. P., & Docherty, J. P. (Eds.). (1993). *Psychodynamic treatment research.* New York: Basic Books.

Mirkin, M. P. (1994). Introduction. In M. P. Mirkin (Ed.), *Women in context* (pp. 1–5). New York: Guilford Press.

Mishne, J. M. (1994). *The evolution and application of clinical theory: Perspectives from four psychologies.* New York: Free Press.

Mitchell, S. A. (1988). *Relational concepts in psychoanalysis.* Cambridge, MA: Harvard University Press.

Mitchell, S. A. (1991). Wishes, needs and interpersonal negotiations. *Psychoanalytic Inquiry, 11,* 147–170.

Mitchell, S. A. (1993). *Hope and dread in psychoanalysis.* New York: Basic Books.

Morris, R. J., & Magrath, K. H. (1983). The therapeutic relationship in behavior therapy. In M. J. Lambert (Ed.), *Psychotherapy and patient relationships* (pp. 154–189). Homewood, IL: Dow Jones-Irwin.

Mowbray, C. T. (1995). Nonsexist therapy: Is it? *Women and Therapy, 16,* 9–30.

Mowrer, O. H. (1964). Freudianism, behavior therapy, and "self-disclosure." *Behaviour Research and Therapy, 1,* 321–331.

Multon, K. D., Patton, M. J., & Kivlighan, D. M. (1996). Development of the Missouri Identifying Transference Scale. *Journal of Counseling Psychology, 43,* 243–252.

Normandin, L., & Bouchard, M. A. (1993). The effects of theoretical orientation and experience on rational, reactive, and reflective countertransference. *Psychotherapy Research, 3,* 77–94.

O'Neil, J. M., Helms, B. J., Gable, R. K., David, L., & Wrightsman, L. S. (1986). Gender-role conflict scale: College men's fear of femininity. *Sex Roles, 14,* 335–350.

Orlinsky, D. E., Grawe, K., & Parks, B. K. (1994). Process and outcome in psychotherapy—noch einmal. In A. E. Bergin & S. L. Garfield (Eds.), *Handbook of psychotherapy and behavior change* (4th ed., pp. 270–376). New York: Wiley.

Orlinsky, D. E., & Howard, K. I. (1986). Process and outcome in psychotherapy. In S. L. Garfield & A. E. Bergin (Eds.), *Handbook of psychotherapy and behavior change* (3rd ed., pp. 311–381). New York: Wiley.

Orlinsky, D. E., & Howard, K. I. (1987). A generic model of psychotherapy. *Journal of Integrative and Eclectic Psychotherapy, 6,* 6–27.

Orr, D. W. (1988). Transference and countertransference: A historical survey. In B. Wolstein (Ed.), *Essential papers on countertransference* (pp. 91–110). New York: New York University. (Original work published 1954)

Padesky, C. A. (1996). Developing cognitive therapist competency: Teaching and supervision models. In P. M. Salkovskis (Ed.), *Frontiers of cognitive therapy* (pp. 266–292). New York: Guilford Press.

Patterson, C. H. (1984). Empathy, warmth, and genuineness in psychotherapy: A review of reviews. *Psychotherapy: Theory, Research, and Practice, 21,* 431–439.

Patton, M. J. (1994). Components of the counseling relationship—An evolving model: Comment of Gelso & Carter (1994). *Journal of Counseling Psychology, 41,* 310–312.

Patton, M. J., Kivlighan, D. M., & Multon, K. D. (1997). The Missouri psychoanalytic counseling research project: Relation of changes in counseling process and outcome. *Journal of Counseling Psychology, 44,* 189–208.

Patton, M. J., & Meara, N. M. (1992). *Psychoanalytic counseling.* New York: Wiley.

Peabody, S. A., & Gelso, C. J. (1982). Countertransference and empathy: The complex relationship between two divergent concepts in counseling. *Journal of Counseling Psychology, 29,* 240–245.

Peck, M. S. (1983). *People of the lie.* New York: Simon & Schuster.

Perls, F. S. (1947). *Ego, hunger, and aggression.* New York: Random House.

Perls, F. S. (1958). *Gestalt therapy.* New York: Julian.

Perls, F. S. (1969). *Gestalt therapy verbatim.* Lafayette, CA: Real People Press.

Perls, F. S. (1973). *The Gestalt approach.* Palo Alto, CA: Science and Behavior.

Perls, F. S., Hefferline, R., & Goodman, P. (1951). *Gestalt therapy.* New York: Dell.

Perls, L. (1976). Comments on new directions. In E. W. L. Smith (Ed.), *The growing edge of Gestalt therapy* (pp. 221–226). New York: Brunner/Mazel.

Persons, J. B., & Burns, D. D. (1985). Mechanisms of action in cognitive therapy: The relative contributions of technical and interpersonal interventions. *Cognitive Therapy and Research, 9,* 539–551.

Phillips, F. B. (1990). NTU psychotherapy: An Afrocentric approach. *Journal of Black Psychology, 17,* 55–74.

Pine, F. (1990). *Drive, ego, object, and self: A synthesis for clinical work.* New York: Basic Books.

Piper, W. E., Azim, H. F., Joyce, A. S., McCallum, M., Nixon, G. W. H., & Segal, P. S. (1991). Quality of object relations vs. interpersonal functioning as predictor of therapeutic alliance and psychotherapy outcome. *Journal of Nervous and Mental Disease, 179,* 432–438.

Polster, E., & Polster, M. (1973). *Gestalt therapy integrated.* New York: Vintage Books.

Poznanski, J. J., & McLennan, J. (1995a). Afterthoughts on counselor theoretical orientation. *Journal of Counseling psychology, 42,* 428–430.

Poznanski, J. J., & McLennan, J. (1995b). Conceptualizing and measuring counselors' theoretical orientation. *Journal of Counseling Psychology, 42,* 411–422.

Prochaska, J. O. (1979). *Systems of psychotherapy: A transtheoretical analysis.* Homewood, IL: Dorsey Press.

Prozan, C. K. (1993). *The technique of feminist psychoanalytic psychotherapy.* Northvale, NJ: Jason Aronson.

Pulver, S. E. (1991). Psychoanalytic technique: Progress during the past decade. *Psychoanalytic Inquiry, 11,* 65–87.

Rabin, H. M. (1995). The liberating effect on the analyst of the paradigm shift in psychoanalysis. *Psychoanalytic Psychology, 12,* 467–482.

Raskin, N. J., & Rogers, C. R. (1995). Person-centered therapy. In R. J. Corsini & D. Wedding (Eds.), *Current psychotherapies* (5th ed., pp. 128–161). Itasca, IL: Peacock.

Raue, P. J., Castonguay, L. G., & Goldfried, M. R. (1993). The working alliance: A comparison of two therapies. *Psychotherapy Research, 3,* 197–207.

Reich, A. (1951). On countertransference. *International Journal of Psychoanalysis, 32,* 25–31.

Rhoads, J. M., & Feather, B. F. (1972). Transference and resistance observed in behavior therapy. *Journal of Medical Psychology, 45,* 99–103.

Rhodes, R. H., Hill, C. E., Thompson, B. J., & Elliott, R. (1994). Client retrospective recall of resolved and unresolved misunderstanding events. *Journal of Counseling Psychology, 31,* 473–483.

Rice, L. N. (1983). The relationship in client-centered therapy. In M. J. Lambert (Ed.), *Psychotherapy and patient relationships* (pp. 36–60). Homewood, IL: Dow Jones-Irwin.

Richardson, M. S. (1997). Toward a clinically relevant model of counseling research: Comments on Patton, Kivlighan, & Multon (1997) and Gelso, Kivlighan, Wine, Jones, & Friedman (1997). *Journal of Counseling Psychology, 44,* 218–221.

Richardson, M. S. (in press). Transference. *Encyclopedia of Psychology.*

Robbins, S. B. (1989). The role of contemporary psychoanalysis in counseling psychology. *Journal of Counseling Psychology, 36,* 267–278.

Robbins, S. B. (1995). Attachment perspectives on the counseling relationship: Comment on Mallinckrodt, Coble, & Gantt (1995). *Journal of Counseling Psychology, 42,* 318–319.

Robbins, S. B., & Jolkovski, M. P. (1987). Managing countertransference feelings: An interactional model using awareness of feeling and theoretical framework. *Journal of Counseling Psychology, 34,* 276–282.

Robertiello, R. C., & Schoenewolf, G. (1987). *101 common therapeutic blunders: Countertransference and counterresistance in psychotherapy.* Northvale, NJ: Aronson.

Robins, C. J., & Hayes, A. M. (1995). An appraisal of cognitive therapy. In M. J. Mahoney (Ed.), *Cognitive and constructive psychotherapies* (pp. 41–65). New York: Springer.

Rogers, A. G. (1991). A feminist poetics of psychotherapy. In C. Gilligan, A. G. Rogers, & D. L. Tolman (Eds.), *Women, girls, and psychotherapy: Reframing resistance* (pp. 33–53). Binghamton, NY: Harrington Park.

Rogers, C. R. (1942). *Counseling and psychotherapy.* Cambridge, MA: Riverside Press.

Rogers, C. R. (1951). *Client-centered therapy.* Boston: Houghton Mifflin.

Rogers, C. R. (1957). The necessary and sufficient conditions of therapeutic personality change. *Journal of Consulting Psychology, 21,* 95–103.

Rogers, C. R. (1961). *On becoming a person.* Boston: Houghton Mifflin.

Rogers, C. R. (1975). Empathy: An unappreciated way of being. *The Counseling Psychologist, 5*, 2–10.

Rogers, C. R. (1977). *Carl Rogers on personal power.* New York: Delacorte Press.

Rogers, C. R. (1980). *A way of being.* Boston: Houghton Mifflin.

Rogers, C. R. (1986). Client-centered therapy. In I. L. Jutash & A. Wolf (Eds.), *Psychotherapist's casebook: Therapy and technique in practice* (pp. 197–208). San Francisco: Jossey-Bass.

Rosenberger, E. W., & Hayes, J. A. (1998). *Through a looking glass somewhat clearly: A case study of countertransference.* Manuscript in preparation.

Rosso, S. M., & Frey, H. D. (1973). An assessment of the gap between counseling theory and practice. *Journal of Counseling Psychology, 20*, 471–476.

Rothstein, M. M., & Robinson, P. J. (1991). The therapeutic relationship and resistance to change in cognitive therapy. In T. M. Vallis, J. L. Howes, & P. C. Miller (Eds.), *The challenge of cognitive therapy* (pp. 43–55). New York: Plenum Press.

Russell, M. N. (1984). *Skills in counseling women: The feminist approach.* Springfield, IL: Thomas.

Ryan, E. R., & Cicchetti, D. V. (1985). Predicting quality of alliance in the initial psychotherapy interview. *Journal of Nervous and Mental Disease, 173*, 717–725.

Ryan, V. L., & Gizynski, M. N. (1971). Behavior therapy in retrospect: Patients' feelings about their behavior therapy. *Journal of Consulting and Clinical Psychology, 37*, 1–9.

Safran, J. D., Crocker, P., McMain, S., & Murray, P. (1990). Therapeutic alliance rupture as a therapy event for empirical investigation. *Psychotherapy, 27*, 154–165.

Safran, J. D., & Greenberg, L. S. (1987). Affect and the unconscious: A cognitive perspective. In R. Stern (Ed.), *Theories of the unconscious* (pp. 191–212). Hillsdale, NJ: Analytic Press.

Safran, J. D., Muran, J. C., & Samstag, L. W. (1994). Resolving therapeutic alliance ruptures: A task analytic investigation. In A. O. Horvath & L. Greenberg (Eds.), *The working alliance: Theory, research, and practice* (pp. 225–258). New York: Wiley.

Safran, J. D., & Segal, Z. V. (1990). *Interpersonal process in cognitive therapy.* New York: Basic Books.

Salvio, M. A., Beutler, L. E., Wood, J. M., & Engle, D. (1992). The strength of the therapeutic alliance in three treatments for depression. *Psychotherapy Research, 2*, 31–36.

Schafer, R. (1983). *The analytic attitude.* New York: Basic Books.

Schlachet, B. C. (1984). Female role socialization: The analyst and the analysis. In C. M. Brody (Ed.), *Women therapists working with women* (pp. 56–65). New York: Springer.

Schwaber, E. A. (Ed.). (1985). *The transference in psychotherapy: Clinical management.* New York: International Universities Press.

Segal, Z. (1988). Appraisal of the self-schema: Construct in cognitive models of depression. *Psychological Bulletin, 103*, 147–162.

Sexton, T. L., & Whiston, S. C. (1994). The status of the counseling relationship: An empirical review, theoretical implications, and research directions. *The Counseling Psychologist, 22*, 6–78.

Sharkin, B., & Gelso, C. J. (1993). The influence of counselor-trainee anger proneness on reactions to an angry client. *Journal of Counseling and Development, 71*, 483–487.

Sherman, M. (1965). Peripheral cues and the invisible countertransference. *American Journal of Psychotherapy, 19,* 280–292.

Shlien, J. (1997). Empathy in psychotherapy: A vital mechanism? Yes. Therapist's conceit? All too often. By itself enough? No. In A. C. Bohart & L. S. Greenberg (Eds.), *Empathy reconsidered: New directions in psychotherapy* (pp. 63–80). Washington, DC: American Psychological Association.

Singer, B. A., & Luborsky, L. (1977). Countertransference: The status of clinical versus quantitative research. In A. S. Gurman & A. M. Razdin (Eds.), *Effective psychotherapy: Handbook of research* (pp. 433–451). New York: Pergamon Press.

Singer, E. (1970). *Key concepts in psychotherapy* (2nd ed.). New York: Basic Books.

Singer, J. L., Sincoff, J. B., & Kolligan, J., Jr. (1989). Countertransference and cognition: Studying the psychotherapist's distortions as consequences of normal information processing. *Psychotherapy, 26,* 344–355.

Skinner, B. F. (1948). *Walden two.* New York: Macmillan.

Skinner, B. F. (1971). *Beyond freedom and dignity.* New York: Free Press.

Sloane, B., Staples, F., Cristol, A., Yorkston, N., & Whipple, K. (1975). *Psychotherapy versus behavior therapy.* Cambridge, MA: Harvard University Press.

Smith, A. J., & Siegel, R. F. (1985). Feminist therapy: Redefining power for the powerless. In L. B. Rosewater & L. E. A. Walker (Eds.), *Handbook of feminist therapy* (pp. 13–21). New York: Springer.

Snyder, W. U., & Snyder, B. J. (1961). *The psychotherapy relationship.* New York: Macmillan.

Spence, D. (1982). *Narrative truth and historical truth.* New York: Norton.

Spence, D. (1987). *The Freudian metaphor.* New York: Norton.

Springmann, R. R. (1986). Countertransference: Clarifications in supervision. *Contemporary Psychoanalysis, 22,* 252–277.

Steenbarger, B. N. (1992). Toward science-practice integration in brief counseling and therapy. *The Counseling Psychologist, 20,* 403–450.

Sterba, R. (1934). The fate of the ego in analytic therapy. *International Journal of Psycho-Analysis, 15,* 117–126.

Stern, A. (1924). On the countertransference in psychoanalysis. *Pschoanalytic Review, 11,* 166–174.

Stiles, W. B. (1993). Quality control in qualitative research. *Clinical Psychology Review, 13,* 593–618.

Stiver, I. P. (1994). Women's struggles in the workplace: A relational model. In M. P. Mirkin (Ed.), *Women in context* (pp. 433–452). New York: Guilford Press.

Stolorow, R. D. (1991). The intersubjective context of intrapsychic experience: A decade of psychoanalytic inquiry. *Psychoanalytic Inquiry, 11,* 171–184.

Stolorow, R. D. (1994). The intersubjective context of intrapsychic experience. In R. D. Stolorow, G. E. Atwood, & B. Brandchaft (Eds.), *The intersubjective perspective* (pp. 3–14). New York: Jason Aronson.

Stolorow, R. D., Atwood, G. E., & Brandchaft, B. (Eds.). (1994). *The intersubjective perspective.* New York: Jason Aronson.

Stolorow, R. D., Brandchaft, B., & Atwood, G. E. (1987). *Psychoanalytic treatment: An intersubjective approach.* New York: Analytic Press.

Stolorow, R., & Lachmann. F. (1984/1985). Transference: The future of an illusion. *Annual of Psychoanalysis, 12/13,* 19–37.

Stone, L. (1961). *The psychoanalytic situation.* New York: International Universities Press.

Strong, S. R. (1968). Counseling: A social influence process. *Journal of Counseling Psychology, 15,* 215–224.

Strupp, H. H. (1980a). Success and failure in time-limited psychotherapy: A systematic comparison of two cases: Comparison 1. *Archives of General Psychiatry, 37,* 595–603.

Strupp, H. H. (1980b). Success and failure in time-limited psychotherapy: A systematic comparison of two cases: Comparison 2. *Archives of General Psychiatry, 37,* 708–716.

Strupp, H. H. (1980c). Success and failure in time-limited psychotherapy: A systematic comparison of two cases: With special reference to the performance of a lay counselor. *Archives of General Psychiatry, 37,* 831–841.

Strupp, H. H. (1980d). Success and failure in time-limited psychotherapy: Further evidence: Comparison 4. *Archives of General Psychiatry, 37,* 947–954.

Sullivan, H. S. (1954). *The psychiatric interview.* New York: Norton.

Sweet, A. A. (1984). The therapeutic relationship in behavior therapy. *Clinical Psychology Review, 4,* 253–272.

Tageson, C. W. (1982). *Humanistic psychology: A synthesis.* Homewood, IL: Dorsey Press.

Trop, J. L., & Stolorow, R. D. (1997). Therapeutic empathy: An intersubjective perspective. In A. C. Bohart & L. S. Greenberg (Eds.), *Empathy reconsidered: New directions in psychotherapy* (pp. 279–291). Washington, DC: American Psychological Association.

Van Wagoner, S. L., Gelso, C. J., Hayes, J. A., & Diemer, R. A. (1991). Countertransference and the reputedly excellent psychotherapist. *Psychotherapy: Theory, Research, and Practice, 28,* 411–421.

Wampold, B. E., Mondin, G. W., Moody, M., Stich, F., Benson, K., & Ahn, H. (1997). A meta-analysis of outcome studies comparing bonafide psychotherapies: Empirically, "all must have prizes." *Psychological Bulletin, 122,* 203–215.

Waterhouse, R. L. (1993). "Wild women don't have the blues": A feminist critique of "person-centered" counseling and therapy. *Feminism and Psychology, 3,* 55–72.

Weinshel, E., & Renik, O. (1991). The past ten years: Psychoanalysis in the United States, 1980–1990. *Psychoanalytic Inquiry, 11,* 13–29.

Weiss, J., & Sampson, H. (1986). *The psychoanalytic process.* New York: Guilford Press.

Whitley, B. E. (1985). Sex role orientation and psychological well-being: Two meta-analyses. *Sex Roles, 12,* 207–225.

Williams, K. E., & Chambless, D. L. (1990). The relationship between therapist characteristics and outcome of in vivo exposure treatment for agoraphobia. *Behaviour Therapy, 21,* 111–116.

Wilson, G. T. (1995). Behavior therapy. In R. J. Corsini & D. Wedding (Eds.), *Current psychotherapies* (5th ed., pp. 197–228). Itasca, IL: Peacock.

Wilson, G. T., & Evans, I. M. (1977). The therapist-client relationship in behavior therapy. In A. S. Gurman & A. M. Razin (Eds.), *Effective psychotherapy: A handbook of research* (pp. 544–565). Oxford, England: Pergamon Press.

Winnicott, D. W. (1949). Hate in the countertransference. *International Journal of Psychoanalysis, 30,* 69–75.

Wisch, A. E., Mahalik, J. R., Hayes, J. A., & Nutt, E. A. (1995). The impact of gender role conflict and counseling technique on psychological help-seeking in men. *Sex Roles, 33,* 77–89.

Wolf, E. S. (1988). *Treating the self: Elements of clinical self psychology.* New York: Guilford Press.

Wolf, E. S. (1991). Advances in self psychology: The evolution of psychoanalytic treatment. *Psychoanlaytic Inquiry, 11,* 123–146.

Wolowitz, H. M. (1975). Therapist warmth: Necessary or sufficient condition in behavioral desensitization? *Journal of Consulting and Clinical Psychology, 43,* 584–585.

Wolpe, J., & Lazarus, A. (1966). *Behavior therapy techniques.* New York: Pergamon Press.

Worrell, J., & Remer, P. (1992). *Feminist perspectives in therapy.* Chichester, England: Wiley.

Yalom, I. D. (1980). *Existential psychotherapy.* New York: Basic Books.

Yalom, I. D. (1989). *Love's executioner and other tales of psychotherapy.* New York: Harper.

Yontef, G. M. (1979). Gestalt therapy: Clinical phenomenology. *Gestalt Journal, 1,* 27–45.

Yontef, G. M., & Simkin, J. S. (1989). Gestalt therapy. In R. J. Corsini & D. Wedding (Eds.), *Current psychotherapies* (4th ed., pp. 323–361). Itasca, IL: Peacock.

Young, J. E. (1990). *Cognitive therapy for personality disorders: A schema-focused approach.* Sarasota, FL: Professional Resource Exchange.

Yulis, S., & Kiesler, D. J. (1968). Countertransference response as a function of therapist anxiety and content of patient talk. *Journal of Consulting and Clinical Psychology, 32,* 414–419.

Zamostny, K. P., Corrigan, J. D., & Eggert, M. A. (1981). Replication and extension of social influence process in counseling: A field study. *Journal of Counseling Psychology, 28,* 481–489.

Zetzel, E. R. (1956). Current concepts of transference. *International Journal of Psychoanalysis, 37,* 369–376.

Index